CHRISTIANS, MUSLIMS, AND ISLAMIC RAGE

CHRISTIANS, MUSLIMS, AND ISLAMIC RAGE

WHAT IS GOING ON AND WHY IT HAPPENED

CHRISTOPHER CATHERWOOD

ZONDERVAN™

GRAND RAPIDS, MICHIGAN 49530 USA

We want to hear from you. Please send your comments about this book to us in care of zreview@zondervan.com. Thank you.

ZONDERVAN™

Christians, Muslims, and Islamic Rage
Copyright © 2003 by Christopher Catherwood

Requests for information should be addressed to:
Zondervan, *Grand Rapids, Michigan 49530*

Library of Congress Cataloging-in-Publication Data

Catherwood, Christopher.
    Christians, Muslims, and Islamic rage : what is going on and why it happened /
Christopher Catherwood.
        p. cm.
    Includes bibliographical references and index.
    ISBN 0-310-25138-9
    1. Islamic—Relations—Christianity   2. Christianity and other religions—Islam.
3. International Relations.   4. Security, International   I. Title.
BP172.C325 2003
297.2'83—dc21
                                      2003008405

This edition printed on acid-free paper.

Christopher Catherwood asserts the moral right to be identified as the author of this work.

All Scripture quotations, unless otherwise indicated, are taken from the *Holy Bible: New International Version*®. NIV®. Copyright © 1973, 1978, 1984 by International Bible Society. Used by permission of Zondervan. All rights reserved.

Interior design by Beth Shagene

Printed in the United States of America

---

03 04 05 06 07 08 09 /❖ DC/ 10 9 8 7 6 5 4 3 2 1

This book is dedicated to
Larry and Beth
Betsy and Lamar
Claude and Leigh
And to my very favourite
University of Richmond graduate
My incomparably loveable and brilliant wife
Paulette

CONTENTS

Acknowledgments

Most authors end their acknowledgments page by thanking their long-suffering wives and families. Here I am going to break with tradition and start with them. None of this would have been possible without the constant, magnificent, and completely wondrous support of my wife, Paulette. She has been my constant companion and muse these many years – she is the woman in Proverbs 31 very happily embodied in contemporary form. No thanks to her can ever be enough.

Second, I am writing this in a beautiful old English house just outside Cambridge, the exterior of which is nineteenth century but the inside of which goes back to the Middle Ages. My office is a great room, entirely remodelled by my wife, in the home of my ever supportive and encouraging parents, Fred and Elizabeth Catherwood. Many a Zondervan book was written in a chair in my office, by my maternal grandfather, the distinguished Welsh preacher Rev. Dr D. Martyn Lloyd-Jones, someone who has continued to inspire me in the years since his death. To my parents, therefore, I give the warmest possible thanks for their kindness in allowing me back into the family home to write this book.

I used to be an editor in Christian publishing before returning to academic life at Cambridge University in England and at the University of Richmond in Virginia. As a result I know how critically vital editors are to the success of any book. To the great team at Zondervan responsible for putting this book together, I give heartfelt thanks and praise, especially to Tim Beals, whose support at a key stage in the process made all the difference, and also to Andy Sloan and Angela Scheff.

None of the process that led to the book being written would have been possible without the original grant from the Rockefeller Foundation to spend a glorious sabbatical, free of any teaching responsibilities, as a Fellow at the Institute on Violence and Survival in Charlottesville, Virginia. The Institute is part of the Virginia Foundation for the Humanities and Public Policy, itself an affiliated part of the University of Virginia. My time there was invaluable, and my debts of gratitude to the foundation director, Rob Vaughan, to the institute's director, Roberta Culbertson, to the many kind people who gave me rides to the office each day, and to that great southern gentleman and scholar, and also fellow Evangelical, Professor Larry Adams and his wife, Beth, I am more than grateful. I would never have won the Fellowship without the close support of two true friends, Professor A.E. Dick Howard of the University of Virginia and Professor John Treadway of the University of Richmond. Both of them are the kind of larger-than-life characters that make life so enjoyable for all who know them.

Cambridge, England, is a great place to work, not just in terms of scenery, but also because, like the University of Virginia, it is a place where there is a huge overlap between the University and Evangelical communities, with numerous academics being also Christians. I am especially indebted to the kind support of so many people that it is difficult to know who to include without sounding like an Oscar acceptance speech in which the awestruck winner thanks as many people as possible in the time available! So I will start with my college, St Edmund's, whose Master Sir Brian Heap is a fellow Evangelical, and whose support over many years is something to be treasured. Many other Fellows have been very kind in lots of different ways, including Dr Brian Stanley, Dr Simon Mitton, Dr Geoffrey Cook, Dr Denis Alexander, Dr Frank Carey, Professor Bob White, Moira Gardner, and many more besides.

The Centre of International Studies is a splendid academic institution with which to be associated. My warmest thanks go to

Dr Philip Towle, a true and effortlessly helpful friend over many years, and to Professors James Mayall and Christopher Andrew for the great support they have given in more recent times. I also have the pleasure of teaching classes for the University's Institute of Continuing Education for some time, including on the subject of Islamic extremism. I am more than grateful to Graham Howes, not just for providing me with good pupils but to the personal kindness and support he has given both me and my wife (who also teaches for the institute) over many a year.

Finally, on the teaching side, I am most fortunate in teaching for the Institute of Economic and Political Studies, which is not part of the University, but an affiliated institution linked to many prestigious American universities for their students to study in Cambridge. The director, Professor Geoffrey Williams, is a much liked and internationally respected expert on terrorism, and for me to teach geopolitics (which includes Islamic extremism) during the semester in which I was writing this book was both invaluable and fun. My thanks to him and his wife, Janice, are profound.

As always, while all the above have been helpful, any mistakes in this book are my own.

This is a book by a Christian author. Many people worldwide have prayed for me during the writing process. It was always so encouraging to know when I would sit pouring over books on Islam in the Lloyd-Jones chair or began the task of putting fingers to the word processor that I was being assiduously prayed for in many different countries. The list is too long to mention them all, but having such Christian stalwarts and renowned experts at peacemaking and defending human rights such as Mike Morris of Peaceworks in Britain and Sam Ericsson of Advocates International in the USA has been a rare privilege. In my church warmest thanks go to our Vicar, Mark Ashton (also a Zondervan author), for his effortless prayerful encouragement.

Paulette and I also give many thanks to our church small-group Bible study, especially for the remarkable way in which that week's passage so often turned out to be precisely relevant to some aspect of this book. Special thanks go here too to Richard

Reynolds, who has not only prayed faithfully, but, as a leading British bookseller, took me one year to the London International Book Fair. There I was able to have a conversation with Paul van Duinen of Zondervan that led to this book being commissioned and written.

This book is dedicated to my wife and her many friends from her days at the University of Richmond. I now have the considerable joy of teaching there every year – including on the subject matter of this book – and of being a Writer in Residence each summer in their history department. Warmest thanks are due to the many great friends I have made there over the years: Professors John Treadway, Hugh West, Harrison Daniel, Ernest Bolt, and John Gordon, all of whom have been enormously encouraging to the visiting Briton down the corridor. The folk at the School of Continuing Studies have consistently given me such great pupils: for this and many kindnesses, I thank Pat Brown, Jim Narduzzi, David Kitchen (and Michelle Cox), and Cheryl Callahan.

And isn't it wonderful to have a heavenly Father who has provided me with such great people in my life? The fact that we can call God our Father and have that kind of relationship with him is one of the things that stands out most strongly in our Christian knowledge of God in comparison with the much more remote inscrutable god whom Muslims worship. Let us all pray in confidence that the lands that were once populated by so many of God's people in the Middle East will, in his love and providence, hear the sound of the Gospel clearly again and turn to it as their ancestors did before them.

Before You Begin

An important orthographic note

This book is written in English, in the Latin script. The original names of many of the people and places in this book were written in Arabic script. Unfortunately, there is no unified way of transliterating them into English. Thus, I have gone with one particular spelling throughout, though I have read books on Islam and on the Middle East that use two spellings for the same person or identical place.

For example, some books use *Koran* while others use *Qu'ran*, which is the spelling that I use here. Those of you who read French will often see another spelling, *Coran*. Since the original is in Arabic, there is no single correct English spelling. I have also referred to the founder of Islam as *Mohammed* (which is also the choice that my computer's spell checker says is correct), but you probably have seen him referred to as *Mohammad* instead. Just to make life complex, the Turkish spelling of his name is often written as *Mehmet*.

Even recent names such as Osama bin Laden's terrorist group, *Al Qaeda*, are spelled differently – many British papers call his organization *Al Qaida* for example, and I have seen yet others still. The situation becomes more complex at transliterating Persian/Iranian names into English, since they are often both Persian and Arabic in origin at the same time.

In addition, while Arabic is the universal sacred language of all Muslims, the spelling of some technical words differs from one Muslim country to another. For example, an Islamic school is a *madrasa* in classical Arabic, but it is known as a *medrese* in Turkish (the language of the Ottoman Empire) and as a *madrassa* (i.e., with two s's) in most other parts of the Islamic world, including the Pakistani madrassas in which the Taliban were trained.

So I must apologize to my readers if my spelling is sometimes different from what you have seen!

A note for
specialist readers

This is a book for the *general reader*. So important is this subject that it is deliberately aimed at as broad of a spectrum of readers as possible. This means that it does not have the normal academic accoutrements such as endnotes or footnotes – the kind of tools I use when writing specialist books.

When it comes to writing books of original scholarship, it is vital to avoid plagiarism, a sentiment that is surely morally correct. So it is important to state here that I am not claiming to be original in the sense that I have done primary document research in Arabic language materials of the kind necessary to get a PhD. This is a work based upon secondary sources, all of which are listed in the bibliography at the end of the book. I have, unless otherwise indicated, not knowingly reproduced the exact wording of any of these works, but I have unhesitatingly picked their authors' brains! Sometimes I have done this through accepting one of a particular author's notions while rejecting his or her other interpretations. With writers such as Bernard Lewis, I have found myself in strong agreement with nearly everything that he says, as specialist readers of this book will soon notice.

What can claim to be unique, perhaps, is the synthesis – the selection of ideas made in this book has, to my knowledge, not been made by anyone else. (Many very helpful Christian books have been written on Islam, but their purpose is often different, and they were written before 11 September 2001.)

I trust therefore that academic readers will forgive the absence of the usual technical details. While academic readers are used to them, most people who will, I pray, be reading this book are not. If you want to follow up my ideas and read volumes, both specialist and popular, in the process, please turn to the books listed in the bibliography. I should say here that not all of them are sympathetic to us as Evangelical Christians. But I hope that I have interpreted them accurately in trying to describe to today's often perplexed Christians exactly what is going on in our troubled world in these times.

Introduction

Can you, depending on your age, remember where you were when John F. Kennedy died? When his brother Bobby was shot? When Armstrong took that historic leap for mankind and landed on the moon? When the Berlin Wall fell and that grim symbol of Communist oppression collapsed? When you heard the news of Princess Diana's fatal car crash? (Having dinner with my parents just like a grown-up, taking the entrance exam to my secondary school, at school, glued to the TV set, and being woken by my father-in-law and told to turn on the TV, respectively!) No one under twenty will of course remember the first three. Since I am now teaching university students born in 1982, I realize that they were only seven years old when the Iron Curtain fell, something that, although I am still only in my forties, makes me feel truly old!

An unforgettable day

It goes without saying though that if you are old enough to read this book, you can certainly remember where you were on that traumatic and history-making day, September 11, 2001, or, to many Americans, simply 9/11. (In Britain we put the day first, so that day was 11/9/01 or 11 September. But in this book we will use 9/11 for convenience.) I was in Charlottesville, Virginia, a Rockefeller Fellow at the University of Virginia's now rather appropriately named Institute on Violence and Survival. I had just injured myself, falling down a flight of stairs in the dark, so I was recuperating at home on my sofa. Just after eating breakfast, my American wife, Paulette, phoned me from Britain, where she had seen the first plane crash into the World Trade Center on the BBC lunchtime news. I turned the TV on to see the second plane crash into the other tower and, since I was in Virginia, hear what to us was the equally terrifying news of the Pentagon plane. Since I was not fully able to walk, I had the next thirty-six hours to do nothing else than to watch TV, absorbed by the unbelievable horror. I am British, but being there on so dreadful a day made me feel every bit as American as my wife. My one respite was being met by my wife's old university friend Professor Larry Adams, an eminent political scientist, Christian author, and, significantly for that moment, Project Director of the Critical Incident Analysis Group. Needless to say, his email, phone, and fax never stopped!

As soon as I was able to get to the office a few days later, I realized that being in an institute dedicated to the study of violence and how to survive it was now an extraordinarily relevant place to be. The book I was writing there on violence and mass murder in the Balkans suddenly had to expand to cover the death of 3000 people in the United States on a single day. It was not until some days later that I discovered that an American Jewish friend of mine, working close to the Twin Towers, had successfully managed to escape, even though his own building subsequently disintegrated too. I mention Bob's survival not just to show that I had a human connection with the carnage but also, as we shall see, because it is important to give clear evidence that, contrary to many of the strange post-9/11 rumours circulating in the Arab world, there were plenty of Jewish people killed or otherwise affected on that infamous day.

Two big questions were soon being asked by everyone – in the University coffee bars, at the many "teach-ins" the University authorities put on for their stunned students, in the homes of many concerned and perplexed fellow families, as well as on every TV show and news bulletin. The first being, "Why do they hate us?" and the second, "Has the world changed?" For my fellow

Christians in Charlottesville, a third question also exists: "How could God allow this to happen?"

Getting beyond 9/11

There is a sense in which, now that we are in the years past 2001, we need to get beyond 9/11. Since that date I have tried to buy as many of the important books on the subject as possible, making a lot of bookstore owners and authors very happy, and my bank manager rather worried. While this book does use the events of that day as a suitably dramatic beginning, it is not yet another one of the countless 9/11 books groaning upon the shelves. What we are doing here is looking at a spiritual battle that has been going on now for over 1300 years, in which the carnage of the Pentagon (which I saw in smouldering ruins not long after the event) and the Twin Towers are but a comparatively small passing event.

One of the things that was most interesting for me on 9/11 and in the weeks afterwards was being British in the midst of an American national trauma. What was also significant was being an Evangelical Christian in a place where my fellow American Evangelicals were trying to distinguish between their response as devastated patriots and as Christians whose faith made them part of the global community of all races and nations of God's people here on earth. (One of the reasons why I dedicate this book to my wife and to her old University friends – all of whom are Christians – is that my discussions with them, over many a meal and often into the night, were so useful in trying to work out a common, specifically Christian rather than just American, approach to these events.)

The key questions this book aims to answer

One of the key themes of this book is that the world did *not* change on 9/11. Rather, Americans found themselves in a wider struggle, from which the Atlantic had hitherto been big enough to protect them, and in which the rest of the world had been engaged for some time. As for the struggle between Christianity and Islam, that has been going on in one form or another since the seventh century, and only to the West's advantage since the twentieth.

British and other non-American English-speaking readers will not be surprised by what I have just written. The week before I wrote this, literally hundreds of Christian Nigerians, many of them English-speaking, were massacred by Islamic extremists on the basis of an article written by a non-Muslim journalist in a local newspaper. We shall look at such events in more detail as this book unfolds, but the thing to note here is that mass murders of Christians living in mid and northern Nigeria date back well before September 2001. In fact Jerusalem was the first major Christian city to be conquered by Muslim armies in AD 638, a full 1363 years before the attack on the Pentagon and Twin Towers. We will see that there is some truth, in terms of both history and the present, in what President Bush said in a mosque in Washington, DC, shortly after the disasters in that city and in New York, when he proclaimed Islam to be a religion of peace. But we shall also see that the situation is in fact considerably more complicated than that. It is to make all these big issues understandable, and to give the long-term perspective, that I wrote this book.

It should become increasingly easier for people to see the big picture after the initial trauma of 9/11 wears off. Although I will not be concentrating on those events, I will be using some of the protagonists as well-known and particularly appropriate illustrations of various Islamic points of view. Many Muslims abhor what happened on that day and are not violent themselves. But they may understand why the perpetrators did what they did because, in a less dramatic way, they share some of the same Islamic rage. What causes that rage and what that same rage is in broader perspective will be one of our key themes.

Although this is not another 9/11 book, it might be helpful in this introduction to start with that tragedy before we go on to look at the big picture. For, as Christians, we know from the Scriptures that ultimately ours is a spiritual battle and not a physical one, and that we are all part of God's family, his redeemed people worldwide. What happens to our brothers and sisters in Christ in Nigeria, in Indonesia, where Christians are also being massacred, in a real sense "happens" to us too. Yet that Muslim family next door seems so nice and mild – and they really are so friendly! We can't see them killing anyone, and their local imam at the mosque in town is standing shoulder to shoulder with our church minister in opposing value-free biology lessons to our thirteen-year-old children. Why are they so pleasant and yet people sharing their Islamic beliefs are killing Christians in the name of their religion?

Let's first look at how we responded as Britons, Americans, or whatever our nationality is, before going on to see that what is truly important is how to think *as Christians* living as part of God's global family on earth.

But we do need to look at some 9/11 issues

I am British, but in addition to my Virginian wife and many American in-laws, I also have a brother who married a Midwesterner and lives in Ohio. I teach in Cambridge, England, but also in Richmond, Virginia. Although I now feel thoroughly Anglo-American in many ways, there are still things about my wife's country that surprise me. One of those things that struck me forcibly was the extent to which Americans, up until 9/11, were remarkably – and, one could add, fortunately for them – insulated from the nasty world outside. The tragedy that hit them with such violence was something completely outside of any of their experience, even for those who had lived through World War II.

Surviving the Blitz: how the British got used to horror

This was true, for example, of my wife's delightful Uncle Lacy, a fellow Evangelical and a senior deacon in his local Baptist Church in Charlottesville. He had spent the day of his sister's wedding –

my late mother-in-law – bobbing up and down in a little boat crossing the English Channel to land upon the beaches in Normandy. He is very much one of what Americans, with much justification, describe as the Greatest Generation. Uncle Lacy went on to fight in the Battle of the Bulge, and returned home in 1945 as one of the many unsung heroes of the liberation of Europe. Yet his sister and her husband – my wife's parents – married in the total safety of Virginia. At no stage during that whole terrible conflict did they come remotely near danger of any sort.

So while it was Americans who made all the difference in the Allies winning World War II, those Americans who did not serve overseas were not in the direct line of fire, even though most of them had loved ones and friends who were. A few German U-boats might have sunk ships off the East Coast, but for those living in the main continental part of America, that is as near as it got. This is not in any way to downplay the horrors of Pearl Harbor. Those killed there in 1941 were as American as those in the continental part of the United States. Furthermore, as we all know, millions of Americans served in the war, and tens of thousands laid down their lives in the service of freedom.

My wife, Paulette, and I live near the American cemetery in Cambridge, where there are hundreds of graves of US service personnel whose actual graves are unknown but who made the ultimate sacrifice to beat the forces of tyranny. Paulette has another uncle, Woody, who served near Cambridge in the US Air Force, and many of his friends are buried there. So it is not as if the United States did not become actively involved – far from it! But the key thing here is that because of the size of the Atlantic on the one side, and because Japanese planes and ships never made it in remotely large numbers as far as California on the other, mainland United States was never itself struck by enemy action throughout the war. The United States was in the war, but not in the same manner as those of their Allies who lived close to their enemies.

During the same time Uncle Lacy was in Normandy and Uncle Woody was in a USAF base in East Anglia, my mother was in London itself, suffering, with thousands of others, the worst of the Blitz. During that terrible time, the capital had its full share of the worst that Hitler's bombers and, later on, rocket scientists could invent, including the terrible V1 and V2 missiles. These raids caused widespread devastation and killed thousands of people, nearly all of them non-combatant innocent civilians. In one raid on London, the minister of one of London's biggest churches, Rev. Dr D. Martyn Lloyd-Jones of Westminster Chapel, was in the middle of a sermon when an enormous bomb blast hit an Anglican chapel not many yards away. Thankfully, the worst damage he received was the ceiling plaster falling on his pulpit and on the congregation below. Had it been a direct hit, no one would have had the opportunity to read his great series on Romans (Zondervan) or this book, since he was my grandfather and his wife and daughter – my grandmother and mother – were seated not far away! Because of these bombings, my mother therefore spent much of the war away from home – an experience made famous by C.S. Lewis, in his Narnia stories, since the heroes and heroines of that story are evacuees from home when they discover the famous cupboard.

Just a few weeks before September 2001, a large terrorist bomb exploded and destroyed buildings near my parents' London apartment. It was the work of a splinter group from the IRA, the Irish terrorist organization whose bombs had killed more people during the course of "the troubles" in mainland Britain and in Northern Ireland than died in the Twin Towers in New York. When I asked my mother if she had been terrified by being so close to such an explosion, she replied calmly, "Oh no. I was in the Blitz."

Yet in comparison to the truly massive carnage of continental Europe during World War II, London and the rest of Britain had it comparatively very easy. We remember, as we should, the six million totally innocent Jews, all civilians and non-combatants, who were massacred in the Holocaust. While enormous numbers of Britons died, either on the battlefield or as a result of bombing raids like the notorious attack on Coventry, Britain itself, other than a few offshore islands, was not occupied. Jews who made it to Britain therefore survived. But we forget that many millions of other people died during World War II. Hitler regarded Slavic peoples no differently from the way in which he saw Jews. As a result, during the four-year war between the Third Reich and the Soviet Union, over twenty million Russians died, which is over three times as many people as Jews who perished in the Holocaust. As with that genocide, the bulk of those were civilians put to death in barbaric ways on Nazi orders.

Consequently, Europeans became all too familiar with large-scale death very close to home. While many of us living on this side of the Atlantic thought that we would never again see such carnage in Europe on that scale again, the wars that followed the breakup of the former Yugoslavia showed that we were tragically wrong. Tens of thousands of people died in those wars, and, once again, the majority of deaths were civilians not soldiers. In one day alone, in the town of Srebrenica in Bosnia, *seven thousand* completely innocent Bosnian civilians were slaughtered – over twice as many as all the casualties in the United States on 9/11. (The fact that all the victims were Bosnian Muslims, murdered by troops professing to be Serbian Orthodox Christians, has a significance that we will examine later on.) The massacre of Kosovar Albanian Muslims in the town of Racak was one of the main causes for which many British and American Air Force pilots risked their lives in Kosovo in 1999 to prevent further genocide from taking place. On our side of the Big Pond, even my generation is still forced reluctantly to become familiar with the loss of life on a terrible scale.

We are horribly used to terrorism as well. At this time of writing, the cease-fire in Northern Ireland is still holding. But for many years the IRA terrorized not just that unfortunate province, but also the mainland as well, in an attempt to make British retention of Ulster so unpopular that there would be pressure on the Government to withdraw. What the terrorists did not realize, among other things, is that they were bound to kill real Christians in their outrages. In one bomb explosion in Northern Ireland, the murdered nurse's father was able to speak publicly of his daughter's outstanding faith in Jesus Christ. Another bomb went off in a London railway terminal at rush hour – designed to maximize casualties. But one of the victims was a Christian businessman, and his wife was able to give a testimony on prime-time television news of her forgiveness, through Christ, of her husband's killers.

I should add here that while the IRA did not hesitate to kill lots of innocent people in their cause, they never wanted to slaughter people on a truly massive scale. Really large death tolls would have been politically counterproductive. This is not the case with today's Islamic terrorists – they have no such qualms and actually want to massacre people on a vast scale for reasons that we shall see.

Dodging the bullets from London to Beirut

Thankfully I only ever heard one big IRA bomb, and the main impact on my life was that of inconvenience, when the entire rail and underground (subway) network was shut down as a result of bomb warnings. I was, however, in London, unfortunately, just feet away from one of the rare instances in England of Middle Eastern terrorism, when gunmen from inside the Libyan Embassy started to shoot at the demonstrating crowd outside, killing a British policewoman in the process. Except for such incidents, British police are not normally armed, so it was especially disconcerting to see heavily equipped special firearms units suddenly appearing on every nearby available roof. I was stuck in the library in which I had gone to work most of the day, while the negotiators did their best to prevent further casualties from taking place.

The nearest that I have come personally to a violent death occurred in the heartland of Islamic violence, the Middle East. Rather foolishly perhaps, I visited a cousin of mine and her husband in Beirut, right in the midst of the long and savage Lebanese civil war. Alison's husband, Chris, taught at the famous American University in Beirut, which was on the Muslim side of the Green

Line that divided Muslim Beirut and Christian Beirut. Alison and Chris lived only yards from the American Embassy – the one that blew up with hideous loss of life. I met many brave American missionaries while I was there. They had not expected to come to a part of the world in which Christ had walked only to spend much of it in a bomb shelter! Sometimes the bombing raids were carried out by Israeli Air Force planes, against some Palestinian or Islamic militia nearby – we will see later why I make that distinction – and the experience of having to shelter from *Israeli* bombing was one the missionaries found stranger still.

As many will recall, hundreds of US civilian diplomats and Marines lost their lives in various atrocities in Lebanon. But while Americans were deeply shocked, the violence was *over there*, not next door, at home. In retrospect, the US deaths there and in 1998 in East Africa should have been a wake-up call that the American geographical immunity from the nasty world outside was coming to an end. We knew soon after the 1998 attacks that a militant and anti-American organization called *Al Qaeda* (the Arabic words for *The Base*) was overtly behind them. But when the same organization hit the United States *on American soil* on 9/11, it was a massive psychological shock against a nation that was completely mentally unprepared.

Here I should say that many Europeans, in saying, "Oh, we're used to terrorism," while being literally right, were also being extremely blasé. While the atrocities in the Yugoslav wars eclipsed those in the United States in casualties, no Western European country had seen terrorism on the 9/11 scale. Nothing done by the IRA in Britain, the Red Brigades in Italy, the Baader Meinhoff Gang in Germany, or Islamic extremists in France even approached the death toll in Washington, DC, and New York. It is one thing to read about atrocities overseas in the newspapers, even if Americans were the victims in Lebanon or East Africa. It is quite something else to see them happen on one's own soil.

So how do we begin to look at the three key questions I posed earlier: Why do they hate us? Did the world change on 9/11? Where was God on that terrible day?

So what is the answer to these key questions everyone is asking?

There is a real sense in which the whole of this book aims to answer these three questions. We will do so in large measure by taking them out of the specific events of 2001 into the much wider perspective of Islam and Christianity, with a history of nearly 1400 years. The worrying matter of Islamic rage is, I will argue, very much of a twentieth and now twenty-first century phenomenon. As for where God was, that is a massive theological discussion – not so much about the problem of suffering but about the nature of God himself. To us as Christians, that should be the most important issue. If you see everything that happens in the light of who God is and why he acts as he does, then all else becomes much clearer when seen in spiritual perspective. As I shall show at the end of this book, that is a cause for supreme and confident optimism. It may seem strange that a subject such as rage and violent death could be viewed like this, but if we know God fully and understand his Word properly, *ultimate* optimism is surely the correct answer.

"Why do they hate us?" is a perfectly natural, human question to pose. It is also understandable that Americans – the principle victims in September 2001 – should ask that in relation to their own country. We will go into much more depth shortly as we look at what Osama bin Laden said both then, in 1998 (following the embassy attacks), and again in November 2002 just before the massacre of the Israeli tourists and their Kenyan hotel staff in the Mombassa attacks. So what follows here is an *hors d'oeuvre* to introduce some of the basic themes that will follow.

What I will show is that the "us" is not by any means just the United States. What bin Laden hates is as much related to a feud about the direction in which Islam should go as his visceral dislike of all Western values. Please note that it is the *values* that such people hate – not the technology. The Al Qaeda terrorists might have used box-cutter knives to hijack the planes on 9/11, but the members of Al Qaeda have shown that they do not hesitate to use the latest technological equipment when it suits their purposes. Furthermore, we should remember that Al Qaeda is a symptom of a much wider malaise – even if we get rid of the specific individuals behind it, there will be thousands more eager to take their places. What we are dealing with is what *New York Times* columnist Tom Friedman is surely right to describe as the "Muslim basement," the terrorists one level below the much discussed "Muslim street," or Islamic public opinion in general.

For this is not a war between Arabs and the United States or Muslims versus America. Rather, it is the latest manifestation of a deeper struggle between one set of values and another. That is why I am calling the chapter on these issues "A Clash of Values," because the secular way of looking at the issue – the famous "clash of civilizations" theory – is, for Christians, much too simple a way of seeing the matter.

The man from whom bin Laden and all similar extremists gained their Islamicist ideology, Sayyid Qutb, was executed in 1966 by fellow Egyptians under the Arab socialist and nationalist leader Gamal Abdel Nasser. (*Islamicist* is the term we will be using for Muslims for whom Islam is a political ideology as well as a religious faith.) Nasser was certainly no friend of the United States, but he was as strongly opposed to Islamic extremism as we would be, because such fanatics directly threatened his own regime. Qutb was in turn as much against Nasser and secular Arab socialist nationalism – which he termed *jahiliyya*, or unbelief – as he was against the West, if not even more since most Egyptians were supposed to be Muslims and should therefore know better. Furthermore, as we shall see, Qutb actually spent quite some time living in the United States. It was precisely because of what he saw and experienced in America that he was so against her. He was particularly outraged, for example, by something we would regard as entirely innocent, such as co-ed dances at a local church!

The post-9/11 talk of "They hate us for our freedoms," including such statements made by President Bush, really isn't accurate, because Muslim extremists actually reject the concept of freedom inherent in all of the Western world today. Just look at Taliban

Afghanistan, a country where such religious ideologues took power. How free was that? So the "us" certainly includes America, but the people they hate go far beyond the shores of the United States, as the November 2002 statements attributed to bin Laden make very clear. America is the specific target of this hate, I will argue, only in that the United States is seen as the embodiment of the West and all that it stands for.

So did the world change that terrible day – or just America?

Did the world change on 9/11? As we have just seen, America most certainly did, with the end of her centuries-long geographical immunity from the horrors of the outside world. For the first time, it was American civilians, rather than soldiers or diplomats, who died en masse. However, I rather agree with former Oxford and Yale professor Sir Michael Howard, who rejected the idea that *the world* changed that terrible day. What I would say instead is that the United States found herself dramatically pitched into the nastier world outside, and into the kind of struggles that the rest of the world have been facing for centuries. Seven thousand dead one day in Srebrenica, three thousand dead on another in New York and Washington, DC – welcome to the sad and dreadful world of mass murder. (For Europeans like myself who are sympathetic to America, the fact that the United States was now engaged with the rest of us, rather than lurching back into a form of isolationism, was definitely a silver lining to the cloud, but that is another story . . .)

Furthermore, Osama bin Laden and those sharing his worldview were harking back on that infamous day to something very ancient – the way in which Muslims see the world divided essentially into two. This is the division between the *Dar al-Islam*, translated into English as the House or Abode of Islam, and the *Dar al-Harb*, the House or Abode of War. Everyone is either under Islamic rule or in the land of non-believers, the House of War. America may have been fortunate not to notice this until 2001, but Jerusalem discovered it in AD 638 when conquered by Islamic invaders, and Spain discovered it in AD 711 when the Islamic invasion of the Iberian Peninsula began. There is in modern Islam a considerable difference of opinion as to what the notorious word *jihad* really means. Moderate Muslims, such as the distinguished writer Akbar Ahmed, emphasize the *internal struggle* part of the word – the daily effort every Muslim undergoes to live a pure and holy life. On the other hand, extremist Muslims such as Sayyid Qutb, and his recent followers in Al Qaeda, interpret it literally in terms of *holy war*, from the vast conquests of the seventh century to the carnage of September 2001 or November 2002. The problem, as we shall see, is that the word *jihad* can actually mean *both* and that the Muslim scriptures, the Qu'ran, can be interpreted equally legitimately to mean either and/or both at the same time. But in the violent sense of it, as espoused by the proponents of *external* Muslim rage, America joined a struggle in 2001 that is over 1300 years old. (Many Muslims feel a deep sense of anger at America as the sole superpower, but their rage is *internal* – they would never believe in taking innocent life because of it.)

So where was God on 9/11?

Many helpful booklets have been written about where God was on 9/11, and I do not want to supplement them here. Much of the rest of this book aims to answer this vexed cry. But to answer it briefly here, the correct response is surely to say that he was where he has always been – in heaven and in control. Tens of thousands of people in recent years have died in hideous floods, in places such as Mozambique and Bangladesh. They may have died as a result of freak weather conditions rather than because of the deeds of evil men, but they are no less dead as a result! Far more people die tragically in driving accidents *every year* than at Srebrenica or on 9/11. Yet we probably do not doubt God's omnipotence or love as a result of them – unless it is *our* country that is ravaged by a flood or a member of *our* family who is killed in a car wreck. Perhaps it was the sheer enormity of the evil behind the 9/11 tragedies, plus the massive psychological shock that such an event was taking part in the hitherto immune United States that jolted so many on that sad day.

But if you look at the story of the children of Israel in the Old Testament, or read about the appalling opposition and persecution that Christians had to face right from the start in the New Testament, you see that for Christians the world often is truly a terrible place. Not only that, but such suffering comes to the righteous often precisely *because* they are righteous (2 Timothy 3:12; 1 Peter 4:12). The ultimate example of innocent suffering is of course Christ himself, who took the punishment for our sins (1 Peter 2:19–24). But God's people have suffered horribly throughout the ages and in many countries today. There is a real sense in which the absence of the suffering of Christians in places such as the United States or Britain is the exception rather than the rule. Hundreds of Christians were massacred by Islamic mobs in northern Nigeria the week before I wrote this, but you can be sure that most of the media that you read makes little or no mention of the fact.

Yet as I found in visiting fellow Christian students in pre-1989 Communist Europe or a church leader in China just after the horrors of the Cultural Revolution under Chairman Mao, believers who go through such appalling times often have a very real sense of God's presence with them even through dire experiences quite beyond both their (and our) ability to comprehend. They know exactly where God is – with them! They know, as did the persecuted Christians we read about in the New Testament epistles, that however dire things may seem, God is always in control.

I was often reminded of this while attending conferences in the 1970s, organized by the International Fellowship of Evangelical Students (IFES) in an Austrian castle owned by InterVarsity Christian Fellowship of the United States. It was not just that there were lots of students from countries where Christian activity was actively discouraged or persecuted, though that was indeed the case. But as a historian I was interested in the castle's past and discovered that it had been owned by people during the

Counter-Reformation who had vigorously persecuted Protestant Christians, many of whom had been incarcerated in its inhospitable dungeons and sometimes held there before being put to death. They must at times have wondered where God was. If they did, one could not blame them. If they prayed for their captors, they never lived to see their prayers answered. Yet four hundred years later, Schloss Mittersill is now owned by Evangelical Protestant Christians. Students come from literally all over the world in order to freely study the Gospel there. The prayers of the persecuted *were* answered, but four centuries later.

As Christians, we need to be extremely careful in our response to suffering. How we have all cringed, for example, when a well-meaning parent of many healthy children says to someone whose only baby was stillborn, "Don't worry, God understands." It sounds so trite, however good the intentions. Likewise, saying, "I know 9/11 was dreadful, but God is in control," to a traumatized American might seem to be equally inappropriate, especially coming from a more jaded British perspective. But as woolly as such sentiments might appear to be, the *spiritual* truth behind them *is* true, however shallow the words might sound coming from the lips of someone who has not suffered in the same way.

One of the problems is that as humans we often want instant answers. Yet as we see from the terrible experiences of Job, God has answers but often chooses not to give them to us. Job never found out the reasons for his ordeal. When God answers him, it is not to respond by saying, "Well, Job, this all comes as a result of Satan saying that he wanted to test a man faithful to me, and I knew you could cope." Not at all! God responds by telling Job about who he, God, is. This is why the problem of suffering is really a question of the character and nature of God. I can remember as a student debating the issue of so-called "unanswered prayer" over coffee late into the night. My response – then as now – to what Scripture teaches is that there is no such thing! God *always* hears and answers our prayers. It is just that he always does so in *his* way rather than ours. How often have we had cause to thank God for not answering requests in the past the way we then wanted him to? I am thankful to God daily for my wife. I am now *especially* thankful that I did not marry other people whom I knew in the days before my wife and I met each other. We all pray for things that we want at the time (including people we may fancy), but as God has better plans for us, he hears our prayers, but answers them better than we could ever imagine. Many married couples can surely identify fully with this!

There is a sense in which I am writing this book because of a serious illness I had eight years ago. Looking back, it is clear that God used that illness of physical exhaustion, unpleasant though it was at the time, to change my direction and lead me back into academic life, teaching Christian human rights and an active Evangelical response to the issue of Islamic and similar forms of religious terror. If this book is at all helpful to anyone, as I pray that it will be, it could be said to be an indirect result of that illness back in 1994 in a way that I could not possibly have seen at the time.

When Zhou En-lai, a Chinese Communist leader in the last century, was asked what he thought of the French Revolution nearly two hundred years earlier, he replied that it was too soon to say! Likewise, we may never know what might *ultimately* be the result of a disaster such as 9/11.

I teach the history of the period 1918-89 to students in Britain and the United States. One of the key textbooks, written by Yale professor John Lewis Gaddis, is entitled *We Now Know*. In this book about the Cold War, one of the important things Gaddis writes is that now that the Cold War is over, after nearly fifty years of conflict, we now know how to describe it properly. But we can only do so precisely because it is over. We *now* know, for example, who won and why it ended. But by definition we could not do that while we were still in the middle of it. We now know, for example, that it ended comparatively peacefully, with the liberation of Central Europe, and without World War III. But no one could have predicted that even a few years before the end. As a result, as Professor Gaddis points out, all histories of the Cold War written *during* it, even as late as the 1980s, are inevitably distorted.

It is rather as if someone wanted to write the definitive history of World War II, but did so in 1941, before America entered the conflict and made ultimate Allied victory inevitable. A history written *that* year would probably and rightly have been rather gloomy! Something published in 1946, after VE-Day and VJ-Day, would naturally have a very different perspective.

We are probably at the beginning of a new global struggle, of a different kind from anything we have seen before, as *this* book will aim to show. That has not stopped respectable commentators and journalists on both sides of the Atlantic from making prognoses on whether or not the West will win the war on terror. Some of them might be exactly on target, while others might be writing pure gibberish. But with the experiences of the Cold War history in mind (Who could have imagined even in 1989 that the great Soviet superpower would have vanished by 1991?), I am quite wary of making predictions, even though I am inevitably asked to make them. But there is one thing of which we can be 100 per cent guaranteed and absolutely certain, beyond any human doubt whatsoever: God *is* in control, and *he* will win! That, I trust, is something *all* Christians can agree upon.

Depending upon which pundit you read in the newspapers, the war on terror could be over soon, it might be even longer than the almost fifty years of the Cold War (historians notoriously disagree with each other about exactly when it began), or it may far outlast our lifetimes. At this stage of writing, we have no idea! Thankfully, we know that God does, and that we can trust him securely in whatever may prevail, whether the struggle gets far worse or ends swiftly. So however depressed you might become reading some of this book, remember that there is a happy ending.

CHAPTER 1

How Christians Should Think about the Past

This book is going to begin by looking at the key issues that enable us to understand the nature of the Islamic world today. If we look at, for example, the alleged statement of Osama bin Laden on 13 February 2003, we will see a lot of references to history, to battles fought over 1300 years ago. If we are going to understand the present, we must first study the past, however strange this might seem. The first three chapters do exactly this. We will look at how we as Christians should look at history. We do, after all, have a faith firmly rooted in real events that took place thousands of years ago and have eternal spiritual significance. Jesus was born in a manger, he had a genuine ministry here on earth in what is now the Middle East, and he died on the cross and rose from the dead. In addition, Jesus was the authentic Son of God whose death redeems those from their sins who have faith in him. Christianity is a historical, fact-based religion – one we know to be the truth.

But being creatures of the present, we too easily forget, in the bustle of twenty-first century life, how much what happens now owes its origin to events long gone. As Christians we should not make this mistake, and this chapter should equip us to look at history through biblical spectacles.

Islam, Christianity, and the debate over the past

Besides studying our own religion, there are other reasons why history is important. One is that Islam also claims to be a history-based religion, and in some sense that is true as well. Mohammed really did exist as a provable historical figure in a part of the world not far away from Palestine. He gathered disciples around him, and within a century of his death his teaching had spread over thousands of miles into a major religion. All this is historically verifiable and makes Islam a history-based religion.

Furthermore, Muslims today frequently argue with Christians on the basis of history and on genuine events that took place incontestably in the past. It was joked that Mohammed Atta, one of the 9/11 hijackers (probably the brains behind the executive part of the operation), was mentally more at home in the seventh century – the era of the Prophet Mohammed's life – than he was in the twentieth (or twenty-first). To the purveyors of Islamic rage, past history – whether historical triumphs such as the seventh century conquests, historical grievances such as the Crusades, or the twentieth century European occupation of the same territories – is at the heart of the hatred they have toward what they deem to be the Christian West.

A specifically Evangelical view of history

One of the reasons why the Bible is so vital to us as Christians is that we see directly in the inspired words of the writers exactly what God said to people, and, in some cases, such as Job, what he says in heaven as well. This is not that Job himself knew, but we do, since the author of that book reveals it to us. (We will look at the different ideas of inspiration between Islam and Christianity elsewhere.) We can read what God said to people as diverse as Abraham and Peter, and, of course, the gospels themselves contain the direct teachings of Christ himself, God the Son.

However, for those of us who are Protestant Evangelicals, direct written revelation finished there. That is, we would argue, because the Scriptures are all sufficient. The Reformers called it *sola scriptura*, Scripture alone is our guide and no human institution or individual can match the unique authority of the Word of God.

But for most of us, especially those who come from the Reformed end of the Evangelical spectrum, God is still very much at work in the world today. So it is not that God is somehow less active than he was in biblical times – far from it. But since we don't have new Scripture, because we don't need it, we are not able to say why God does what he does, why he permits things that puzzle us, and why events go one way in one country, and the exact opposite somewhere else. We can guess, but we could be quite wrong.

Protestants often wonder why God waited so long to bring about the Reformation. Catholics, needless to say, ask why it happened at all! Within the history of the Reformation itself, for instance, interesting interpretative questions arise. Secular historians point to the significant detail that Luther began his ministry not long after the invention in Europe of the printing press. This meant that Lutheran pamphlets could be circulated in enormous numbers rapidly in a way that made their widespread distribution much easier than when all manuscripts had to be handwritten. Looking at the juxtaposition of Luther coming to realize some vital spiritual truths and the means to get them easily available to tens of thousands of people, it is hard to think otherwise than it was God who inspired men like Caxton and Gutenberg to invent the European version of the printing press, even though those two men would have had no idea of the spiritual impact of their discoveries when they made them.

Where Protestants disagree with one another

So far most Protestant readers can agree. As this example shows us, secular historians can get the details right – the invention of the printing press greatly helped the rise of Protestantism – even if they don't get the spiritual message. We need not read only Christian historians to be able to thank God for things he has done.

However, the early Reformers fell out with each other on theological issues from early on – Luther and Zwingli on the nature of Communion, most Reformers with the Anabaptists on the role of the state, and so on. Inevitably, this means we become increasingly partisan in how we imagine God to have been at work. Baptists, for example, were often persecuted viciously by their fellow Protestants, let alone by the Catholic Church. Christians with an Arminian view of the doctrine of salvation love to tell how Calvin was responsible for the death of Servetus. In turn Reformed Evangelicals, like me, point out that it was amazing that in such a bloodthirsty age, when professing Christians often put other professed believers to death, Calvin can only be said to be involved in one judicial execution and not hundreds.

Our interpretation of the past becomes steadily more partisan, with each one of us convinced we are right, but with many of our fellow Christians disagreeing with us, and often passionately. Those in the Reformed wing of Evangelicalism often have what is called a providential view of history – we can see God's providence at work as the centuries unfold. This could be a major reason why so many of us in our different denominations are so drawn to the study of history. However, if one looks at British or American history, we can see that the spiritual antecedents of some Americans or Britons were persecuted by the spiritual forebears of others. Baptists in Virginia were persecuted by the Anglican establishment there, something that many a twenty-first century Baptist remembers to this day. Knowing many Virginian Baptists and Anglicans, I doubt if either side would think that that persecution was a good thing today.

Being in large measure a Calvinist, I can find myself sympathizing on numerous doctrinal issues with the New England Puritans, but I would certainly never even begin to agree with their putting Quakers to death for what they felt was their mistaken theology. While at Thanksgiving we can rightly celebrate and thank

God for his providential care of the early Christian settlers in America, we surely can't claim that *all* they did was blessed by God. Yet in doing what they did, they completely and sincerely believed that what they were doing was very much in the will of the God whom they loved and served. So in saying that some things in the past are providential, we must always examine ourselves and ask whether all our fellow Evangelicals – or whoever – would feel the same way. Printing we can agree upon, but persecution is something about which we must lovingly differ.

The terror of the Crusaders

I am deliberately mentioning Protestant demeanours first so that no one can think I am describing the hideous Catholic mistake I am about to mention out of prejudice. I am referring to the Crusades, a historical act that still, both fairly and unfairly, vitiates relations with the Muslim world to this day and was used extensively by Osama bin Laden in his tirades against the West in 1998 and in 2001.

When I wrote a book about Billy Graham back in the 1980s, he graciously agreed to help me by inviting me to spend a week with his team in Orlando, Florida, where he was actively evangelizing in collaboration with the local churches. The name of that event? The Central Florida *Crusade*. In Britain there is an active interdenominational Christian youth group of many years standing: *Crusaders*. When an American president or British prime minister wants to tackle the terrible social problem of widespread drug abuse, what is such a government campaign called? A *crusade* against drugs. All this goes to show that in the West, both in Christian and in secular circles, we regard the word *crusade* as something benign and wholly positive, whether used evangelistically or in support of a social programme with which all right-minded citizens should agree.

Yet, as we have seen, bin Laden accuses the West (and gains massive street credibility in the Islamic world) of being *crusaders*, something the Muslim world regards in the exact opposite way, as a profoundly evil event that shows the true extent of Western perfidy and wickedness. The terrible truth though is this: When we look at what the Crusaders actually did, both bin Laden and moderate Muslims who like to engage in friendly dialogue with Christians *are actually right*.

Some of the worst examples of mass slaughter from the Middle Ages were the Mongol invasions of the twelfth century, when thousands of innocent people were massacred wholesale during the Mongol conquests of most of the Eurasian land mass. We look on them now with horror – as did many of their descendants, such as the famous Emperor Kublai Khan in China or the Mughal Emperor Akbar in India. But when you read accounts of how the Crusaders invaded the Holy Land at the end of the previous century, you discover that there is no difference between them and the Mongol horde who attacked the world a few generations later. Even Western eyewitnesses talk of Crusaders wading deep in blood after the seizure of Jerusalem, since the so-called Christian knights slaughtered everyone in sight, Muslim, Jew, local Arab Christian, man, woman, and child alike. It was total carnage, and it was all done in the name of reclaiming the holy places for Christian rule. Whatever the considerable wrongs of the Muslim conquests of the seventh century, no Muslim army came anywhere near the Crusader level of atrocity. When the Kurdish Muslim prince Saladin eventually reconquered Jerusalem for Islam, he was careful to spare all the inhabitants, Christian or not, and local Arab Christians and Jews were able to live in the Holy Land for centuries afterwards.

This is very different of course from the romantic version that we learn about in the West as children. Although King Richard the Lionheart was one of England's most unsavoury and violent of kings, both personally and morally, it is for his bravery in the Crusades and for his patronage of music that we tend to remember him now. In the tales of Robin Hood, he is seen as the heroic good king, not as the psychopath he undoubtedly was.

Unfortunately, it was a pope who launched the two centuries of crusades against Islamic rule of Palestine. He did it in God's name, to which the assembled multitudes shouted, *"Deus lo veult,"* or "God wills it!" Even though Christians today would never condone such violence in the name of Christ, we are still being blamed for it centuries later. When President Bush launched his retaliatory attack on Afghanistan in 2001, bin Laden and others did not hesitate to depict it to their fellow Muslims as a Christian crusade against Islam, with Bush as the crusader in chief. Such is the memory that medieval, supposedly Christian, atrocities have sustained for over seven hundred years since the last Crusaders left the Holy Land in 1291, with the fall of Acre, the last major Latin city in Palestine.

Why we are accused of the Crusades today

So when Muslims today attack people in the West for what happened in the Crusader era, there is a real historical sense in which they are right. A person can, if he or she wishes, say truthfully that the Crusades to recapture and hold Jerusalem were not the only crusades of the twelfth century. We tend to think of the medieval Crusades as being solely against Muslims. This is, in fact, not the case. The Albigensian Crusade, which took place in what is now the south of France, was against French heretics. In the eleventh and twelfth centuries many Europeans – the Cathars in Mediterranean France and the Bogomils in the Balkans – supported a version of the ancient Manichaean religion. The northern French Crusaders crushed the Cathar religion during the Albigensian Crusade with every bit as much savagery and ferocity as the eleventh century Crusaders slaughtered Jews, Muslims, and Arab Christians alike in the Holy Land and Egypt.

In other words, it was not that the Crusaders particularly or necessarily hated Muslims; it was that they were equally barbaric to everybody! This is not to defend the Crusaders in Jerusalem, but to point out that European warfare at this time was frequently bloodthirsty – and, one can thus add, not at all in tune with the teachings of Christ. Christian Just War teaching evolved after these sanguinary times, and by the later Middle Ages made very clear that civilians were never deliberately to be touched. So we cannot and should not ever defend the excesses of the Crusaders, whether in the Middle East or the South of France.

We are still paying for the mistakes the Crusaders made

There is surely an equally important theological point to be made. Western writers have pointed out that the Crusaders were doing no more than trying to reclaim lands that had been Christian ruled until the Islamic invasions. This is true but in a slightly more complicated form.

When Pope John Paul II went on a pilgrimage as part of the Jubilee celebrations in 2000, he had to do more than apologize for the Crusades in the Arab countries that he visited. (We will soon see why this kind of apology is always unfairly one-sided.) He had to apologize for them in Greece as well. His visit there suffered from virulent Greek Orthodox protesters demonstrating volubly against his presence since they also have bad memories of the Crusades – and in their case also with good reason. The Fourth Crusade in 1204 was supposed to recapture Jerusalem from the new Islamic rulers. But because of the greed of the Venetian and Genoese merchants, it captured the Byzantine Empire's capital of Constantinople instead. The new Latin Empire did not last long, for a Byzantine emperor was back in their old capital by 1261. But the materialist greed of the Crusaders had fatally weakened the one great Christian state that had acted as a bulwark against Islamic invasions of Eastern Europe for over six hundred years.

The Byzantine Empire never fully recovered from the Fourth Crusade, and by 1453 it ceased to exist. Constantinople became Istanbul, the capital of the new and Islamic Ottoman Empire. The Ottomans had conquered most of the old Byzantine Empire by this date anyway, and went on to seize all of the Balkans as well as the already Islamic lands of the Middle East and North Africa.

Countries like Greece had to endure nearly five hundred years of Muslim Ottoman rule, and some parts of present-day Orthodox Eastern Europe were under Islamic rule until right into the twentieth century. Since the popes in the Middle Ages tended to be unsympathetic to the Eastern Orthodox Byzantines, Western Catholic nations were often rather slow to help against Muslim incursions. So in 2000 the Greek Orthodox were in effect blaming the present pope for the activity – or rather complete lack of it – of popes six centuries before!

Looking at the matter historically, the protesters had a good case: The Crusader destruction of the Byzantine Empire lead to centuries of Islamic rule throughout the Balkans. Much of the bitterness and large scale bloodshed in that region in the 1990s, in which thousands of innocent European Bosnian Muslims were slaughtered by Serbs, goes back to a twentieth century desire for revenge for fourteenth and fifteenth century Muslim conquests. Seven thousand Bosnian men were murdered by Orthodox Serbs in one single orgy of killing in Srebrenica, and Catholic Croats massacred the inhabitants of the village of Ahmici. (I look at this in more detail in my book *Why the Nations Rage*.)

In addition, the Holy Land had been ruled by the Byzantine Empire before the conquest of Jerusalem in 638, rather than by Western Europeans. So while it is true to say that the area was reconquered, it was not reconquered by the people who had once ruled it but by complete outsiders – the Crusaders of Western Europe. But the main theological objection to the Crusades is that by using military means to place Jerusalem back under Christian rule, the Crusaders were using the methods of Islam and not those of the Scriptures.

How the Crusaders were using the tools of Islam

One of the reasons I thank my small-group Bible study ("house group" in British English) in the Acknowledgments is that the Bible passage so often became relevant to writing this book. Just before writing this chapter, we looked at the Beatitudes in Matthew. Christ is already presupposing that those who follow him will be persecuted and reviled for his sake, as swiftly happened after Pentecost and as has happened to countless Christians ever since. His kingdom, as Christ said himself, is *not* of this world, which is why his disciples did not fight. This is one of the key themes of this book and one of the most critical differences between Christianity and Islam.

The important thing for us to understand here is that Christians do not need a Christian state in order to be effective and faithful Christians. (See my book *Whose Side Is God On?*) In fact, as we see from the first centuries of early Christianity, the blood of the martyrs was the seed of the church. This maxim has proved true in recent times with the phenomenal growth of the church in China since 1951, when all the Western missionaries were expelled and the state often savagely persecuted Christian believers.

On the other hand, as the historian Bernard Lewis shows us in his excellent work *What Went Wrong*, this is not at all the case with Muslims. Nowadays millions of Muslims do live in non-Islamic countries, mainly in Western Europe but also many in the United States as well. But when this was a comparative rarity, there was much searching theological debate among the Muslim theologians as to whether they ought to be there, which is one reason why Islamic countries took so long to have permanent embassies in Western countries. Muslims do not separate church and state, so a regime in which an individual Muslim lives ought to be one following the Islamic faith.

As we have seen, both Christians and Jews were able to live in comparative freedom in Islamic regimes, whether in El Andalus in the West or in the Middle East under the different Muslim states that existed there. Their *dhimmi* status (protected monotheists) did not give full civil rights as we would understand them now, and they could not evangelize. They also had to pay extra tax and could not hold leading positions. But in comparison to active persecution, their *dhimmi* status, while not pleasant, was comparatively mild. Obviously, as the Jewish writer Bat Ye'or has written in *The Decline of Eastern Christianity under Islam*, this was to lead to a rather defensive, inward-looking church. This is unlike the thriving Nigerian churches of today, where proximity to Islam seems to be enlivening it rather than inducing a state of permanent torpor. But the key point is that the Arab and Coptic Christians of the medieval Middle East, as well as not being persecuted, did not need a Christian regime in order to survive. Early Christianity grew despite the savage persecution of the Roman emperors, and Christianity *by definition* does not need a sympathetic regime to grow and prosper.

God's true people are now everywhere

We know where Christ is now – in heaven! And, through the Holy Spirit, Christ is with his people, wherever they are. God's people are his worldwide church in all places and among all nations. So while the Muslims have to pray toward Mecca and try to pay a physical pilgrimage there once in their lifetime, there is no such requirement for Christians. This is not to downplay the considerable pleasure to be had in visiting the places where Jesus once lived or that King Solomon built, or to take an active interest in the current affairs of present-day Israel. But Christianity is not a religion of *place* but of *spiritual relationship*. We are one in Christ. Of course, it is nice if we live in a country in which Christians are not persecuted. But as the New Testament shows, official hostility has frequently been the fate of Christ's followers from the very beginning.

So should it have mattered that Jerusalem was in the hands of Muslim rulers? Surely the *spiritual* answer is no – God is not constrained by who rules in a particular country. He does not and never has needed governments sympathetic to his people to be able to carry out his purposes. But, as we see elsewhere, this was not what the Crusaders believed. They did not have proper theological understanding of the truly global nature of God's church.

They knew dimly that there were Christians as far afield as Ethiopia and China under Christian rule in the former but not at all in the latter. But for all intents and purposes, Christianity was to the Crusaders a geographical entity, which we now call Christendom, a Western Europe under the spiritual jurisdiction of the pope. (The Catholic Church had long since split theologically from the Byzantine controlled Eastern Orthodox Church, with the formal split occurring in 1054.) So the Holy Land therefore needed to be under Christian control, and in particular under that of people in spiritual obedience to the pope, since Eastern Orthodox Christians were regarded as heretics. The medieval church had plenty of shrines and venerated places, as does the Catholic Church today, with sites such as Lourdes and Santiago di Compostela still being visited in large numbers.

But as well as giving reverence to the physical sites where Jesus had been instead of solely to Jesus himself, the Crusaders made another drastic error. This was to use military force – Christian holy war or crusade. As we have seen, this is something completely alien to the entire Christian faith. The weapons of our warfare are spiritual not literal and physical, because it is a spiritual battle that we are fighting (2 Corinthians 10:4; Ephesians 6:12). Bloodshed is something that is inflicted upon martyrs, not by sword-wielding Christians. So where did the concept come from? It has to be seen as a medieval, Western version of the Muslim jihad, or Islamic holy war, of the kind that we saw sweep across so much of the world in the seventh century. Military jihad, sometimes called the *lesser jihad*, is a Muslim concept. It is certainly not anything Christian. The early apostles preached the Good News – the book of Acts mentions no weapons.

In a sense, the Crusaders were using a Muslim tactic against their Islamic enemies – paying them back in their own kind. "You invaded our territory in the seventh century, so we will invade yours in the eleventh!" So while it is fun to read tales of medieval daring, and to mourn the loss of the Crusader kingdoms of *Outremer*, we surely cannot have any spiritual regrets that the Crusades ended up in failure. When discussing the Crusades with a

Muslim, it is right, tactfully but firmly, to point this out. What, after all, were the Muslim conquests of the Middle East? In terms of time, whereas the Crusaders were only briefly successful, Islamic rule of the region was to last, the Crusader interlude excepted, from 638 to 1917, or well over twelve hundred years. But the methodology – military invasion – was the same. The *real* difference is that what the Crusaders did was entirely contrary to all the tenets of their professed faith.

Just because the Crusaders claimed to be Christians – and, one can hope, some of the less violent may truly have been – that does not mean that we have to try to defend them. Would today's Christians want to defend the Borgias, the immoral papal family of Renaissance times? The principle is surely the same. It is Jesus and the Christian faith that we must defend, not atrocities committed contrary to all biblical teaching but carried out by those who claim his name. Massacres, from eleventh century Jerusalem to twentieth century Srebrenica, may have been committed by those proclaiming themselves to be Christians fighting against Islamic incursion. But evil is evil, and perhaps all the more so if it discredits the name of Christ, the Prince of Peace.

The effect of the Crusades on the Islamic world

As Bernard Lewis has pointed out in several of his books, the loss of Jerusalem to Frankish knights did not *at that time* draw much attention in the Muslim world. The region was then split between Sunni rulers (of whom Saladin, the successful Muslim commander who beat the Crusading armies and recaptured Jerusalem for Islam, was one) and the breakaway Shiite Fatimid Caliphate based in Egypt. There was a sense in which, in terms of internal Islamic power politics, the Sunni Muslim recapture of Egypt, which was then an economically and strategically more important region, was far more vital than the comparatively brief Crusader rule over Jerusalem. (Although the Crusaders were finally expelled altogether in 1291, Frankish rule over Jerusalem itself lasted for less than a century.) Far more serious, in addition, was the loss of El Andalus – Moorish Spain – in a slow reconquest that continued until final Spanish victory in 1492. Knights from the medieval Iberian kingdoms of Castile and Aragon were never expected to crusade in the Holy Land, on the basis that they were fighting the Muslims sufficiently at home.

Lewis is convincing when he says that the real significance of the Crusades arose in the nineteenth and twentieth centuries, and it is since then that Muslims have spoken about them with such wrath and deep feeling. There is a sense in which, in order to discuss the Crusades with a Muslim, it is more important to read David Fromkin's best-seller *A Peace To End All Peace* about the Franco-British carving up of the Ottoman Empire after World War I (in which Winston Churchill played an eminent role) than Sir Steven Runciman's famous multivolume history of the Crusader kingdoms. What really hurt the self-esteem of the Muslims in the Middle East was the decision made by the victorious Allies in 1918 (with America not taking a direct part) to partition the old Ottoman Empire between Britain, France, and Italy.

The historic roots of present Islamic rage

For the first thousand years or so in the confrontation between Islamic and Christian countries (note: not Christianity!), the Muslim powers held the initiative. What really happened in the twentieth century was that the loss of that initiative, which in a way the Muslim powers lost in the period 1683–99, only came home to roost when the West effectively gained it with the fall of the Ottoman Empire in 1918 and the abolition of the caliphate by a secularized Turk, Kemal Ataturk, in 1924. Up until 1683, when the invading Ottoman army failed to capture Vienna and then had to sign a treaty relinquishing territory to the West in 1699, one could convincingly argue that Islamic powers had held the initiative against Christian professing countries ever since the Muslim invasions began in 632. That is 1051 years of Islamic preponderance! (Strictly speaking, the Muslim Ottomans also failed to seize Vienna in 1526 as well. But since they successfully conquered most of Hungary at that time, and since the Muslim Mughal emperors in India were equally successful, I agree with Bernard Lewis that the later date is the better one.)

Then from around 1683 to 1917, when British and Australian forces under Field Marshal Lord Allenby captured Jerusalem, the balance slowly but surely began to swing the other direction. With final Allied victory in 1918, the formal demise of the Ottoman Empire in 1922 and the end of the Ottoman Caliphate in 1924, the advantage clearly switched to the Western camp. Note that I don't say the "Christian camp" – the Western powers, such as Britain, France, and Italy did not divide up the Middle East in the name of Christ. The separation between secular action and Christian endeavour was by this time very clear in the West, and these countries were acting in their own interests and not those of the Gospel.

So why do they hate us now?

The loss of face in the Middle East was massive, and indeed there are those who would argue that it has never recovered even to this day, as Fareed Zakaria wrote, for example, in the post-9/11 article "Why They Hate Us" in *Newsweek*. Up to the twentieth century there is a case for saying that the medieval crusading interlude – a comparatively brief blip in twelve hundred years of Muslim power and domination – was no more than a temporary inconvenience swiftly ended by the superior generalship of the great Saladin. No long-term harm was done to the basic Islamic overlordship of the Middle East, and to the Muslim rule of Jerusalem, a city which is third in importance to Muslims after only Mecca and Medina. Even the loss of the Balkans from 1830, when the southern part of Greece gained its independence, to 1913, when most of the region was regained to European rule, could perhaps be looked upon with some equanimity. But in

1918–22 the one remaining Muslim superpower ceased to exist.

Turkey, under the Westernizing rule of Kemal Ataturk, was lost to proper Islamic rule. (As I write this, an Islamicist party has won power in the 2002 Turkish elections. But even that new government has insisted that it wants to continue as a full democracy, in its membership of NATO and in its desire to join the predominantly Christian European Union.) The Turks, by beating a Greek army in 1922–23, were able to recapture some lost territory (including the biblical city of Smyrna) and regain some of their losses. This is a significant reason why, Zakaria argues, Turkey is a predominantly Muslim country that is today friendly to the United States, Europe, and the state of Israel.

From Western colonization to Islamic rage

Much of the Arab core of Islam was under Western rule. In the period from 1918 until after World War II, Britain kept Egypt (annexed in 1914 but in practice much earlier), and took Palestine, Jordan, and Iraq (a hitherto non-existent country effectively invented out of bits of the old Ottoman Empire by Winston Churchill). France took Syria and Lebanon, while Italy kept Libya and various islands in the eastern Mediterranean. The promises made by the victorious British soldier known to us as Lawrence of Arabia that there would be a great Arab kingdom were all dashed. Iraq and Jordan did have kings, but they were under firm British protectorate rule through the League of Nations. The fact that the French were from the same part of Europe as the Frankish knights who had led and largely dominated the Crusades was an especial humiliation. The two holy places of Mecca and Medina *were* under Arab rule, that of the Hashemite clan of Mohammed himself, and the same family as the new puppet kings of Iraq and Jordan. But Hashemite rule did not last long; in 1924 that part of Arabia, the Hijaz, was conquered by the Al-Saud clan, under whose rule it remains today.

So while the Crusades could be forgotten about as a fleeting misfortune up until 1918, after that date they became seared into Muslim memory as a savage infringement of Muslim land – the *Dar al-Islam*. But this was because the same Europeans whom they had beaten in the twelfth century had now beaten them in the twentieth. Rough-hewn Crusaders from Western Europe always looked down on their fellow knights in *Outremer* whom they thought had gone soft and decadent by taking up advanced Islamic ways of living. In medieval times, as we describe elsewhere, Islamic civilization in terms of material comfort, hygiene, medicine, and technology in general, was far in advance of anything European. But by the twentieth century that had ceased to be the case, and Western predominance in all these fields became all too apparent after the fall of the Ottoman Empire. Islam no longer had the cutting edge.

George Bush, the great Crusader?

This, then, is the reason why present-day Islamic extremists, of which Al Qaeda is only the most violent manifestation, use the past to kill people in the present. Muslim states should be ruled by believing Muslims. A state that was under British mandate – as Iraq and Jordan were after 1918 – is thus not fully Islamic. The same effectively applied to Egypt. When that country was taken over by Arab socialists such as Nasser in the 1950s, it was, as we saw in looking at Sayyid Qutb, *still* in infidelity, *jahiliyya*. To the Islamic purists today, it remains in that fallen state, as does Saudi Arabia itself, ruled not by righteous Muslims but by the hereditary and Western-dependent House of Saud. In helping the Saud dynasty, the United States is perpetuating infidelity at the heart of Islam itself. They are, in that sense, no different from the Crusaders of centuries ago. Once a land is Islamic, it should, the purists feel, *always* be Islamic. This is why bin Laden expressed such sorrow at the loss of El Andalus – even though this was now well over five hundred years ago! The Crusades did not really matter at the time to the Islamic world, but now they have become a potent symbol of decline, of the West's recent predominance over the Islamic East.

This is why the Crusades are at one and the same time a source of present-day wrath but also a complete red herring. The mind-set of General Allenby in liberating Jerusalem in World War I, or of President Bush in the early twenty-first century, could not be further from the bloodthirsty mentality of the medieval Crusaders. But to the militant Islamic mind, all these things symbolize the breach of the *Dar al-Islam*, the sacred, once-Islamic land of the Muslim faith. In the Middle Ages the Crusades were a temporary inconvenience – Islamic forces shortly after went on to create an enormous Ottoman Empire in the Balkans and defeat the ancient Christian power of Byzantium. But now the humiliation of Islam looks permanent and complete. Since an Islamic power can never be wrong, the present situation must be accounted for by blaming someone else. How better than to link the twenty-first century West with the eleventh century Crusaders?

Now that we have looked at a Christian perspective of the past, we now need to go on to look at the particular events of the past that have led to the Islamic rage of the twenty-first century. How did Islam begin as a world conquering empire? What is the golden age to which Al Qaeda and other Muslim extremists look back upon with such fondness? Chapter 2 will show us the first few centuries of the great Islamic/Christian divide.

CHAPTER 2

The Rise of Islam

One of the key things about the three so-called Abrahamic faiths – Christianity, Judaism, and Islam – is that they are all based on the interaction between revelation and historical events. We will now look at the early history of both the Christian and Islamic faiths.

The difference between the origins of Islam and of Christianity

There are three reasons why we should look at the origins of Christianity and Islam. First, because, as Bernard Lewis and others have so rightly pointed out, the enormous difference between their origins are in and of themselves very telling. The second reason is because of the way in which history has been distorted in the present and become a football in the debates between Muslims and Christians to this very day. The final reason is because of the way in which past events, especially in the past 150 years or so, have turned to Islam's disadvantage, and contributed in no small measure to the very Islamic rage that is causing so much damage today.

You cannot understand Al Qaeda and much of what Osama bin Laden is saying unless you grasp the considerable influence his interpretation of history, and that of his fellow extremists, has had on what they are doing now in the twenty-first century.

In his many books, Lewis has what one can best describe as a recurring theme – the dramatically divergent historical origins of the Muslim and Christian faiths. (Professor Lewis is himself Jewish, so as well as being an easy historian to read, he is also spiritually objective in that sense between the two.)

Christianity – a persecuted faith

In essence, what Lewis shows is that Christianity began as an illegal religion in ancient Rome, persecuted from the very outset. It had a leader who, from the viewpoint of secular history, was executed and off the scene by the time that the faith he originated began to spread beyond the narrow confines of his followers.

As Christians, of course, we would look at it differently – Jesus was put to death on the cross for our sins, rose again from the dead, and went to heaven at the Ascension to sit at God's right hand. We know that the early church was filled with the Holy Spirit, who enabled them to spread the Gospel over astonishing distances early on. But the main *effect* looked at from a historical perspective is the same. For, whether one looks at it from a secular or spiritual perspective, several things stand out: Jesus was not physically present on earth when the church began to spread, and his followers were zealously persecuted, first by the Jewish authorities and then by the Romans, who ruled nearly all the areas in which Christianity first grew.

Furthermore, the methodology used by the church was entirely pacific. It was through personal evangelism and through preaching, and in all cases through peaceful persuasion. Since the church was soon illegal – Christians would not worship the emperor as a god, and they soon lost the special dispensation given to Jews – there was no other means available.

Even more important, in using peaceful persuasion, and in relying on the power of the message and the working of the Holy Spirit, the early Christians were following in the methodology of their founder, Christ himself. For Jesus made it clear when he said, "My kingdom is not of this world. If it were, my servants would fight" (John 18:36). Jesus, the Prince of Peace, was not a man of war, nor did he need a physically violent means of spreading the message. It is true that the New Testament often uses military imagery – spiritual warfare, battling against sin, the Christian in full armour – but the point about all theses instances is that they are referring to *spiritual* battles.

Islam – the crucial differences begin to appear

In relation to militant Islam, it cannot be emphasized strongly enough that Christianity did not begin as a state religion. The early disciples were a spiritual community of believers living in a politically hostile environment. When blood was spilt, it was Christian blood shed because many members of the early church had been martyred for their faith.

Later on in this chapter we will see the devastating consequences that took place when Christians forgot their founding principles and allowed Christianity to be linked to a political entity, the Roman Empire.

Where Christians in the past got things wrong

Here we must admit two things. The first is that when Muslims attack the terrible things that so-called Christian states have done, they are sadly often right. Indeed that is something that we as present-day Christians can agree with without denigrating from the truth, because one of the effects of the self-styled Christian countries is that real Christians were often persecuted as savagely as Muslims, Jews, and complete non-believers. The United States would not exist as it does today without the large numbers of godly Christians who fled persecution not by pagan or Islamic regimes, but from countries calling themselves Christian.

Second, it will be fair to reply that the reasons why such Christian states were so wrong is that they were making the same basic error as do all Islamic regimes, namely linking spiritual truth to political and military power. In other words, if the Christian states were wrong, so too are Muslim countries that even today persecute people not of their own faith.

But after admitting the validity of the Muslim riposte, we should then return to the origins of the Christian faith itself. We can show clearly from the Scriptures that Christianity as properly understood – as opposed to a false kind of Christian understanding that gives the faith a bad name – is completely separate from political states of any kind, however benign.

The spiritual and political results of separating church and state

We can do what the secular British (and American) news magazine *The Economist* did to good effect on its website after 9/11. It argued, with considerable persuasion, that the total freedom of worship granted to Muslims in the United States is the very reason why Islamic states should give similar freedom to non-Muslims in their own countries – and for other reasons that we will explore in more depth later in this chapter. There are few countries in the world that are as actively Christian as the United States. (For Americans who decry how non-Christian America still is, try living in Europe, which really is effectively "post-Christian.") But, as we shall see, there were good *spiritual* reasons as well as secular ones that led America completely to separate church and state.

As I write this an American Christian medical missionary recently has been murdered for trying to spread the Gospel in an Islamic country. *The New York Times* columnist Thomas Friedman made an important point in commenting on this tragic incident. He wrote an open letter to leaders of Islamic countries saying that the American was killed for something that was entirely legal for Muslims to do in the United States – the proselytization of believers of other faiths to your own. There is what the experts call a powerful degree of *asymmetry* between what we permit in open Western societies and what is forbidden in closed Islamic countries – especially those to which the United States is allied, such as Saudi Arabia.

I described in my book *Whose Side Is God On* the contrast between Britain who has both an established church and low actual church attendance and the United States who has total separation but an immensely strong Christian population. Surely that is no coincidence. America has a thriving church because she has returned to the biblical pattern of separating what belongs to God from what is Caesar's. It is the Scriptures we must defend, the clear teaching of Christ and the apostles, and not what some medieval or other Western ruler decided to do. Since the message of the Bible is one of peace not violence, this puts us in a much stronger position than a Muslim, who often has all sorts of untoward things to defend.

Islam – a very different story

For Islam, it is a different story. The Muslim faith is one where faith and state were inexorably intertwined from the outset. Mohammed was both a spiritual and military/political leader from the beginning. Two years after his arrival in Medina in 622, he found himself at war – the much commemorated Battle of Badr in 624, in which he was able to beat his enemies. In his city-state of Medina he was, in effect, both pope and emperor all rolled into one, the head of state and the founder of his new faith.

We will later look at how you can interpret the Qu'ran in many different ways, since, from an outsider's point of view, it is a book written in different places and circumstances, depending on the needs of the moment. Consequently, decent-minded, moderate Muslims will always look to the benign parts of the Prophet's teaching.

Many such people are active in promoting what peace-orientated pro-Western Muslim leaders call the "Dialogue of Civilizations." This is a deliberate counterbalance to the gloomy thesis propounded by Harvard professor Samuel Huntington in his famous book *The Clash of Civilizations*. This theory presupposes that future wars will be between what he calls "civilizations," namely cultural/political entities that are based to no small extent on the national religious beliefs of the peoples within them. (We shall explore this fascinating theme later on, since both the theory and its author became fashionable after 9/11.)

Moderate men such as President Khatami of Iran, and the distinguished American-based Pakistani writer, Akbar Ahmed, have been keen advocates for peace and for bridge-building Western-Islamic world dialogue. As these men are sincere, what they are supporting is in many ways a good thing.

But the problem is that they are basing it on their particular interpretation of Islam – a Shia one with Khatami and a Sunni one in the case of Professor Ahmed – that does not always bear a relationship to the early history and teaching of their own faith. (If you want an easily readable account of Islam by a leading moderate, you cannot do better than read Professor Ahmed's well-written books.) Both of them look, understandably, to Islam's Golden Age, when Islamic civilization was far more advanced than the West, and far more tolerant of the Christians and Jews in their midst than Europeans were of their Jewish and other non-Christian populations.

However, when I read Ahmed's books – the story of the creation of the Taj Mahal in the then Muslim ruled Mughal Empire of north India, for example, or the moving lyrics of Moorish troubadours in Islamic-ruled Spain – I am reminded of British books that tell how the British Empire brought peace, medicine, and the rule of law to so many parts of the world. It is not simply that without the wise, tolerant, benevolent third Mughal emperor, Akbar, in the fifteenth century that the British would have found the conquest and consolidation of India far more difficult to accomplish three hundred years later. It is surely that like the Mughals – invaders from central Asia – we, the British, should never have been invading these countries at all. Invading and conquering other peoples is wrong, and it is not necessary to spreading the Gospel.

We should also remember that the West never conquered China, yet faithful American, British, and other missionaries spread the Good News of Jesus Christ all over that vast country. Today, not only does the church still survive there, despite decades of intermittent Communist persecution, but its biggest growth has been since Mao expelled the Western missionaries in the early 1950s. Few countries have been as evangelistically active as the United States, yet America's overseas colonies have always been tiny. God may have used the European lust for empire in the nineteenth century for godly men and women to proclaim the truth worldwide, for he also used pagan rulers in Old Testament times for his purposes as well.

To put it another way, just because some good things came out of many of the Islamic conquests in past years, that does not mean that moderate Muslims can legitimately explain them away. For it is indisputable that by Mohammed's death in 632 he was not only the spiritual leader of a dynamic new faith, but also the political/military ruler of most of what is now the Arabian peninsula. While some of this expansion can be attributed to his enthusiastic converts, much of it, including that of the formerly predominantly Jewish and Christian regions, was not by words but by the sword – moving that final *s* from the end of the word to the beginning makes all the difference.

After Mohammed's death, the Islamic empire spread faster and wider than any other set of conquests in history before or since. Even the Mongol warrior, Genghis (or Chinggis) Khan, whose empire spread from the Polish border to the Chinese coast never ruled so wide and geographically disparate a kingdom, and the British Empire was not geographically contiguous and took longer to assemble. From the Atlantic coast of Spain in the west to what is now the Pakistani borderlands in the east was under the single sway of the Prophet's successors, the Caliphs.

When Iraq was a Christian country

Iraq was heavily populated by Christians and Jews – Jews who had, in the most part, lived there continuously since the days of the Babylonian exile, and Christians who claimed biological descent from the Assyrians of Old Testament times. There was an enormous Christian-Jewish population, obviously, in what we now call the Holy Land, and the same was true of Egypt as well. Many of the descendants of those seventh century Jews continued to live there until the twentieth century.

There are still Christian churches of various kinds in the region – Saddam Hussein's equally notorious Deputy Prime Minister, Tariq Aziz, is from Iraq's tiny Assyrian Orthodox Church minority. Until recently there were large numbers of Palestinian Christians, many of whom have now emigrated to the United States (72 per cent of Arab Americans in 2001 were, according to *The Economist*, of Christian, not Muslim, origin). Likewise, depending on whether you use official government or unofficial Christian estimates, 6 to 12 per cent of Egyptians are even today members of the Coptic Christian community. While many of them are members of the Coptic Orthodox Church, a theological descendant of a semi-heretical early Christian group, the Monophysites, many Coptic Christians are actively Evangelical, a happy legacy to a large extent of years of faithful evangelism by American Presbyterian missionaries.

In the seventh century it was very different: The entire region was filled with Christians and Jews. Because the area has been under Islamic sway for so long, we tend to think that it has always been like that, which is far from being the case. The Islamic invasions were against lands that were heavily Judaeo-Christian. One should add that there were also large smatterings of paganism, as in Mohammed's own land of Arabia. Since this part of the world was near the now fast declining Sassanian Empire, there was also Zoroastrianism, the ancient religion of Persia, again going back to Old Testament times.

Explaining away an awkward past

One of the sad things I found in my research for this book was the way in which authors of Christian background try to explain away the conquests in ways in which secular, Muslim, or Jewish writers do not. (Eagle-eyed readers will spot this from some of the books listed in the bibliography.) There is a sense in which some of them want to be politically correct in order to show that professing Christians are not prejudiced.

With others, mainly Evangelicals, they are rightly keen to do nothing to hinder effective evangelism among Muslims, and so they therefore go out of their way to avoid what they think is creating needless offence. Here their motivation is impeccable, and their reasoning is nothing but spiritual, but one has to say that their grasp of history is distinctly shaky. That is why I have often found entirely secular history books more helpful, since their main aim is to find out what actually happened, without any need to make the discoveries more palatable.

And, when it comes to issues such as the Crusades, both professed Christian and overtly Evangelical writers are absolutely right to say that such activities were entirely wrong, for reasons that will become apparent. So, on the basis of my interpretation of the many fascinating works of Princeton historian Bernard Lewis, and of books like *The Cambridge Illustrated History of the Islamic World*, we have to say that the massive Muslim wars of conquest were exactly that. They had, in effect, the sword in one hand and the Qu'ran in the other.

How to think through some thorny issues

In addition, I do not think that one is being in any sense anti-Islamic, unthinkingly pro-Western, or politically incorrect in saying all this. For example, today it is politically correct to say that imperialism is wrong. With that statement I would agree. But if it is wrong for Westerners to have conquered large parts of the globe in the nineteenth century, surely it was equally wrong for the Arab Islamic armies to have done exactly that in the seventh. Conquest is conquest! As we have just seen, the rationale for the European conquests – medicine, law, civilization – are exactly the same that can be given for the seventh century Muslim invasions, which similarly brought huge technical, legal, and medicinal benefits to those they conquered.

Ironically, for example, in light of the present-day harsh treatment of women in much of the Middle East in Taliban Afghanistan, women in the lands of the Islamic conquest enjoyed property rights that were not to be granted to women in the West for centuries. Now Western women have fullest possible such rights, but until the nineteenth century, all married women's property in many European countries, like Britain, became the automatic property of their husband upon marriage. In Islamic countries, a woman kept her title rights to at least half of it and sometimes the whole of it both during her marriage and after her husband's death.

However, can the limited emancipation of women be regarded as a legitimizing factor for the Muslim conquest of, say, Jerusalem in AD 638? (The fact that what we call the Holy Land was under Christian rule until around this time was a major factor in launching the Crusades around 450 years later.) The answer has to be no. It is unlikely that the invaders were thinking of bringing the benefits of Arabic enlightenment when their great conquests began. A mix of the desire for power and booty, along with a passionate conviction that they were doing the will of Allah is surely more convincing a reason, with the later benefits being a happy by-product rather than the main cause.

When Spain was Muslim ruled: El Andalus

One thing we forget, in thinking that the Arab lands from Morocco to Iraq were not always Muslim, is that countries that are at present counted as being in the Christian world were under Muslim rule as well. Any American of Spanish, Portugese, or Sicilian descent has ancestors who were under Islamic rule – and in the case of Spain, for nearly eight hundred years. The Spanish region Andalucia is named after the original Islamic word for their Spanish conquests: El Andalus (sometimes written as *Al Andalus*). Numerous Spanish words have North African Muslim (or Moorish) origin, and some, like alcohol, have come down to us in English. A great deal of Spanish and Latin American culture is in large part derived from the Moorish era in Spain, and through the large Spanish Empire of many years later has thus spread worldwide. (The same could be said, to a more limited extent, of Sicilian culture, which was reclaimed from Muslim rule much earlier.)

The conquest of the Iberian Peninsula (now Spain and Portugal) began in AD 711. By AD 732 they had conquered nearly all of it and had also successfully seized much of what is now the Mediterranean coast of France as well. It was only one battle that stopped them from getting even further, and conquering the whole of Western Europe as well. This was the Battle of Tours, sometimes called the Battle of Poitiers, since the actual site is somewhere between those two French towns. Here the forces of the victorious Frankish King Charles Martel finally beat the Islamic invaders and saved the rest of Europe from Muslim conquest. As the famous British eighteenth century writer Edward Gibbon described it, had the battle gone the other way, the university halls of Oxford in England would not be the dreaming spires we all admire. Rather, they would now be the dreaming minarets of Islamic scholars teaching the Qu'ran to the students of a Muslim England. It was, as one historian wrote about another such famous battle, a close run thing.

From the Atlantic Ocean to the Indian Ocean – one big Islamic empire

In 732 Mohammed had been dead for a mere century. He could probably never have imagined that his followers would have conquered so vast a swathe of territory. It was an empire that stretched from Spain in the West to the borders of India in the

East, a territory far bigger than anything ruled over by the Romans. Not only that, but in one sense it still exists, now nearly fourteen hundred years since his death. North Africa, Iraq, Egypt, Palestine – these were once Christian countries. Now they are part of the *Dar al-Islam*.

With the exception of the slither of Holy Land taken briefly by the Crusaders in the Middle Ages – and in the case of Jerusalem itself for less than a century – it was not until our own times that these lands were ruled by anyone other than Muslims. The loss of Spain by 1492 in Western Europe was balanced by the conquest of the Balkans in the same century by the Ottoman Turks, so what was lost in one part of Europe was compensated for by gains in another.

Christianity suffers for a past mistake

In the fourth century, Christians had arguably made a major mistake, one that it would take until the Reformation to begin to rectify – and, one could argue, was not corrected even then. This was the decision, understandable after centuries of persecution, for Christianity to become the official religion of the Roman Empire.

This is not to make a particularly Protestant point, since, as I will show, once the Reformation began, many Protestant countries made exactly the same error. The doctrine that I am addressing here is that of the relationship between church and state. I deal with this from an internal Christian point of view in another book *(Five Leading Reformers)*. Here we are looking at it from the way in which it affected relations between Muslims and Christians.

Once the state becomes involved in the Christian church, it soon gives itself the right to be involved in internal doctrinal disputes as well. If the church is an official part of the state, the secular rulers want the kind of church that will not create either political trouble or become a source of political rivalry. In dictatorships especially – Rome was no democracy – this is even more important, since the state is, in essence, ruled by a single all-powerful individual.

So as soon as Constantine made Christianity legal – technically speaking it was not until later that it formally became the official faith – he began to intervene in what were purely spiritual and doctrinal matters. Furthermore, he was doing so not as an ordinary Christian, if he ever truly was converted, or as a church leader, but as the emperor.

While we would probably be happy to go along with most of the theological decisions of the early councils of the church, we can thank God for enabling them to turn out the way they did, because in reality these were effectively as much political decisions as doctrinal. Indeed, some of Constantine's successors supported what we would now regard as heresy, such as on the matter of Christ's true nature, the Arian controversy. Thankfully, the good guys won in the end. But I think we could ascribe it as much to divine mercy, to God preserving his church, than to the councils themselves, since the political pressure put on such gatherings is all too apparent from the record.

Christians persecuting other Christians and other tragedies

As a tragic result of making just one version of the Christian faith the official religion in individual countries, the Christians were soon persecuting other Christians over doctrinal disputes. Some of the disputes are interesting, since they mirror twenty-first century dilemmas. For example, there was the question of, as the state decreed, readmitting to Christian fellowship those who denied Christ during persecution – something still part of a debate between the so-called house churches and the government-sponsored Three-Self Patriotic Movement Churches in China to this very day.

But rather than sort them out on a discussion basis, the full power of the Roman Empire was used actively to persecute those who took the unofficial view. Whatever we might think of people whose denominations are different from our own, I trust we would not want to imprison them, let alone put them to death.

But imprisonment, exile, and sometimes even death were the results of Christianity becoming part and parcel of the Roman Imperial state. Even if an emperor was personally godless or immoral, and many of them were, he still had an enormous say in what happened in the church. He appointed the leaders as well – something that the Byzantine Roman emperor continued to do for over a thousand years, until the conquest of the Ottoman Turks finally ended the Eastern Roman Empire in 1453. (The city they seized was officially called Constantinople – the *polis* or city of Constantine, since he founded it. We in the West forget that the Eastern Roman Empire – Byzantium – outlasted the Western Roman Empire by nearly a thousand years.) This is called *caesaro-papism* – Caesar (the emperor) merging in his person many of the powers held later on in the West by the pope.

Even in the twenty-first century in Britain, the prime minister has the final say in who is appointed to high office in the Church of England, as Tony Blair showed in 2002. Such state power over the church is a direct descendant of the Faustian bargain struck between church and state in the reign of Constantine.

Islam – a by-product of Constantine?

The fact of government-supported Christians persecuting dissenting Christians was, in the three centuries that followed Constantine, to have the direst of indirect results. Today, we would be mainly in theological agreement with the majority of fellow Christians on most issues, and so would have avoided persecution. Many of the key issues upon which Protestant and Catholic Christians agree today were fought out at many meetings, or church councils. But the point here is that Christians, or in the case of those with more extreme views, outright heretics, were being actively punished *by the state* for their views.

Furthermore, in the case of the group we now call the Nestorian Church, they were, whatever their undeniable quirks, spreading Christianity to the uttermost ends of the earth, as Christ had commanded. Not only that, but they were doing it the old fashioned way, through missionary endeavour and cross-cultural evangelism. Nestorian missionaries got as far as China, and were still there centuries later when Marco Polo came to visit what was then the Mongol Yuan Empire there. That is not to say that more theologically orthodox Christians were not also involved in mission, but so far as the lands east of the Roman Empire were concerned, the Nestorians were the main group involved for a long time. One of the reasons why they could travel so far east is that the Sassanian emperors of Persia did *not* persecute them. This is a sad reflection – professed Christians fleeing a Christian empire because a Christian emperor persecutes them with the blessings of the Church.

So when Islam erupted on the world in the seventh century, some Christian groups were actually glad. No longer would their fellow Christians be persecuting them. To the Muslims, all Christians – (Western) Catholic, Nestorian, (Eastern) Orthodox – were the same. They were all *dhimmi*, monotheists, permitted by the Qu'ran therefore to practise their faith, and sometimes known as a result as Peoples of the Book. Such Christians did not, therefore, have full civic rights. But then they didn't have in effect such rights already under Byzantine rule. All the Muslim conquests did was to substitute one kind of oppression for another, and for all intents and purposes Islamic oppression was less obnoxious to them than to be harassed by the church and state authorities.

This is a tragic reflection on what the Constantinian combination of church and state could and clearly did do. In time, whole swathes of the world that had been predominantly Christian, at least in allegiance, ended up going over to Islam. Today there are still the remnants of these ancient Christian churches, but, as the well-known writer Bat Ye'or has shown us, they are a sad and rather inward looking spectacle. Only the Coptic Church in Egypt survives in comparatively large numbers; and there, thankfully, many Coptic Christians have turned to a more active biblical Evangelical faith.

When Christianity became a religion of place

Christianity is a universal faith, not limited to any one ethnic group or geographical area. This is because it is universally true! But the other effect of the Constantinian settlement is that, over time, it became a religion of *place*. This is what we now call *Christendom*. In the West we rather arrogantly think of it as applying just to Western Europe, but, properly understood, it originally encompassed a Catholic Western Europe and a Byzantine Eastern Europe. That is not to say that Christians didn't exist elsewhere – as I mentioned earlier, Marco Polo was astonished to find Nestorian Christians as far east as China. There were pockets of Christianity in places like Egypt and Lebanon (from whom today's Maronite Christians descend). Likewise, there was also a tiny Christian church in southern India, the ancestor of today's Ma Thoma churches. A church also existed in Ethiopia. But for a very long time Christianity was, for all intents and purposes, a European religion. Certainly within Europe, within Christendom, the feeling existed that this was the area in which Christians dwelt.

That is also not to say that evangelism did not take place. Much evangelism happened in Europe, especially after the fall of the Roman Empire, when brave missionaries took the Gospel to the pagan tribes of present-day Germany or England. We all know the exciting tales of St Patrick, the missionary to Ireland. Some parts of modern Europe did not become Christian until comparatively late, until the tenth or eleventh centuries. The evangelistic zeal of the book of Acts was not dead, but the main point is that it was still done almost overwhelmingly within Europe.

One of the greatest tragedies was when, during the time of the Crusades, William of Rubruck was sent out to the court of the Great Khan, all the way over in Mongolia. The Great Khan, a near descendant of the infamous Genghis Khan, asked the pope to send missionaries so Christianity could have a fair hearing in his now vastly increasing realm. But there was no official response to the request. In time, many of the Khan's descendants converted not to Christianity but to Islam, such as in Iran. Since the Mongols were the conquerors not the vanquished, in their case conversion was entirely a matter of choice and not of compulsion. They *chose* Islam. Often the only Christians that they saw were the rather feeble descendants of the early Nestorian missionaries, who, as William of Rubruck realized, were already in a sorry state.

My book *A Crash Course in Church History* looks at this in more detail. But I think it is fair to say that it was not really until the Reformation and the discovery of the Americas that European Christians engaged in serious missionary activity *outside of Europe*. Meanwhile, the Mongol rulers of Persia, the Il-Khans, had converted to Islam, as had those Central Asian Mongols from whom Tamerlaine (Timur-I-Leng) and the great Mughal emperors of India descended. Present day Indonesia and West Africa were turning to Islam not through the sword but through traders and merchants bringing their Muslim faith with them. They had remembered that theirs was a universal faith. The Christians, who were supposed to have such a faith themselves – and the true one at that – had not.

In other words, when Christianity was a persecuted religion under pagan Roman emperors, it spread all over the place like wildfire. When it became inexorably linked with the state, it remained in Europe. It was not until the sixteenth century that the Catholic Church began serious evangelism beyond Europe's borders. Even there, as anyone who has seen the film *The Mission* will know, entirely European politics made a major difference in how Latin America was evangelized – nor did it help, in such places, that Christianity also came with Western conquest. We recall today the great eras of Protestant mission. But when did they begin? Not until the *eighteenth century!*

So we had churches in Egypt, Syria, and Ethiopia ossified and concentrated more on survival than expansion. We had churches under recent Islamic conquest in lands such as the Balkans. And finally, we had in Western and Central Europe a church that was growing, that was evangelistic, but only within the confines of its own geographical area.

The sad fact remains that Christianity did not rediscover its real, universal roots until the cozy world of Western Christendom was broken asunder by the Reformation. But by the time that had happened, much of Eastern Christendom, which had formally split from the West in 1054, was now under the yoke of Muslim Ottoman rule, not to escape until the nineteenth century. This was because Christianity thought of itself as the religion of a *place*. If you lived in Europe, you were a Christian; and, by and large, the reverse applied as well. Power was shared, in much of Christendom, between a spiritual leader, the pope, and a secular ruler, the Holy Roman emperor, who, as medieval popes did not hesitate to point out, owed their *spiritual* allegiance to the papacy. The pope himself was a secular ruler, being directly sovereign over large portions of central Italy, right up until Italian unification in the late nineteenth century. (The Vatican City state is the remnant of the old papal states, and explains why, until 1978, the pope was invariably an Italian.)

Meanwhile, while our European ancestors were fighting each other in many different kingdoms and principalities, Islam was emerging as a gigantic superpower.

The Golden Age of Islam

The Ummayid caliphs ruled from Spain to the Himalayas, and, when they were deposed in the Middle East, continued to rule over most of today's Spain for a few centuries more. The Abbasid caliphs – best known to us in imaginary tales such as *The Thief of Baghdad* or *A Thousand and One Nights* – were in fact very real and immensely powerful. Not all the later caliphs ruled as much in practice as in theory, and sometimes breakaway caliphates arose, such as the Shia Muslim Fatimids in Egypt or the later Ummayid caliphs in Spain. But there was a great commonality of Muslim-ruled territory over this vast expanse of land, one that was not broken up by the occasional political secession. All these territories were part of an enormous multiethnic, multiracial *Dar al-Islam*, or House of Islam. You could go from Spain to Iran and be effectively part of the same country all the way.

Take the great medieval explorer, judge, and general all-around polymath, Ibn Battuta, whose *Travels* are even more astonishing (and better authenticated) than those of the better known Venetian, Marco Polo.

An Islamic empire from Morocco to East Asia

The extraordinary thing about Ibn Battuta is that he was able to go from present-day Spain and Morocco to what is now China nearly without even leaving Muslim territory. In East Asia, much of this was the result of conversion growth, brought by Arab traders and other Islamic merchants to what is now Malaysia and Indonesia. With the latter, the fact that such an enormous country – well over 130 million people – is predominantly Muslim should surely be a reproach to the failure of Western lands to send counteracting missionaries for over five centuries after the Islamic missionaries first arrived.

By the time of Battuta, the great Islamic state of El Andalus was beginning to fade, a victim of the military success of the Christian *Reconquista* under the kings of Aragon and Castile. The Golden Age of Andalus – in which a leading Jewish thinker like Maimonides was able to thrive alongside more orthodox Muslims such as Averröes – shows how Muslims at that time were far more tolerant to non-Muslims, Christians included, than European Christians were to the Jews and Muslims within their own borders. (As writers have commented since 1998, when Osama bin Laden first became known in the West, his public nostalgia for the halcyon days of Islamic rule in Spain are rather ironic, since they practised a tolerance of non-Muslims of a kind he finds abhorrent.)

So history, then, is important, not just because of the way in which it explains the present, but because of the lessons that it teaches us. The Bible is filled with history, and as Christians in the twenty-first century, we reject the study of the past at our peril.

CHAPTER 3

The Rise and Fall
of Islamic Superpowers

Nowadays, we take it for granted that the West is globally at the top. No power on earth even approaches that of the United States, for example. But this has not always been the case. Right up until the twentieth century there was an Islamic superpower, ruling not only over the Middle East, but also much of North Africa and, crucially, over large swathes of Southeast Europe as well. This was the Ottoman Empire, which on two occasions nearly reached into Central and Western Europe as well. Yet in 1918 it lay shattered and defeated, a loss that Osama bin Laden and many in the Muslim world mourn, with much bitterness, to this very day. This chapter examines the rise and fall of that great empire, and its all too present consequences for us in the twenty-first century.

New Islamic empires
arise as old ones fall

However, for all the losses in the West, there were substantial gains in the East. In what is now India, different Islamic groups, often based in what is now Afghanistan, were making inroads into Hindu territory. By the fourteenth century, the Mughals, descendants of the great warrior Tamerlaine (Timur-I-Leng), were conquering large parts of northern India. Emperor Akbar is one of the most revered of all Muslim Indian rulers, and in some shape or another the Mughal Empire was to last until finally extinguished by the British in the eighteenth and nineteenth centuries. The Taj Mahal is perhaps one of the most famous tombs in the world, and is renowned everywhere as an object of beauty. It is also the most lasting memorial to the period of Islamic rule in India, since most of the subcontinent was overrun by the early eighteenth century. (Only Britain ever succeeded in conquering all of it.) Samarkand in Central Asia became one of the most fabled cities in the world, a monument to the great Islamic states of that region.

More ominously for the Christians in Europe, another powerful Islamic empire was slowly beginning its long decades of conquest. This was the Ottoman Empire, which lasted right up until the twentieth century and was to be one of the largest and most successful empires of all time.

One of the biggest mistakes of the Crusaders was that in 1204 instead of trying to launch another attack on the Holy Land, they decided to plunder and conquer the Orthodox Christian Byzantine Empire. In so doing, and in creating a brief Latin empire for only fifty-seven years, they fatally weakened the one Christian power capable of preventing a Muslim invasion of Europe through the Balkans. Already much of what is now Turkish Anatolia had been conquered by new Muslim invaders from Central Asia – the Seljuk Turks. In time they were succeeded by an even more successful ethnic Turkish dynasty, the Ottomans.

The rise of the Ottoman Empire

By 1345 the Ottomans had already begun their conquest of the hitherto Christian Balkan Peninsula. Perhaps the most famous of their battles – even though it was actually a draw – was that of Kosovo in 1389. Here the Ottomans with, it has to be said, some Christian allies, fought a Serb army under the Serbian prince Lazar. While the Serbian kingdom did not fully fall to Ottoman rule for some years afterwards, this was to prove a psychological blow from which the Serbs never entirely recovered. Even as late as the 1990s, Serbs were still massacring tens of thousands of completely innocent Bosnian Muslims as part of a warped revenge for this defeat over six hundred years ago. This time the murders were being done by nominal Christians, something that we should not forget as we contemplate the large-scale deaths at the hands of Islamic extremists in New York and Washington, DC. The crusader mentality of blood and gore has not altogether vanished.

By the fifteenth century, while the Islamic world was losing El Andalus, countries familiar from news bulletins in the late twentieth century – Bosnia, Serbia, and Greece – were being vanquished by Muslim invaders. At the Battle of Mohacs in 1526, even a Hungarian army was routed, and most of present-day Hungary was to fall to Muslim rule until the end of the seventeenth century. Here Protestants received much more freedom from the Muslim rulers of Transylvania than Hungarian and German Protestants received from the Catholic Habsburg rulers of the rump Hungarian kingdom over the border in what are now Slovakia and Croatia, which the Ottomans failed to capture. In 1453 the great Byzantine city of Constantinople also fell, ending over a thousand years of Christian imperial rule and empire. That part of the world has never been regained for Christianity, even though there is still an Orthodox patriarch in what is now called Istanbul. The old bulwark of Eastern Christianity against Islamic invasion was no more.

In 1529 even Vienna, the capital of the great Catholic Habsburg dynasty, was under siege, although in this case the attempt failed and the West survived to breathe another day. As with the Battle of Tours/Poitiers in 732, it was a close run thing – had Vienna fallen, then all of Central and Western Europe would have been wide open to Islamic invasion, just as Luther was beginning to preach the Protestant message. Here one could say that the permanent Muslim threat to Western and Central Europe actually helped the nascent Reformation. This was because the Holy Roman Emperor Charles V was too busy trying to defend his

Austrian, Italian, and Spanish domains against Islamic invasion to find time to crush the growing Protestant theological rebellion in his German domains.

So by 1529 Spain was free from Islamic rule, but the Balkan Peninsula was under it for the first time. Islam now spread from the Atlantic coast of Morocco in the west to the islands of Indonesia in the east, the greatest extent it had ever reached. Nearly all of this vast arc of Muslim population was also under Muslim political rule, with the two gigantic Ottoman and Mughal Empires ruling over millions of people, whether over Christians in Eastern Europe or Hindus in India.

The Ottomans were also able to recreate much of the old Abbasid Empire, ruling from the border of Iran in the east to Morocco in the west, with only Spain (now Christian) and Iran (still Muslim, but under its own rulers) eluding them. The Ottomans also resurrected the old Ummayad and Abbasid title of *Caliph*, which meant that the Ottoman sultan had a kind of spiritual as well as political control over most of Islam. (The Ottoman Caliphate existed right up until 1924, when the now secular Turkish Parliament abolished it – a source of great sorrow to Osama bin Laden and those of his way of thinking even today.)

The Ottoman conquests are a good riposte to anyone who asks, "What about the Crusades?" For there can be no justification for what was nothing other than a pure war of military imperialistic conquest. The Crusades, as I have argued, were not right, but then nor was the Ottoman invasion of Christian Southeast Europe either!

Dhimmi status – Christians in the lands of the Ottoman caliphs

In Islamic Europe and the Holy Land, the Christians were given *dhimmi* status. This meant that they were not given full rights and were unable to hold high office. But as "people of the book," or members, along with Jews, of a monotheistic faith recognized by Mohammed, they had special protected status, which in practise varied according to the Islamic state in which they found themselves. As Bat Ye'or, a writer much admired by many American Evangelicals, has shown, this had a thoroughly emasculating effect on many of the Christian remnants in that region. The once great Christian churches of Iraq, for example, are now pale shadows of what they had been in the past. (The fact that Iraqi Christians have never been as persecuted as their fellow believers in Saudi Arabia is something that we should recall when we think and pray about that region.)

The Ottoman Empire's Christian subjects were divided up in what were called *millets*. These were groupings arranged not according to nationality but *religion*. (I explore this at much greater length in my book *Why the Nations Rage*.) Your identity was a *religious* one – Orthodox, Catholic, Jewish, and, of course, Muslim. This meant, in the Christian Balkans, for example, that the Greeks, Romanians, Serbs, and Bulgarians would all be lumped together in the *Orthodox millet*, whose spiritual head was the Orthodox patriarch in Istanbul. This tended to favour the Greeks, something that was later to be a cause of nationalism in the nineteenth century, as the Greeks, Serbs, and other groups began to rebel and demand independence.

Here I should say that although Ottoman rule was not nearly as enlightened as the Ummayad rule had been in El Andalus, the Ottoman Turks were at least entirely nonracist. *Anyone* who converted to Islam could hold office, and this meant that many Slavic Europeans, and assorted dark-skinned races in or near Africa, could hold even the highest positions in the empire, as high as Grand Vizier itself.

In Bosnia and Albania, many European Ottoman subjects therefore converted to Islam. There is an often vitriolic debate among nationalist historians today in the Balkans as to exactly who today's Bosnian Muslims are in terms of ancestry. Tens of thousands of entirely innocent Bosnian Muslims were massacred in the 1990s by Serbian supposed Christians, in revenge, according to Serb extremist interpretations, for the fact that the ancestors of those Bosnians had converted to the religion of the hated

Ottoman Turkish rulers. This is something that should appal us today, and it is a shame that more Christians were not in the forefront of condemning the massacres of evil men who carried out their deeds in the name of our faith, according to their rather warped view of their past.

Here is a puzzle for you: Why do people like Osama bin Laden and other contemporary Muslims keep blaming us for the Crusades, which began over nine hundred years ago, and yet not denounce us for very recent massacres, some – like at Racak, as recently as 1999 – of innocent Muslims by Serbian Orthodox soldiers? Remember too that the Crusaders also massacred local Jews and Arab Christians as well as Muslims. They were utterly indiscriminate in their slaughter – whereas the victims at Srebrenica in Bosnia and Racak in Kosovo were entirely Muslim.

Missing out on the enormous developments in the West

Up until 1683, when they failed to capture Vienna, the Ottoman Empire was one of the most powerful on earth. Rulers such as Suleiman the Magnificent were feared everywhere, especially in Europe. Right up until the eighteenth century, the so-called Barbary Corsairs from North Africa would raid European coastal towns for white slaves. It was the Ottoman Muslim Empire that seemed to have the military advantage. The effects of this can be seen in Eastern Europe to this day. As people from there often moan, they were Europeans, but, being under alien Muslim rule, completely missed out on the Renaissance, the Reformation, the European discovery of the Americas, the scientific revolution of the seventeenth and eighteenth centuries, and the Industrial Revolution. That is a lot to miss!

Militarily the Ottomans might have had the upper hand, but as that last paragraph shows, it was in Western Europe where the enormous epoch-making changes were taking place. Nowadays, even the most secular of scientists will happily admit that Christians in places such as Poland and Britain played critical roles in the scientific discoveries of the sixteenth and seventeenth centuries. (In other words, many of the key breakthroughs were made *before* the Enlightenment of the eighteenth century, by which present-day humanists set so much store.) Whereas in the Middle Ages many of the amazing scientific and medical developments were being made initially by Muslims, such as Avicenna, and then travelling to the West, now the big discoveries were being made in the West – and staying there. As Bernard Lewis has shown so clearly in his important book *What Went Wrong*, the lands of Islam were sunk in complacency and torpor. The initiative was now very much with the Christian West, psychologically also helped, many historians feel, by the interaction with the entirely different non-European civilizations of the New World. The old Islamic advantage was long past.

The slow decline
of the Islamic empires

As previously mentioned, the Ottoman Turks had failed in their attempt to capture Vienna in 1683. By 1699 they had to sign a treaty to their disadvantage for the first time in their long history. Likewise, in South Asia the great Mughal Empire was beginning to pass its peak and to fall into British hands, starting with the victorious general, Clive of India. The Russians, similarly, were making strides further east, although here it would take into the early nineteenth century before they were able effectively to rule large swathes of formerly Islamic lands.

By the nineteenth century, the Ottoman Empire was nicknamed the "Sick Man of Europe." Some of Greece was able to gain independence in the 1830s, though the present-day borders of Greece date from the 1920s. Other parts of the Balkans slowly followed, with increasing degrees of autonomy and then outright independence, from the 1850s right up until the Second Balkan War in 1913. But for the British, who were deeply concerned with Russia becoming too powerful, the "Sick Man" would have died much sooner. (When asked whether this policy had been a good thing, the great Victorian statesman Lord Salisbury said that Britain had "backed the wrong horse"!) In the Crimean War of 1854–56 and then in the massive war of Balkan liberation of 1876–78, it was only British intervention that saved the Ottomans from losing most of their empire to the Russians.

The British were not completely altruistic, however. They and the French, aided by Rothschild money, constructed the Suez Canal, which linked the Mediterranean to the Red Sea. This meant that British forces, instead of having to circumnavigate Africa to get to their empire in India, could now take a much shorter route along the canal. Although Egypt and the Sudan nominally remained under Ottoman rule, they were, in effect, British colonies with a semi-puppet local king, the Khedive. The first Khedive, Ali Pasha, and his family were actually from Albania and started life as street tobacco sellers. Their rise is a classic example of the essentially classless nature of Muslim Ottoman society, in which anyone of talent could get to the top.

The last of the dynasty, the rather corrupt King Farouk, was deposed in 1952, in a coup that eventually led to the famous Arab socialist and nationalist leader Gamal Abdel Nasser coming to power. Recently my wife and I stayed in a beautiful old bed and breakfast in the Cotswolds. The husband of the couple who owned it seemed very upper class and frightfully English. But he was in fact an exiled member of the Egyptian royal family. He gave up his claim to the throne because he and his British wife are keen Christians! So while he lives in a cottage and not a palace, he will be going to a far better place one day than any of his illustrious ancestors.

By the start of the twentieth century, all the great Islamic empires of South and Central Asia had disappeared, under the rule of either the British or the Russians, with Afghanistan being an uneasy buffer zone between these two great empires. Only the Ottoman Empire remained, still ruling over the Middle East and a considerable part of Balkan Europe. Fatefully for them, the British and Russians had reconciled their differences by 1907. In two vicious wars, the First and Second Balkan Wars of 1912–13, the Turks lost most of the European territory that they had hitherto retained.

Then in 1914 the Ottomans made their fatal mistake. World War I had just broken out. Instead of siding with their old nineteenth century ally, Britain, they joined the war instead on the side of the German Empire. This soon proved to be a military disaster, despite their occasional victories, such as at Gallipoli, a terrible battle in which many Australian and New Zealand soldiers died. The British, under General Allenby, started off from British-ruled Egypt and began a campaign of slow conquest of the Ottoman Empire. Meanwhile, a psychologically strange but strategically brilliant young officer, T.E. Lawrence, was seconded to foment an Arab rebellion against the Turks. This proved phenomenally successful, and as anyone who has seen the film will know, he was soon being called Lawrence of Arabia.

The desert revolt and the great betrayal

Theologically speaking, from an Islamic perspective, the war was an interesting one. The Turkish sultan was the Caliph of the Faithful, so in theory obedience to him was a Muslim command. However, most Arabs decided to support the rebellion, since its Arab leader was Feisal, the sharif of Mecca. Feisal was the head of the Hashemite part of the Quraishi clan, the family from which the Prophet himself came. The sharifs were also Mohammed's direct blood descendants (as are the current rulers of Morocco), and this gave them enormous prestige in the Arab world. Feisal was the Custodian of the two holy places, Mecca and Medina, and this further added to his aura.

So while Allenby's British and Australian troops were liberating Jerusalem, Lawrence and Feisal were successfully overthrowing the centuries-long Turkish rule over the Arab peoples. But unknown to Feisal and possibly not to Lawrence, things were not that simple. For during the war, before the Americans joined the Allied side in 1917, the British and French had seen war with the

Ottoman Empire as a wonderful way of expanding their own respective domains. The French Monsieur Picot and the British Sir Mark Sykes came together and in the now infamous Sykes-Picot agreement carved up the Ottoman Empire between Britain and France.

Woodrow Wilson, the American president, was a man of firm moral views. Because of this, and because also of the consequent founding of the League of Nations, Britain and France could not simply annex these new territories to their empires outright in 1918, when the Ottoman Empire was finally defeated. (Some of that empire also went briefly to Greece and to Italy, but that need not detain us here.) So instead, what are now the states of Iraq, Syria, Lebanon, Israel, and Jordan became what were known as League of Nations mandates. Technically, the League itself ruled the mandated territories, but, as everyone knew, *in practise* they were ruled by the power given the various mandates, which for the countries of the Middle East meant Britain and France. (The United States also received some mandates, mainly small formerly German-ruled islands in the Pacific.)

Iraq, a country now very much in the news, had not existed as such for centuries, since that region had long been a buffer zone between the Ottoman and Iranian Empires. Its present-day boundaries are those of three former Ottoman *vilayets*, or provinces, and the modern state was invented by Winston Churchill, who was then Britain's Colonial Secretary. Much of Syria and Lebanon had been under Crusader rule in the Middle Ages, so went rather appropriately to the descendants of the Franks, the French. Britain gained the lion's share, since now, as well as ruling Egypt, she ruled the lands on the other side of the Suez Canal as well.

Furthermore, in 1917 the British Foreign Secretary, the Earl of Balfour, had made an official declaration permitting Jewish return to the Holy Land – hence the term the Balfour Declaration. Britain did not keep its full promise. Jewish emigration to Palestine remained a contentious issue right up until World War II, with the result that many more Jews died in Nazi hands than need have done. As a result of the Balfour Declaration, the dynamic nature of the Middle East was to change irrevocably, with results that echo to this very day.

The main point from our angle is the sense of enormous betrayal that Feisal and the Arab peoples got in 1918 when they discovered that there would not be the large Arab state for which they had fought so hard against the Turks. Feisal had thought that he would be ruling in Damascus. Instead, that was to become a French territory. The Middle East had ceased to be part of one empire only to become divided between two others. Not only that, but at least the Turks, whatever their faults, had been good Muslims. The British and French were Christian powers. For the first time in centuries, much of the Islamic heartland, including the third-holiest Muslim city, Jerusalem, would be under infidel rule. This was a major trauma to the Muslim Arab psyche.

Churchill did his best to make it up to the Hashemite dynasty. One of Feisal's sons became king of Iraq, and another one king of Transjordan (now just Jordan). The Hashemites had had no links with Iraq, since they came from the Hijaz, the part of what is now Saudi Arabia that borders on the Red Sea. Not only that, but Iraq was seen as an artificial creation. The northern part is Kurdish – the Kurds being the big losers of the 1918 settlement, since they were the one major Middle Eastern group not to end up with a homeland of their own. The central part, from which Saddam Hussein's family came, is Sunni Arab; the southern part is also Arab, but Shia Islamic in religion. Not surprisingly, the Iraqi Hashemites essentially survived only with British support, and when that ceased to be possible, they were overthrown and massacred in 1958. The Jordanian Hashemites are still quite present in Jordan, with the half-British King Abdullah on the throne, a Western-friendly descendant of Mohammed.

But the settlement of 1918–22 was very different from what the Arabs had envisaged, even though two of the Hashemites ended up on newly created thrones. The two Hashemite kings and the king of Egypt were seen as European stooges, and places like Palestine, Syria, and Lebanon were under direct Western rule. The great free Arab nation for which everyone had yearned was not to be. Self-determination, the watchword of Woodrow Wilson to the newly free Czechs, Poles, and other now-independent nations, clearly did not apply to the Arabs.

It is this betrayal more than the subsequent state of Israel, which did not come into being for another thirty years, that is the ultimate source of Arab rage. This is certainly the feeling of Fareed Zakaria, in his seminal *Newsweek* article "Why They Hate Us." Though the Turks were able to drive the Greeks out of Anatolia, the Greeks of the biblical city of Smyrna, who had been living there for thousands of years, were expelled – the city is now Turkish and called Izmir.

Uniquely, of all the nations defeated in 1923, Turkey was able to have a brand-new treaty with the West, and regained much of its lost territory. The new and victorious dictator, Kemal Ataturk (who had also won, as had Mustafa Kemal, at Gallipoli), abolished Islam as a state religion, introduced the Western alphabet, liberated women from the veil, and eliminated the Islamic fez hat for men. In Turkey, as Zakaria rightly shows, Westernization was associated with military victory and success. In the rest of the Islamic world, it went hand in hand with Western colonial domination and Arab humiliation.

The Hashemites may have gained Iraq and Jordan, but, important for our own times, they lost their ancient domain, the Hijaz. This was conquered in 1924 by King Abdul Aziz ibn Saud – usually known to us simply as Ibn Saud – the leader of the Saudi dynasty. His family had ruled the interior of Arabia for centuries, but he did not rule the coast and, more significantly, the two holiest shrines, Mecca and Medina. His conquest of them meant that not only did he now rule most of Arabia, now renamed Saudi Arabia after his family, but also the two holy places as well. This gave his family huge Islamic legitimacy, even though, unlike the Hashemites or the rulers of Morocco, he was *not* a blood descendant of the Prophet Mohammed. (Fatally, perhaps, he also conquered what had in the past been part of Yemen, the desert kingdom in which myrrh and frankincense had been produced since biblical times. The overwhelming majority of the Saudi 9/11 hijackers came from this conquered province.)

From the Arab humiliation to Osama bin Laden

This profound post-1918 sense of Arab humiliation and betrayal is crucial if we are to understand Osama bin Laden and the other extremists of the twenty-first century. We find some interesting references in bin Laden's speeches, for example (following a BBC and *Guardian* newspaper translation), what he said on 7 October 2001:

> What America is tasting now is something insignificant compared to what we have tasted for scores of years. Our nation [the Islamic world] has been tasting this humiliation and this degradation for more than 80 years.

Note the phrase "for more than 80 years." It is not more than *fifty*, which would tie in with the creation of the state of Israel, but *eighty*. This takes us back to World War I and the Franco-British decision to carve up the Ottoman Empire. It also harks back to the abolition of the Ottoman Empire in 1922 and the end of the Caliphate in 1924, these last two acts being not those of a European, but of a Muslim-born Turk, Kemal Ataturk. It was not the West that abolished the last Islamic superpower and the ancient post of Caliph, one that goes back to the Prophet's own immediate successors, but a secularized Muslim.

To extremist Muslims everywhere, of whom bin Laden is merely one among many, this represents double humiliation. Westerners had invaded the *Dar al-Islam*. People who ought to be proper Muslims, like Ataturk, were betraying the true faith. To the godfather of all hard-line Muslims, Sayyid Qutb, this is an especial betrayal. As we will see elsewhere, bin Laden did not really take up the Palestinian cause until well into 2002. He and his kind may dislike "Jews and Crusaders," but the ultimate enemy are the apostates within Islam, and those Westerners, such as the

United States today, who help them. Compared to this, even the existence of the state of Israel is secondary, because the arrival of the Jews in large numbers after the Balfour Declaration is in a sense only part of the deeper humiliation that happened at the same time. Had the Arabs had the state to which they felt entitled, back in 1918, there would, of course, have been no state of Israel.

Is Israel a by-product or the main cause of Islamic rage?

In that sense, Israel's creation is a by-product rather than the prime cause of Arab and Islamic humiliation. Jews had lived in the Arab world for centuries. Until the creation of the Israeli state in 1948, they had mainly done so in peace. As monotheists, they were protected and given *dhimmi* status, as one of the Peoples of the Book. Baghdad, for example, had an enormous Jewish population, and Jews lived in large numbers as far afield as Morocco. We must also not forget that there was no Arab equivalent of the Holocaust – it was white Westerners who massacred millions of Jews. (The Turks *did* slaughter hundreds of thousands of non-Muslims, but it was *Christian* Armenians they submitted to genocide, not their Jewish subjects.)

In addition, although they lived quietly with their majority Muslim neighbours, the Jews were still living as a tolerated minority in what was unquestionably an Islamic state. There was no question who was boss – the Muslim leadership. Jews were fine though, because they posed no threat to the overall Islamic predominance in these regions.

In 1918 when the Jews started to arrive in large numbers in the region we now call Israel, it was at the effective invitation of the British rulers of what had once been Muslim-ruled lands, and land that the Arabs felt should rightly have been theirs. Once more, this is not to take sides about whether the physical place of Israel is the fulfilment of Bible prophecy. Rather, I am describing a historical process and the Arab Muslim reactions to it. This is especially important to restate, since many of the Palestinians who objected to the Jewish settlements were and still are nominally Christian Arabs and *not* Muslims.

Whatever our prophetic views we must always distinguish between the *Palestinian* issue and that of *Islamic rage*, especially since the PLO leader Yasser Arafat does not hesitate to denounce Osama bin Laden, as we see elsewhere.

Bin Laden's dreams of a caliphate restored

Newspaper speculation in 2001 was that bin Laden wanted to be caliph himself. Hence the history that we have been looking at in this chapter has relevance to events in the world today. Unless he does something in the near future – *if* he is alive when you read this – this would now be hard to verify. But in terms of his ideology and that of his followers, the concept of restoring the caliphate does make sense. As Malise Ruthven points out in *A Fury for God*, there is a major element of entirely unrealistic Islamic thinking on this issue. Look again at the Muslim doctrine of jihad and the importance of all this will, I trust, become clearer.

CHAPTER 4

Core Muslim Beliefs

This is a book as much about Muslim rage as it is about Islam itself. It is also historical, since I contend that Islam's challenge to Christianity has existed since its inception nearly fourteen hundred years ago. So a Muslim picking up this book might be puzzled as to why I talk as much about jihad or Holy War as I do about much more peacefully orientated Sufi beliefs. Similarly, the book aims to explain what is going on in the world today rather than being primarily an evangelistic tool to help Christians reach out to the growing number of Muslims living around them.

Therefore, I have not concentrated quite so much on the specifics of Islamic theology as on the effect that those beliefs have had on the wider world down the centuries. We do need, however, to have at least some look at the foundation of Islam itself and on the life of its founder, Mohammed.

Don't insult the opposition!

Recently, some Christian leaders in the United States made derogatory statements about the young ages of some of Mohammed's later wives. They were perhaps mistaken for two reasons. First, insults are not the best way to get the attention of Mohammed's present-day followers. One of the things that I want my readers to come away with is a sense that Muslims around the world are not so much the enemy as they are people in urgent need of salvation in Jesus Christ. Jokes in wartime are often good for morale, as Hitler was the butt of many of them in World War II. But there is a huge difference between the present struggle against terrorism and the global wars of the twentieth century. Then we were fighting *nations* – Germany, Japan, and others. Now we are fighting as much an idea – militant Islam – as a particular people. As we discovered, over 70 per cent of Arab Americans are of Christian not Muslim ancestry. We are not, to a real extent, even fighting governments but groups, terrorists who are citizens of many different countries around the world.

Therefore, we want to "drain the swamp," as many Western leaders put it. One way in which we can do this is to persuade the majority of citizens in Muslim countries that terrorism is not an option and that the West means them no harm. The day I write this chapter, two top Islamic leaders in Indonesia – a single country containing more Muslims than most of the Middle East put together – have come out to *oppose* the compulsory introduction of Islamic Sharia law to that country. As we will see, Islam is no monolith.

As citizens of the West, we want to encourage the so-called "moderate Muslims," such as those just cited in Indonesia, as well as in Egypt, Jordan, and similar places, to help us in the fight against extremism. Insulting Mohammed does not help this cause.

Furthermore, as Christians, regardless of our country of citizenship, we have an altogether more powerful calling: to reach out to the Muslim world with the Gospel of Jesus Christ. This is already difficult enough, humanly speaking, without the additional burden of Christian leaders in the West hurling personal insults at Mohammed. Islamic leaders always take note of such things and use them against those Christians living in Muslim countries, as many Christian friends of mine in various Muslim regions continually tell me.

The second major point to make here is that Islam as a system and false religion is in fact a far more lethal threat than is the particular individual who founded Islam. It is, as I write this, continuing to win converts in many parts of Africa, Asia, and other similar frontline areas. It is ultimately a *spiritual* battle that we are fighting, and not a personal one. The main thing about Mohammed is that he began a religion that has been highly effective over many centuries in preventing people from seeing their need of salvation in Jesus Christ.

So let us now go on to look at some particular facets of Islam.

A religion of a book and a single founder

One of the first things we notice about the Muslim faith is that, like the Jewish and Christian faiths, it is a religion of a *book*. It is also a religion of a particular founder – Mohammed, an Arab born in present-day Saudi Arabia around AD 570.

Those wanting more detail on Mohammed can turn to some helpful Christian books, examining his life from an Evangelical perspective. *Cross and Crescent* by Colin Chapman, *Muslims and Christians at the Table* by Bruce McDowell and Anees Zaka, and *Faith to Faith* by Chawkat Moucarry are only three of a large number of works that are helpful. So too are many secular books, since they are useful in giving us the basic facts. Many of the books that the writer Bernard Lewis has written would come under this category.

This chapter, therefore, aims at highlighting some parts of early Islam, in a way designed to help us see where present-day Muslim beliefs and practises emerge. This period is especially important too in comprehending Islamic rage and Muslim extremism, since many of the recent Islamicist hard-liners look back on this formative period of Islam with an especial awe.

A religion of revelation

Mohammed always claimed that he did not invent Islam, but that it was revealed to him by God (or *Allah*, to use the Arabic name) in visions and through the angel Gabriel (who is known in Arabic as *Jabril*). Westerners have been quite wrong to refer to Islam as Mohammedanism or some variant spelling. So far as Mohammed was concerned, he was merely passing on the final message of God, the true revelation of the same God whom Christians and Jews worshipped, but in the wrong way.

Abraham is as much a figure in the Qu'ran as he is in the Old and New Testaments. To Muslims everywhere today, he too, like Moses and Jesus (or Isa, to give his Islamic name), was a prophet of God. The difference to Muslims is that Mohammed is *the* prophet, the final one in a long sequence, who gave God's ultimate and true revelation.

Hence, since Abraham appears in Islam, Judaism, and Christianity, these three religions are often bracketed together as the three Abrahamic (or Abramic) faiths.

A Christian reminder

Now since this is a Christian book, written by a Christian for Christians, we would of course not look at things quite in that way. For us Jesus is the final revelation of God, and, even more than that, Jesus is God. Ours is an exclusive faith, and, in our present multicultural politically correct age, that is a hard thing to be. But it is something important for us to grasp, if we are to see how others around us see things. Non-Christians do not, needless to say, believe that there is *any* exclusive faith, since nothing is exclusively true.

With most Muslims, although they would passionately disagree that Christianity is exclusively true, they believe equally strongly that *Islam* is exclusively true. One could say then that the good news is that they do, like us, believe in the reality of absolute truth, but the bad news is that they feel it to be Islam and not Christian faith as revealed in Jesus Christ. So as Christians we can look at this two ways. As the Evangelical sociologist once said of his Marxist colleagues, at least they believe in *some-*

thing. But Muslims are also people who need the true revelation of salvation through the Cross.

So it is accurate to say that Christianity, Judaism, and Islam are all revelation-based religions with a book at their core. In *that* sense they are more similar to each other than to Hinduism, Buddhism, or the many nature-worshipping religions in different parts of the world. While as Christians we would contend that only the claims of Jesus are absolutely true, nonetheless that does not make Islam any less of a revelation-based and book-based religion simply because its claims do not match up to those of Christ.

How the Qu'ran is claimed to have been written

Oddly enough, Muslims suggest that the Prophet was probably illiterate, which is strange, since he must have been able to take dictation if he was able to write down the revelations that he was given according to the Muslim interpretation of the Qu'ran's origins. (I should say here that capitalizing the *P* in Prophet does not imply any recognition that what Mohammed said is true. It is simply his title.) This claim is strange since the Qu'ran is one of the finest examples of classical Arabic in existence and, because it is compulsory for Muslims to read, has had the same enormous influence on the Arabic language as the King James or Authorized Version has had on English.

The reason behind this idea that Mohammed was illiterate is the Muslims' belief that the Qu'ran came direct from heaven and may even have co-existed in all eternity with Allah himself (many a theological dispute was had over this latter point during the Golden Age of medieval Islam). It was dictated word for word in the Arabic language. It cannot therefore be changed, and since Mohammed had it revealed to him, he could not by definition have written any of it himself – though this again raises the dictation problem we saw earlier. In reality, it is probable that Mohammed, coming from one of the leading Arab clans, was highly educated and certainly had the ability to both read and write.

This brings us to a major difference between Christianity and Islam. Both of us have books, but there the similarities end. Our Bible was written by many authors over several centuries (and if, like me, you take a more conservative view of Scripture, beginning many centuries earlier than most secular scholars would allow). Each author wrote in a unique style, as biblical scholars are quick to point out.

The Qu'ran too was probably written over the entire active lifetime of Mohammed, after his initial revelations. But regardless of his own involvement, what we read today is an authoritative compilation made not long after his death by loyal disciples. As will become obvious to readers of the Qu'ran, they compiled the revelations according to length, with the longest first and the shortest last. There is, therefore, no easy and continuous narrative such as is found in the Bible, and to outsiders the conglomeration of verses (or *suras*) can appear rather confusing. To Muslims, however, this does not matter, since all of it is part of the revelation of Allah.

The fact that it can only truly be read in Arabic is another major difference. Jews do not mind translations of the Hebrew Scriptures into other languages and nowadays all Christians zealously advocate the translation of the entire Bible into as many different languages as possible, however small the language group might be. Not only that, but as Evangelicals we continually update translations as well, as language use changes. The theological rationale, instilled in us since the Reformation, that everyone needs to read God's Word in a language they can understand, remains strong. However, the Qu'ran is authoritative only in *Arabic*, which is the same as saying that we could only read the Old Testament in Hebrew or the New Testament in Greek. So while all three Abrahamic religions are book-based, there is a huge difference between Judaism and Christianity on the one hand and Islam on the other.

A book of contradictions?

There are many contradictions in the Qu'ran, which shows the different crises and events through which Mohammed was going when he wrote different parts of the book. (Needless to say, since this implies *human* authorship as opposed to divine revelation, most Muslims would not agree with this interpretation.) References, for example, to Jews seem to change dramatically from sura to sura. Since the final arrangement of verses is by size, not by theme or chronology, this makes it all the harder to work out what was written when. As we will see when we consider jihad (or "struggle"), Muslims get around this by saying that some parts of the Qu'ran abrogate or supersede other parts, which still remain part of the inspired whole. This is, for example, how moderate Muslims are able accurately to quote suras that make clear that Mohammed intended his religion to be one of peace. But it is also how Islamic radicals can equally point to the more bloodthirsty verses and claim those as well.

The different suras on the Jews are especially interesting since they also show how Mohammed changed his mind. It was not until his death in 632 that his newly created religion prevailed in the Arabian Peninsula, and for a lot of that time many of his own clan were against him. From 622 (the date when Muslims start their calendar) when he went from Mecca to Yathrib, he was also a secular ruler. As one French historian has put it, Mohammed was very much a mixture of Jesus, the founder of a great faith, and the great Frankish late eighth and early ninth centuries emperor and warrior, Charlemagne. No sooner had Mohammed gained political control of Medina (the new name he gave to Yathrib) than he was fighting wars. His victory at the Battle of Badr in 624 is celebrated even today. Not without significance is the fact that in 1973 the Egyptian attempt to regain the territories lost in 1967 was code-named *Operation Badr.*

The Qu'ran is not the only basis of present-day Islamic faith and practise. Also important are the *hadiths*, the many sayings of the Prophet written down after his lifetime. Here Islamic scholars and schools of thought differ on exactly which hadiths are genuine and which are not. Some of the more controversial Islamic beliefs on peace and war are based on hadiths rather than directly on the Qu'ran itself. Those wishing to establish a hadith as genuine always give its provenance, so its authenticity can be firmly established.

Mohammed and the Jews of Arabia

Among the key people of the peninsula at the time were the Jewish tribes, and their merchants in particular. (We forget that Arabia once had large Jewish and Christian populations, and we should pray regularly that one day it will do so again. DNA research done on contemporary Yemeni Jews suggests that Jews in Arabia were not so much Jews by physical lineage but through conversion – something that the present-day state of Israel regards as perfectly legitimate for citizenship.) At one time it looked as if the merchants were sympathetic to Mohammed, so there are suras that say pleasant things about the Jews. On other occasions, the merchants clearly sided with his enemies, so there are also suras that denounce the Jews with full vigour.

One of the many fascinating things pointed out by *The Cambridge Illustrated History of the Islamic World* is the strong way in which Judaism influenced Islam, far more, as Patricia Crone points out in her article there, than Muslims would like to admit. As she also indicates, we learn a lot in the Qu'ran about Abraham and Moses, but not really much about Mohammed himself. I would add that what the Qu'ran teaches us about the many familiar biblical people it describes often bears little resemblance to what the Old or New Testaments write about them. Moses, for example, appears differently and the account of the Noahic flood is not exactly the same either. As we know, the Qu'ran also denies that Jesus was God, or that he ever rose from the dead.

Two other situations are interesting. First, good Muslims initially were to pray in the direction of *Jerusalem* and not, as at present, toward Mecca. Secondly, the deep-set Islamic belief in the *oneness* of God – Muslims believe that Christians are really poly-theists who believe in three Gods – is strongly Judaic in inspira-tion. Is there a sense, therefore, in which one could say that Islam is Judaism misunderstood and gone severely awry? It certainly lacks any sense of the Messiah, and its view of God is very remote, so unlike that of the Old Testament. But while this view can cer-tainly be stretched too far, it is an interesting reflection all the same.

A religion of works

Islam is very much a religion of law and is the ultimate works-righteousness religion. This law is called *Sharia* by devout Muslims and is firmly based on the teachings of the Qu'ran. Christianity, and the way in which the Bible recommends us to behave, is, by contrast, based as much on principles as on rules and on our per-sonal desire to please and thank our loving God. Islamic law is highly legalistic. This has created major problems in the twenty-first century, since there are many things arising in modern times that were inconceivable in the seventh century. (As I show else-where, the Shiite version of Islam, as practised in Iran, is much more flexible at this point, whatever its other failings may be.)

So when present-day Muslim hard-liners say that they want to impose Sharia law – as in northern Nigeria, or in Indonesia, for example – they are also creating major obstacles for Muslim adherents in their modern societies.

The other problem is that since Sharia law is supposed to come directly from God, it is non-negotiable. Sharia is the official law code of, for example, Saudi Arabia. The difficulty in asking that country to change its law code is that, by so doing, you are in effect asking the Saudis to change something that God has writ-ten. It would be the equivalent of asking Christians or Jews to alter the Ten Commandments. However, with Christianity, the whole point is that we need a Saviour precisely because we know that we as fallen human beings *cannot* keep the law. In Islam, by contrast, the scales are weighed up, and if your good outweighs the bad, you go to heaven; but if it does not, you go to hell. There is, in a tragic way for Muslims, no possible assurance of salvation in so legally based a religion.

The life of Mohammed versus the life of Christ

Another key source of inspiration for devout Muslims is the *sunna*, or the life, of the Prophet himself. Here one can say that while no Muslim believes that Mohammed was divine, there are branches of Shiite Islam that come very close to sanctifying his life to quasi-divine status. It is here that one can notice a marked difference in the kind of lives led by Mohammed and Jesus Christ. This is because, to us, Jesus *is* God. As we saw earlier, as Christians we ought to be careful not to insult the founder of Islam even though there are aspects of his life that were not particularly desirable. But from the point of view of this book, it is not his sex life on which we should concentrate, if in part only because Muslims have come up with many explanations of whom he married and why.

Rather, in the context of Islamic rage and extremism, it is best to concentrate on Mohammed as an undoubted military leader and strategist since this is something of which Muslims today are proud, rather than being in denial. The fact that early Islam was in no small measure spread through Mohammed's genius at military strategy – he was usually outnumbered by his enemies on the battlefield – stands in the starkest possible contrast to Jesus Christ. As Jesus said, *his* kingdom was *not* of this world, otherwise his disciples would have fought to prevent his arrest (John 18:36). (We'll explore this theme further when we look at jihad.)

While most moderate Muslims, such as King Abdullah of Jordan, abhor violence and do so genuinely, it is hard indeed to get around the historic beginnings of the Islamic faith in tribal warfare. Islam today, as King Abdullah and others make clear, does not *have* to be a violent religion. Even Yassir Arafat was against the atrocities of 9/11. Moderate Muslims were upset with Franklin

Graham when he called Islam a religion of violence because, for many Muslims today, violence such as what occurred on 9/11 does not play any part in their own faith. But if one takes the sunna of Mohammed seriously, this is a major problem for those who want to contrast his life with that of Jesus Christ. (To be fair, I should add that Mohammed never did himself commit the kind of atrocity that took place on that infamous day in 2001, which was why so many Muslims were as appalled by it as everyone else.)

Even though Franklin Graham may have been unfair to genuine Muslim moderates, one does have to say, though, that in looking at the lifestyle of Mohammed, Graham nevertheless has a case that Muslims of any stripe must answer. While Christians have done unspeakable things throughout history – the Crusades being only one example – we can, by contrast, look back on Jesus Christ with complete confidence as the ultimate Prince of Peace.

The Five Pillars of Islam

Among the best-known deeds of good works that all Muslims have to carry out are the *Five Pillars of Islam*. Each of these is compulsory if a Muslim wishes to get to heaven. These pillars are held across all the different schools and divisions of Islam.

The first is the *profession of belief:* "There is no God but God (i.e., Allah) and Mohammed is the messenger of God." This is the core belief statement necessary to make in order to be a Muslim. It proclaims the existence of God and that Mohammed is now his messenger.

The second is *prayer five times a day.* The call from the top of the minaret is now world famous, and in many cases it is now tape recorded rather than given by a *muezzin*, the person who makes the call to prayer out aloud. The prayer is always the same: *Allahu Akbar,* or, in English, "God is great." Muslims have to prostrate themselves, and men and women must do this separately. While many do this at the local mosque, others do so wherever they can. All those praying now have to face Mecca – as we saw, it was originally Jerusalem they had to face. Various other prayers are uttered, and on Fridays prayers normally take place congregationally at a mosque. (Women do not have to attend this, which is the cause of concern for some Muslim men today, as they realize that many Muslim women are not as religious as they were in the past.) Sermons are often delivered on Friday, which in most Muslim countries has now also become the official day of rest. In Sunni mosques, these sermons are given by the local *imam*, who is not a clergyman but a specialist in Islamic law and interpretation.

The third pillar is *alms giving*, or *zakat*. This can be looked at in two ways. It is an excellent institution that helps the poor and underprivileged in many Muslim countries, but it is also a sad example of the works-righteousness upon which Islam is based.

The fourth is *Ramadan*, which is the month of fasting. Because the Muslim calendar does not tie in with that of the West, this can be at different times each year, albeit not usually more than by a few weeks. Muslims have to fast during the day, and in very strict countries they cannot even, in theory, swallow their saliva. (More lenient places do permit drinking tea, especially if it is hot.) People may eat at dusk, which varies from place to place, since dusk falls at different times depending upon geography. In one Muslim country in which I once stayed, the authorities sound off a cannon to say that the people are now permitted to eat. Some Muslims then eat a light meal, others a veritable feast. The major feast at the end of Ramadan in many Muslim countries is like the American celebration of Thanksgiving.

The final official pillar is the *hajj*, or the pilgrimage to Mecca, which all faithful Muslims (especially men) are supposed to make at least once in a lifetime. The rituals associated with the hajj are many and too complex to enumerate here. The fact that the pilgrimage has to be made to Mecca has given enormous power to the Saudi authorities. It has also in recent years caused considerable problems, with ultra-Shiite Iranian pilgrims at one time being banned. At another time, extremist radicals seized the holiest sites and had to be removed by military force. The day I write this, the

British government has promised to give financial support for Muslims in the United Kingdom to attend the hajj, as a gesture by the authorities to demonstrate a lack of prejudice against the country's Islamic minority.

In recent years, extremist interpretations of Islam have included jihad, the struggle or holy war, as a sixth pillar, but this is not agreed upon by everyone. While some seventh century Muslims felt this way, most now do not. We deal with this vexed issue in Chapter 6. Five pillar Islam is the norm, and we therefore end this chapter here.

CHAPTER 5

CHAPTER 5

Other Muslim Beliefs

What are the core beliefs that unite all Muslims? This chapter will explain the roots of Islamic faith. One of the things that Muslims always stress to outsiders is that, unlike Christianity, there is just one Islam. In one sense this is correct. There is no equivalent, for example, of the Protestant/Catholic/Orthodox division of Christian faith. All Muslims share the same basic beliefs.

In another sense, though, this is a completely misleading picture. Around 85 per cent of today's Muslims follow the Sunni path of Islam, and around 15 per cent follow the Shia version, which is now based mainly in Iran. Here the basic differences are not so much theological as political, going back to disputes in the seventh century. We must look, for instance, at a critical scenario: The fourth "Rightly Guided Caliph," the title given to the original successors to Mohammed, was Ali, who was Mohammed's cousin and also his son-in-law. While Ali's proximity to the Prophet was not in question, most historians outside of Iran agree that he was not the ablest of political rulers.

What follows might seem a little obscure, but in reality it is vital to our understanding of present-day Islam, since some Muslims, and especially those influenced by Al Qaeda, regard what happened in this time period as if it were yesterday. In addition, if we are to understand Iran, and the mess that is Iraq, we also need to grasp the events of long ago that might at first seem somewhat arcane. Finally, as Christians we regard events that took place two thousand years ago as absolutely vital. The same principle applies for many followers of Islam today, which is why we need to look at some battles and seemingly obscure legal debates of a very long time ago.

The origins of Shiite Islam

Strictly speaking, Islam is a religion of equals, and, in some interpretations of that faith, the notion of hereditary monarchy is unacceptable. (Needless to say, the many hereditary rulers of Saudi Arabia, Jordan, and similar states do not agree.) But to some of the Muslims of the seventh century, the leadership of the new faith ought to be in the bloodline of Mohammed himself. Ali was just such a person. But since he turned out to be such a weak ruler, the Islamic state that was created with such vigour began to be in danger after 632. The Ummayad family was soon plotting to put one of its own on the throne, and before long Ali was assassinated by a fanatic in 661. The Ummayad dynasty began its long rule, initially in Damascus and later on in Spain when the Syrian based branch was overthrown.

The supporters of Ali, however, did not regard things as that simple. Ali's first son, Hassan, was not natural leadership material, but the second son, Hussein, was made of stronger stuff. He fought for what he regarded as his right to the caliphate, but was defeated and killed at the battle of Karbala in present-day Iraq in 680.

Hussein's followers became known as the party (or *shia*) of Ali, hence their present name of Shia or Shiite Muslims. While they are today prevalent in Iran, when the Shiite Fatimid caliphs in Cairo were beaten by the famous Kurdish warrior Saladin in the twelfth century, mainstream Sunni Islam became politically prevalent in the areas it now dominates. It was only, in fact, in the seventeenth century that Shiite Islam became the official religion of Iran, which it has been ever since.

So when you see Iranian fanatics charging through the streets, running stripped to the waist, chanting, and beating their backs with whips, they are doing something that over 85 per cent of Muslims do *not* believe in. What they are doing is commemorating what they regard as the martyrdom of Hussein, who they regard as the third lawful successor of Mohammed. Since Hussein's death was at the hands of those who Sunni Muslims regard as lawful rulers, one can see why Sunni Muslims regard Karbala as a great victory and Shiites as a tragic defeat. While the sight of fanatical Shiites whipping themselves into a bloody frenzy is thus a frightening one, it is important to remember that most of the Muslims you meet in the West who are Sunni would probably share your view. Islam is not as monolithic as we often think of it as being.

Some possible Sunni and Shia differences

When the Ummayad caliphs in Damascus and later the Abbasid caliphs in Baghdad took power, they brought the majority of Muslims with them, which is why most of the Muslim world is Sunni today. This, in turn, also helps to explain why many Iranians, while hating the United States, supported America in Afghanistan, since the Sunni Muslim Taliban suppressed the Shiite Afghans sympathetic to Iran. In addition, theologically it is true to say that Ayatollah Khomeini always referred to himself in broadcasts abroad simply as a Muslim and not as a follower of its Shiite version. But as we saw elsewhere, Shiite Muslims are in general more open to the modern world than their more hidebound Sunni brethren.

Books written by people who have lived in the dominant Sunni world tend to be more sympathetic to that point of view. I have stayed in Islamic countries such as Bahrain or Lebanon where there are large numbers of *both* kinds living side by side. As to whether either Sunni or Shia Islam is more compatible with the modern world, my interpretation is based more on what I have read or observed in general rather than on my own personal experiences. If Iran goes moderate or ceases to be an Islamic state at all, as some hope, then my prediction for a moderate victory in the internal power struggle going on at the moment is correct. If the hard-liners prevail there, or if democracy fails to take off in Bahrain, then perceptive friends of mine like Christian commentator Larry Adams will have been proved right and Islam and democracy will continue to prove incompatible with one another. Read your newspapers and watch these places to find out what will really happen.

As many writers have said, Shiite Islam is *future* orientated. Like Christians, Shiite Muslims await the return of a spiritual leader yet to come back – though in their case an ordinary man, not the Son of God. This anticipated leader is the so-called Hidden (or Twelfth) Imam. Of the four Rightly Guided Caliphs of the period after Mohammed, the Shiites only regard one of them, Ali, as a lawful successor. They give the proper successors (by their interpretation) the name of Imam. This is confusing for Westerners, since it is also the title given in Sunni mosques to the chief interpreter of the law. For example, most Sunni Islamic mosques in Britain or the United States will have their own imam.

Hassan was the second Shiite Imam and Hussein the third. Between then and 980, when the twelfth Shiite Imam vanished, Shiite Muslims recognize twelve lawful successors of the Prophet. Shiite Muslims are therefore sometimes called Twelver Shiites as a result. (A smaller group, of which today's Ismaili Muslims are the main relic, believed only in five lawful Imams. Today the Aga Khan is their leader. He is regarded as important but not as a full-fledged Imam.) Shiite Muslims regard the twelfth Imam as being in hiding, ready to return at a time known only to Allah. Some Shiite Muslims tended to regard the Ayatollah Khomeini as a likely candidate for a reappeared Imam, but his death proved that this was clearly not the case. (Nor did he effectively claim himself to be the Imam.)

Psychologically, this means, as some commentators have written, that Shiite Muslims are always looking to the future rather than to the past. There is, I think, something in this view. However, as Larry Adams has also said, some of the current Sunni/Shiite differences could by now also be cultural. Persian civilization, like Cyrus's, was very advanced even in biblical times. Perhaps it is no coincidence that the Iranians, their modern descendants, have maintained a difference between themselves and the Arab-originated Sunni version of Islam.

The four schools of Sunni Islam

The division between Sunni and Shiite Islam is not the only one within the Muslim religion. Sunni Islam has within itself four different schools of thought, each one of which is practised today. Here again one ought to be careful. These are not along the line of the Catholic/Protestant type of differences. Nor are they of the variety of the divisions between Presbyterians and Baptists, or between an Evangelical interpretation of Scripture and a liberal one.

The dividing lines between these four schools of Sunni Islam are not so much theological as *legal*. This is because Islam is the ultimate in works-righteousness as a religion. If the scales are in your favour, you go to heaven; if they are not, you are bound for hell. Muslims do not have the assurance that Christians do to know within our lifetime as to which of the two we will be going. In other words, the four schools that follow are more like different law codes than theological denominations. Famous Islamic centres of learning, such as the one in Cairo at Al-Azhar, teach all four schools of jurisprudence.

In order of foundation, the four schools are the Hanafi (after Abu Hanifa, who died in 767), the Maliki (after Malik ibn Anas, who died in 795), the Shafii (after al-Shafi, who died in 820), and the Hanbali (after Ahmad ibn Hanbal, who died in 855). All the schools were effectively founded by the end of the ninth century, within three hundred years of Mohammed's death.

Some of the differences would strike us as being somewhat obscure. For example, when it comes to Friday prayers, the Hanafi school stipulates that there must be at least three Muslim men present to form a quorum. The Maliki school insists on twelve being the lowest number, while the Shafii and Hanbali schools insist that the quota must be no less than forty. Clearly, these are not exactly profound theological differences. However, in a works-based religion like Islam, to obey the law in the correct way can make all the difference between going to heaven and ending up in hell, so obeying the right rules in the correct way becomes absolutely vital.

Roughly speaking, the Hanafi school predominates in most of the Arabic Middle East and in South Asia, the Maliki in different parts of Islamic Africa, the Shafii in East Africa and in non-Saudi parts of the Arabian Peninsula, and the Hanbali in Saudi Arabia. The official interpretation of the great Ottoman Empire was Hanafi. (There are variants of these schools in places such as Pakistan, the Deobandi being an example, one that has strong links to the Hanbali school.)

While this geographical distinction is still more or less correct, it is important to say that the stern Hanbali interpretation of Islamic law is now becoming far more widespread, thanks to Saudi petrodollars. No other school of Islamic law has a state behind it that is prepared to spread it and fund it with as much money as with the Hanbali school and Saudi Arabia. A version of Hanbali Islam, rediscovered in the eighteenth century in that country, is also exactly the kind of harsh interpretation so favoured by all the 9/11 terrorists. Hanbali school Islam might until recently have been limited geographically to Saudi Arabia, but in recent times its new strength has made a devastating difference to our own world.

Muslims and the law

Muslims distinguish between two kinds of law: *Sharia*, which is the immutable and absolute law code direct from God, and *fiqh*, which is human-based law that must be fully compatible with that from God.

All of the various schools of thought are legal systems, as well as the basis of true Islamic belief. The word *Islam*, after all, means "submission," and the whole of Islam is about correct submission to the will of God. Theology (or *kalam*) in the sense of truly understanding and appreciating God is not as important as it is in other faiths, especially Christianity or Judaism, where it is central.

The Sufi way of mystical Islam

Excessive Islamic legalism is, in many ways, rather joyless. Many approaches have emerged in Islam of finding a more personal relationship with God, perhaps because of the legalistic basis of the religion as a whole. The best known example of this is *Sufism*, otherwise known as the *Sufi way*. We get the words *fakir* and *dervish* from different kinds of Sufi religious practise. Sufism is often seen as the mystical version of Islam, and its closest parallel is folk Catholicism, of the kind found in remote European valleys or in Latin America. It goes back a long way, but perhaps owes a lot to the great Sufi mystic Al Ghazali, who lived in the eleventh century. Much of Sunni Islam is open to Sufism, and Pakistani Islam is strongly influenced by the Sufi traditions. But in general it is Shiite Islam that is more disposed to Sufism than the mainstream Sunni version, which makes Iran a more Sufi orientated place than Saudi Arabia.

Theoretically, Islam is a religion in which everyone has a direct relationship with Allah. However, in Sufism, as in folk Catholicism, holy men, especially those of the Sufi Orders that believed in isolation and contemplation, were soon regarded by ordinary people as intermediaries between man and Allah. Forms of dancing, such as that practised by the famous Whirling Dervishes, became popular as means of communicating with God. Some historians go so far as to say that some forms of both Christian and Buddhist monasticism were of great influence in the development of Sufi thought. Needless to say, this made Sufism profoundly unacceptable to the more austere forms of Islam, such as the Wahhabi interpretation of Hanbali Islam.

Why we shouldn't always accentuate the negative

There is a tendency among my fellow Evangelicals to believe the very worst versions of Islam to be the only authentic ones available. There is a longstanding historic reason behind this. However, one also has to say, as do many historians and commentators, that because there is no Islamic equivalent of the pope or of the great Reformation "Confessions of Faith," that to declare any one form of Islam *the* authentic version is in fact mistaken.

Consequently, if the friendly Muslim down the street is a passionate Sufi follower, it does not mean that he or she is any less authentically Muslim than Osama bin Laden or any other follower of a more austere Islamic interpretation. Certainly many Hanbali school Muslims would reject Sufism altogether. But well-known Muslim writers, such as Akbar Ahmed and Bassam Tibi (both of whom are easily available in English), would take a different approach.

Nevertheless, if we are looking at Islamic rage, we need to understand these different schools of legal thought. This is because we must consider some of the implications of the different schools before going on to discover why Hanbali Islam has become so prevalent and dangerous.

Ijtihad: the gate of personal interpretation

Here the expression *ijtihad*, meaning personal interpretation, makes all the difference. It is perhaps here that the greatest distinction between most of Sunni Islam and Shiite Islam lie, and where Islam comes nearest to the kind of *theological* differences that distinguish Protestant and Catholic understandings of the Bible.

To all but perhaps the Hanafi interpretation of Islam, the possibility of personal interpretation of the Qu'ran is firmly shut. As we will note elsewhere, the expression is the "gate of *ijtihad* is now closed." This explains why Islamic interpretation is increasingly rigid. It is, one can argue, why the Golden Age of Islam, when Muslim countries were far ahead culturally, medically, and scientifically of the West, is unlikely to be replicated. The great era of the Abbasid Caliphate, for example, was while the gate of *ijtihad* was effectively still open. It may also be, as Bernard Lewis has so persuasively written in his many books, why Islamic empires became increasingly complacent and atrophied in relation to the increasingly dynamic West.

Al-Wahhab and the austere Wahhabi form of Saudi Islam

Reform (described as *islah*) and renewal (or *tajdid*) are legitimate within even Hanbali Islam. Here the Arab reformer Ibn Abd al-Wahhab (1703–97) is pivotal, for it is the reforms he brought to Arabic Hanbali Islam that lead us directly, in a real sense, to present-day Islamic rage and Al Qaeda-style terrorism.

Al-Wahhab was a reformer, based in what is now the Nejd district of Saudi Arabia. He was appalled at what he regarded as the huge amount of syncretistic additions that were being accumulated by Arabic Islam. This to him was especially abhorrent in the heartland of the Muslim faith. In particular, he strongly disliked Sufism and the way that it opened the door to practises alien to core Islamic belief.

Those sympathetic to what he was trying to accomplish in purging Islam of incorrect beliefs have likened what he did to the Protestant Reformation. I am not sure whether one can draw so exact a parallel. It might be better to compare him – if such a comparison is possible – to the Catholics of the Counter-Reformation at the Council of Trent. Whichever parallel is best, what he wanted to do was to restore the Hanbali school of Islam to what he felt was the correct interpretation of Islam at the time of the Prophet.

Some say that al-Wahhab *himself* was exercising individual judgement, or *ijtihad*. However, he would probably have denied such a claim, because he was not trying to discover anything new or, as in the case of the great Islamic philosophers of the Golden Age, trying to reconcile Western thought with Muslim law. In fact, he followed those medieval Arab thinkers who rejected the attempts by the likes of Avicenna and Averröes to bring about precisely such a reconciliation in medicine, philosophy, science, and other disciplines. Rather, he was a *mujjadid*, a reformer or a renewer.

Al-Wahhab was fortunate in that he had a political sponsor – the leader of the Al-Saud clan in Arabia. (In those days, what we now call Saudi Arabia, after the Al-Saud family, was an amorphous conglomeration of several tribal groupings, most of whom owed ultimate allegiance to the Ottoman Sultan hundreds of miles away in Istanbul.) The combination of Wahhabi religious fanaticism and Saudi clan military strategy nearly ended up in the liberation of Arabia from Turkish rule as early as the eighteenth century. As things worked out, such freedom did not come until the twentieth century, when the then ruler of the kingdom of Nejd, Abdul Aziz Ibn Saud (often known in the West simply as Ibn Saud), was able to conquer most of the peninsula by the 1920s.

Along with Saudi political rule came the Wahhabi revivalist form of Islam as the official form of Muslim faith for the newly created kingdom. Commentators often write that, in some sense, the Saudis have had a kind of Faustian pact with the Wahhabis ever since they came to power after World War I. Certainly some regard hereditary monarchy as incompatible with true Islam. (That did not, though, prevent centuries of caliphate rule under the Ummayad and Abbasid dynasties after Mohammed's death.) It is also true that many members of the Al-Saud family do not exactly live pure and unblemished Islamic lives. But there is a sense in which the Wahhabi *ulema*, or Islamic legal experts, give religious credence to what is by any reckoning the Saudi family's dictatorship over their kingdom. Remove the Wahhabis from religious power and the Saudi monarchy might not last too long.

Sayyid Qutb and the longtime causes of Islamic rage

Early in 2003 I read in an American newspaper that simply removing Al Qaeda does not solve the long-term problems of Islamic rage. Since the terrorist threat from that source is the symptom rather than the underlying disease, this is right. The truly deadly result of Hanbali Islam is a whole mentality, rather than just the particular activities of an individual group. Eliminate one, and there will still be countless followers of the same idea.

Perhaps the most eminent and also deadly follower of the Hanbali school in the twentieth century was the Egyptian Sayyid Qutb (1906–66). He has been accurately described as the intellectual father of Islamic rage and can legitimately be said to be the ideological and spiritual inspiration behind present-day Islamic terror. (For those wanting more on him, see the books I have listed by Malise Ruthven and John Esposito.)

Liberal Muslim writers, such as Akbar Ahmed and Bassam Tibi, describe mainstream Islam as a religion of peace – the *Dar al-Salaam*. By their standards of interpretation, they are correct. As Evangelicals, we must guard against our tendency to say that they are wrong about their own religion. For many Islam *is* a religion of peace, even though for other schools of interpretation it is anything but that. We do not have to render *all* Islam violent to make it into an antagonist of Christian faith. As the famous Evangelical preacher John MacArthur writes, *all* non-Christian religion is false. This means that we don't have to say that Islam is innately violent to say that it is false. Even nice-as-pie Islam is false. So too is Buddhism, Marxism, New Age religion, Western materialism, postmodernism, and many other thoughts that come to mind. If we denounce Islam as being *inherently* violent, and we find ourselves then up against a devout Muslim follower of one of the non-violent interpretations, then our legitimate case against the spiritually false nature of Islam is in danger of being undermined (see Chapter 7).

However, if you look at the teachings of Sayyid Qutb and the kind of Islam that he represents, then that brand of Muslim belief is indeed innately and deliberately most violent. To men like Sayyid Qutb, the Islamic world as well as the *Dar al-Harb*, in which the rest of us live, is falling away from true faith. He called this *jahiliyya*, which is the word Mohammed used to describe Saudi Arabia before he came along to put them straight. This means that those supposedly Muslim rulers who do not follow the true path are as guilty as Westerners who deny the truths of Islam altogether. The only way to get rid of such people, whether professed Muslim or not, is through military struggle, or jihad.

Jihad can be interpreted in many different ways, many of them entirely peaceful. The struggle can be an internal one for purity as much as an outward one for military conquest or liberation. But to the followers of Qutb, the answer is normally violent, with results that we saw in New York and Washington, DC, in 2001 or in Bali in 2002.

All this can be read in Qutb's classic *Signposts on the Road*, the book published in 1964 that eventually cost him his life in 1966. To Qutb, the whole world was in a state of *jahiliyya* or spiritual ignorance. What is significant and sobering for us as Westerners is that this view was reinforced by his stay in the West – in New York; Washington, DC; Colorado; and California – rather than diminished by it. So repelled was he by what he saw of the United States that he became more convinced than ever that the whole world was threatened by the nature of modern culture. For on return he felt that not merely was the West saturated by what sociologists call modernity but the Muslim world was as well. This included Qutb's own nation of Egypt, a self-professed Arab socialist regime that was very hostile to the West.

The twenty-first century results of Qutb and his views

It is vital for us to remember that it is not so much the West *as the West* that so enrages those taking Qutb's view, but the West as the prime producer of non-Islamic contamination. They do *not* envy our freedom, because they regard the mentality that freedom produces as decadent and un-Islamic. Furthermore, such people, following the famous medieval philosopher Ibn Khaldun, see great powers rising and falling in cycles. To Qutb the West was so corrupt that it was bound to fall. Since the West's demise was inevitable, it was all the more vital that it be succeeded as the key player in global power by a properly Qu'ran-following Islamic superpower, which is what he wanted to create. But of course to create such a truly Qu'ran-following superstate, it was first necessary to get rid of the apostate, *jahiliyya* nominal Muslim states like his own Egypt.

This is why the proponents of this interpretation of Islam are as against their own regimes as they are opposed to us in the West, why it was by his own country that Qutb was executed, and why the *primary* cause of Al Qaeda is as much against the present regime in Saudi Arabia as against Britain or the United States. This is why the decision by the Saudi royal family to allow Western troops to remain in the kingdom after 1991 was so profoundly abhorrent to Osama bin Laden and those of like mind. (That is not to say that Al Qaeda went on to have other targets – simply to say that the desire to remove what they believe to be an un-Islamic Saudi regime was, many of us would argue, what put them on the road.)

The devastating impact of the defeat in the Six Day War

Arabs often refer to the Six Day War of 1967 simply as *the disaster*. Militarily, politically, and psychologically it was exactly that. But it also had profound implications outside of the Middle East that are with us still. For along with the military defeat came the cultural defeat of Arab socialism and of *secular* opposition to the West. One of the reasons why so many Arabs turned to Mohammed in his lifetime is that he won battles! It was also, arguably, the same for conversions to Islam in the seventh century, in the wake of the great Islamic conquests. "Their God is giving them victories – he must be true!"

Parenthetically, this is why so many nineteenth century Evangelical missionaries were so wary of what are called "rice Christians" – people in poorer countries professing an interest in Christian faith because the West seemed so much more advanced and prosperous. No one wants to wish persecution on anyone, but one of the good side effects of the Communist takeover of China in 1949 was that the "rice Christians" quickly disappeared. Nobody who is in it for the money wants to be part of a faith that brings with it persecution, jail, and all the financial poverty that comes with being a persecuted believer.

Today, being a Christian can bring you death at the hands of Islamic mobs in places such as northern Nigeria and parts of Indonesia. That is surely why Evangelical leaders such as John MacArthur are *biblically* right to say that Scripture-based Christianity does not make any link between *material* well-being and true faith, otherwise the disciples and other early Christians would have been the wealthiest people around in the Roman Empire! Muslims, however, continue to make a strong link between prosperity and Allah's blessing, which is why the events of 1967 were so devastating.

In 1967 it was the massed ranks of Arab armies that were beaten hollow by puny Israel, and not the other way around. In the same way in which many anguished Americans asked where God was on 9/11, so many Muslims asked where Allah was during the Six Day War.

The defeat of Arab socialism and the rise of religious extremism

Sayyid Qutb had been a member of the Muslim Brotherhood, an organization founded in 1928, which was in turn a successor to various earlier anti-British groups founded to resist colonial rule. When Egypt's corrupt King Farouk was deposed in 1952, some of those behind the plot had been sympathetic to or even part of the Brotherhood. But the secular Arab nationalist socialism of Nasser, while not antagonistic to Islam as such, had no time for the religious-based views of those like Qutb. Since Nasser was able to humiliate the old colonial powers of Britain and France in 1956, Nasserite socialism was for a long time seen as the most popular cause in the Arab world. Since Qutb was executed the year before Nasser's defeat, he never lived to see his own ideas become increasingly vindicated in the people's imagination.

Socialism and secularism are Western originated doctrines. Since they had failed to guarantee victory against the West, in the form of its local ally Israel, these two ideologies were seen by many as having failed. Suddenly, the siren song of Qutb and *Signposts on the Road* became to many across the Arab world as *the* answer to what went wrong. For remember, to Qutb it was not just the wicked West that was *jahiliyya* but the apostate regimes in the Middle East as well. A *truly* Muslim regime would never have been defeated in the way that Egypt, Syria, and Jordan were by Israel in 1967.

Going back to the ancestors: the Salafiyya

Qutb's school of Islam is also called Salafiyya, as the British newspaper *The Guardian* discovered in looking at various extremist mosques in the United Kingdom after September 2001. Salafiyya originates from the Arabic word *salaf*, or ancestors. The term is often used in relation to the early Muslims around the Prophet himself in the first century of Islam. Muslims who support Salafiyya are those, such as the people *The Guardian* came across in the Finsbury Mosque in London, who want to restore Islam to the purity of its origins.

One of the things that commentators of all stripes have written about Qutb and his followers is that they have a completely totalitarian mentality. Their solution is an absolutist Islamic state, one in which rightly guided Muslim leaders would rule using only Sharia law.

As Chapters 2 and 3 show, not even the direct successors of Mohammed himself were able to achieve so perfect a state! From both a Christian and secular point of view alike, such a regime is impossible to accomplish. But it is, nevertheless, the goal of the current proponents of what is described as the Salafiyya interpretation of Hanbali Islam.

The siren call of political Islam

The major political reason for the appeal to the Islamic masses of such a utopian version of Islam is the vast majority of states in the Middle East having highly oppressive, totalitarian, dictatorial regimes. Their inhabitants see them as being in league with the West, and with the United States in particular. Since democracy is not perceived to be a realistic option, the only source of viable opposition are groups that follow Qutb, such as the Islamic group that murdered President Sadat of Egypt and later formed a part of Al Qaeda. When it comes to opposition politics, the radical Muslims are the only show in town.

This has massive implications worldwide, as Americans, Australians, and Britons, among others, are only now discovering. The Palestinian opposition to Israel, while often unspeakably violent, is a *local* struggle in a particular geographical area. What is disturbing about the kind of Islam espoused by Sayyid Qutb and his twenty-first century followers is that it is *universal*.

This is why, for example, Osama bin Laden has been known to mourn the loss of Islamic ruled Spain – El Andalus – even though it ended as long ago as 1492. From his perspective, once something is Muslim it is *always* Muslim. Islam is not the faith of a particular region, as Nigerian and Indonesian Christians are discovering daily to their cost. (It is important we stop linking the words "Arab" and "Muslim" in our minds. Indonesia is the most populous predominantly Muslim state in the world by far, and there are also possibly more Muslims in majority Hindu India than there are in most of the Arab Middle East.) Islam is very much a *universal* religion, one that spread, as we have seen, by conversion in places like West Africa and East Asia, as well as by the sword.

So to Qutb, and those of his ilk, Islam is the one true religion that must be spread across the globe, starting with the reform of the *Dar al-Islam* but stretching into the *Dar al-Harb* as well. Some commentators feel that for such Muslims jihad in its full military sense has become like a sixth pillar of Islam. Since it is the wicked, materialist, crusading West that is corrupting Islamic states and preventing the spread of Islam to new territories, then the West too has become part of the enemy. Both despotic governments in the Middle East and democratic regimes in the West are in equal danger from this particular revivalist form of Islam. As writers as diverse as the Muslim and German-based Bassam Tibi (author of *The Challenge of Fundamentalism*) and Mark Juergensmeyer of the University of California Santa Barbara (author of *The New Cold War?*) have shown us in their books, this *is* a religious conflict.

How everything has become a spiritual conflict

To us as Christians, that this is a religious conflict should be obvious. We know from the Bible that ultimately *everything* is a spiritual conflict, one that has already been won on the Cross by Jesus Christ. As Paul's epistles remind us, we are all engaged in spiritual warfare of some kind or another.

However, to the increasingly secular society around us, to those who believe that religion should have disappeared from sight a long time ago, this is all rather a shock. Religion as a force in global affairs should have vanished with the steam engine. In fact, to many secularists it went away longer ago than that, in the era of the Enlightenment in the eighteenth century. The Muslim author Bassam Tibi is unusual in that he is an overt Muslim who also claims that he believes fully in what modernists have described as the "Enlightenment Project," a sociological term which, simply put, means thinking in the manner of the Enlightenment philosophers of the eighteenth century and their successors. But with the rise of such impossible-to-pin-down views as postmodernism, even many secularists realize that we live in what they call a post-Enlightenment era.

As mainstream writers, such as Juergensmeyer and Tibi have shown, you cannot just look at the world through entirely secular lenses anymore. The fact that they are, from our point of view, non-Christian authors makes their case all the more powerful, since, if we said the same things, secular thinkers and commentators would laugh us out of court. Their critique of secular writers who try to insist that the motives behind Islamic rage are *really* just economic or political is thus all the more devastating.

We are now living in a new political era

That is not to say that politics is uninvolved in all this – far from it. But the key point here is that in the Muslim world the sacred/secular divide of the West simply does not exist. To the radical Muslim mind every facet of life is religious, and so their political thinking is suffused with their religious outlook.

The old ways of looking at issues simply do not work anymore. As Chapters 2 and 3 show, after 1648 most governments started to act primarily in *secular* ways – the so-called Westphalian system. Your *state's* interest became your paramount concern. According to people like Henry Kissinger, this remained the case even after the advent of secular ideological states such as the Soviet Union in the twentieth century. States such as the USSR, UK, or US are called *actors* in international relations, and the presupposition among specialists is that all of them are *rational* in what they do. This means, for example, that while the Soviets wanted all the world to become Communist, they did not set off World War III since they knew that the United States had enough nuclear weapons to stop them. Even the most hardened Soviet Politburo members were what is called *rational actors*.

However, we now have a major actor in international affairs for whom things such as national boundaries or state borders simply do not exist. To this mind-set there are only two borders that count – the *Dar al-Islam* and the *Dar al-Harb*, the homes of obedience and war respectively. For, as you will have guessed, it is extremist Islam that I am talking about here. Consequently, some of us are now arguing that the nice, neat theories of international relations of the past 350 years or so – the Westphalian System – simply are no longer relevant! The foreign policy buffs and the generals are going to have to start all over again. We are living in a whole new political era.

If we are to understand this new global order, we *must* understand religion, for it is religiously based. In the old secular sense of the word, groups like Al Qaeda are *non-state actors*. Rather than being an individual country like the old Soviet Union, for example, they are amorphous groups of fanatics in *different* countries but based around similar goals and aspirations. Al Qaeda, for example, is more than just its founder and bin Laden's immediate followers in different parts of the world. Rather, it is a coalition of like-minded Muslims as far afield as Indonesia, East Africa, Western Europe, and the United States, most of whom have probably never met each other but all of whom share the same Islamic dreams. When it came to Hitler in World War II, the invasion and conquest of the Third Reich was enough to end the Nazi menace. Now, in this age of religious nationalism, it is going to be much more complicated.

Dealing with Islamic rage as a political opposition

As I have said throughout this book, Islamic rage is only partly to do with American support for the state of Israel. In large part, people turn to Islamicist groups because there is no one else who dares to verbalize their dislike of the local *Muslim* regime. This in the past has been why many Middle Eastern regimes have not hesitated to permit the publication of the vilest anti-Semitic propaganda, on the basis that if local people hate the Jews they will forget to loathe their own government.

One of the few encouraging pieces of news to emerge from that region in early 2003 was the decision of an Egyptian governmental authority to denounce as forgeries the infamous anti-Jewish work *The Protocols of the Elders of Zion*. This is the ultimate in Jewish conspiracy works, originally forged by the Russian Secret Police in the nineteenth century. Many Palestinian children are taught it as pure truth, and the fact that a leading Arab regime now denounces it is good news, as was the simultaneous decision to recognize the Coptic Christian Christmas as a national holiday.

American leaders have talked about draining the swamp of terrorism. We will look at this in more detail later (see page 189), but here, in the context of the different kinds of Islam, it is important to say that democracy can be a more effective enemy of Hanbali extremism than Western tanks or missiles. Much academic blood has been spilled over whether democracy and Islam are compatible. Places like Iran and Bahrain are still too early on in the experiment for us to know what will happen long term. The great sage and specialist Bernard Lewis, writing in the first issue of *Newsweek* in 2003, sees no reason why they should not be successful, and one can trust that he is right. For *if* he is – and the jury is still out – then there will be few things more effective in draining the swamp than the democratic right to vote out a government that you don't like.

In other words, if you have some degree of freedom, then you don't need to turn to the hard-liners to express what you think of the government. You would then be able to do so freely and certainly at the ballot box. The claim of the religious extremists to be the only means of effective opposition to the local dictatorship will then have been fatally undermined. Furthermore, change will have occurred from within the country and not with the aid of foreign governments or armed forces.

One thing is vital for us to understand as Christians, people whose ultimate citizenship is in heaven rather than with a particular nation here on earth. One of the most worrying developments in recent years is the turning to the radical and often violent versions of Islam among many young Muslims in the West. While they are proud of all that living in Britain, France, or the United States brings them, they have, nonetheless, an instinctive Islamic sympathy with people as unsavoury as Osama bin Laden, Saddam Hussein, or those like them.

The testimony and lessons of a brave convert

At the end of 2002 a brave convert to faith in Christ from a British Muslim background wrote his testimony in the *Times* of London. Why had he converted to Christianity? his father bewailed. Why didn't he sympathize with Al Qaeda, like so many other boys of his age?

While most British Muslims are not of the Hanbali school, there is an instinctive sense of solidarity with those who are good at humbling the West. This is why, as Christians, we must be very careful where our patriotism leads us. The situation in the United States is probably not all that different. If Muslims on our own doorstep are feeling things like this, then that must be a matter for prayerful concern. We must, as Christians whose patriotism and true loyalty is with Christ, do all we can to show our local Muslim neighbours that the West and Christianity are not automatically hand in glove.

A Christian Middle East once more?

There are, as the maps in the first issue of *Newsweek* in 2003 show, large Christian minorities in Egypt, Jordan, and Iraq, but none at all in Saudi Arabia. If *all* these countries feel humiliated by the West, then there are bound to be bad side effects for the local Christians, who will inevitably be tarred with the Western brush. But if such countries begin to have democratic regimes, then the situation could begin to change. Already, as this book shows, the advent of a large measure of democracy in Iran has led ordinary people to become more pro-Western and even see pro-American demonstrations in the streets. If Christian faith is no longer automatically associated with a national enemy, then it will be easier for local Christians and also easier for people to hear the Gospel. Even if it only eases the persecution from Islamic mobs that Christians often face in Egypt, it will surely be worthwhile.

Many at this point may think I am being ludicrously optimistic. But don't forget two things. First, remember that the Iron Curtain came down without World War III. Surely God in his love and mercy was behind so seismic an event. Second, these places in the Middle East were predominantly Christian before the rise of Islam. In addition, countries that were overwhelmingly pagan in 1900, such as Nigeria and Korea, now contain *millions* of Christians. So what is stopping God from acting in the same way in what was once, after all, a largely Christian region?

But Qutb and his like don't believe in democracy

The Hanbali school of Islam, of which Sayyid Qutb and Osama bin Laden are merely two members, is completely incompatible with democracy in any form. If people of that persuasion get into power, then it is all over – unless some violent revolution gets rid of them. For if you believe not in democracy but in the absolutist rule of an inner circle of rightly guided pure Muslims, ruling not in the name of the people but in the name of their interpretation of Mohammed, then freedom does not stand a chance.

What is worrying is the power of Saudi petrodollar money, whose effects we will look at in Chapter 10. It really does matter, from one point of view, which school of Islam predominates. (Spiritually, all of them are sadly mistaken – it is some of the other results that we are considering here.) One of the tragedies about the support that hard-liners receive is that many of those who back them do so because they dislike totalitarian regimes. As the early supporters of Ayatollah Khomeini found out after 1979, they had in effect replaced a despot, the Shah, with an altogether far more ruthless and absolutist dictator, Khomeini. The Islamic Republic executed many more people than did the Shah, as the Russians also discovered in 1917, when they overthrew the Tsar in favour of the Bolsheviks. If the present-day peoples of the Middle East long for democracy, it is not in the followers of Sayyid Qutb that they will find it. In terms of human rights for Christians, it is obviously better to have a regime like the one in Jordan than in Saudi Arabia.

Ultimately, of course, it is not just democracy or a corruption-free government that the people of this region need. They need the Gospel! Not even the worst Iron Curtain tyranny was able to stamp it out during the Cold War, and we should pray the same for the Middle East today.

CHAPTER 6

What Muslims Really Believe

Muslims, as we know, have some strange misunderstandings about what Christians believe, especially about such doctrines as the Trinity. But we as Christians are equally guilty of following strange stereotypes of what Muslims actually believe. At a time of heightened sensitivity, it is all the more important that our understanding of Islamic faith is accurate. Yes, it is true that some versions of Islam think that mass murder is entirely justified – a duty even. But other Muslims are equally sincere in proclaiming their version of Islam to be a religion of peace. Where do they get their different versions?

"Kill the unbeliever where you find him . . ." (Sura 2:256).

"There is no compulsion in Islam . . ." (Sura 2:190–94).

These two contradictory statements are *both* equally valid quotations from the Qu'ran. The first of these is from the so-called *Sword verse* and the second of these is one frequently quoted by moderate Muslims today.

If you are confused about how both of these are part of Islamic sacred scripture, I am not at all surprised! There seem to be a lot of versions of Islam. Read one thing and you fear for your life. Read something else, and you think that Islam is simply just another kind of postmodern, touchy-feely religion in which lots of nice people believe. What is it that Muslims *really* believe? How do you react when you see some nice imam on television say that Islam is a religion of peace, and the next minute there is some spine-chilling *fatwa*, or decree, from Al Qaeda terrorists, wishing death and destruction on the West and all its works? Who is to tell which is right? More important, *Is there a right version at all?*

Finally, how should we as Christians react? For surely part of the problem is that a lot of people doing the interpretation on television and in our newspapers are secular commentators who really don't understand religion of any kind properly, let alone from a biblical perspective. It is not surprising that many Christians are thoroughly confused!

The many and varied versions of Islam

For example, when I read the work of Akbar Ahmed, a former Cambridge academic and neighbour – *Islam Today* (the book of the TV series) – it portrayed a very moderate, peaceful view of Islam. That kindly, contemplative version of Islam is the one practised in many countries around the world. As Professor Ahmed now lives in the United States, one can say that he is typical of many Muslims who are always so friendly when you meet them, and who are genuinely appalled at the terror propagated in the name of Islam today.

I was in the United States when the chilling video came out of Osama bin Laden and some of his cronies, showing them laughing and crowing over the many thousands of deaths in New York and Washington, DC. The problem is that *that too is an expression of Islam.*

So do both the peace lovers like Akbar Ahmed and the mass murderers like bin Laden claim to be the authentic voice of Islam? The answer is yes. But is there by now a *truly* authentic Islamic voice, about which one can say with certainty, "Yes, that is Islam speaking"? The actual answer is that to find such a genuine voice is something that is well nigh impossible to do because *both* sides can legitimately point to parts of the Qu'ran and say – "There you are! *My* interpretation is the correct one!"

For both the suras, or verses, with which I began this chapter are, beyond question, parts of the Qu'ran. Some bits tell good Muslims to slay their enemies, while others advocate peace and neighbourly understanding. Sometimes we as Christians get a bit worried that there are verses in the Bible that *appear* to contradict each other, something as Evangelicals we believe that Scripture should not do. But this is nothing compared to the real problem that Muslims *ought* to face as they expound or exegete the Qu'ran.

Don't always just quote the nasty bits . . .

Before we look at Islam, there is one thing necessary to say here, since this is a book primarily aimed at a Christian audience and written by an Evangelical author. There is a danger, if some recent books are anything to go by, of stereotyping Islam. Liberals tend to believe that those of a similar mind-set in the Muslim world are surely *the* real voice of Islam today. (Karen Armstrong's post-9/11 bestseller, *Islam: A Short History*, is a classic example of this genre.) Likewise, some of my fellow Evangelicals seem to have picked the very worst parts of Islam that they can find and pronounce that *those* blood-curdling portions are beyond question the genuine article! (No names here as one of the offenders is an old friend . . .) As that old friend's ghostwriter said to me recently, moderate Muslims are surely the equivalent, in Islamic terms, of postmodern theological liberals in the church. He went on to elaborate that since Evangelicals don't agree with Protestant or Catholic liberals, surely we should not agree that a moderate Muslim is the authentic voice of Islam. This means that the extremists must therefore be more genuine in their understanding of what Islam *really* believes – Osama bin Laden therefore speaks for Islam in a way that my former Cambridge neighbour Akbar Ahmed does not.

Now as an Evangelical, I am fully and utterly in favour of the Evangelical understanding of *Christianity*. When it comes to what Christians ought to believe, I am fairly died-in-the-wool (or conservative, for the Americans)! But to me, the problem with the approach outlined above is that it is reading *Christian* differences into *Muslim* faith. Even the most non-violent Muslims imaginable would claim to hold a profoundly theologically conservative view of the Qu'ran. They would say passionately that the conservative-liberal division within Christianity is quite alien to them. Furthermore, when you look at *some* parts of the Qu'ran, they are right. It really does say, "There is no compulsion in Islam." In addition, since we don't want to be victims of a terrorist attack, we should, surely, support non-violent "moderate" versions of Islam, if only out of self-preservation!

Surely too, from a Christian point of view, it matters not whether someone is a moderate or an extremist – since either version is a false religion. The entire Islamic world, whether in its Arabian heartland or that delightful Muslim family down the street, stands in need of Jesus Christ as Saviour. There is no need for us always to believe the worst, since either kind of Islam should prompt us to prayer and evangelism.

The reason we often want to believe the worst of Islam is not so much theological but historic. Islamic rulers have in the past conquered many Christian states, from Spain to the Balkans. Christian-Islamic tension did not emerge out of thin air in 2001. It has been going on for nearly fourteen hundred years, and for a thousand years the West was often at a disadvantage in the struggle. Even Britain, which Islamic armies never reached, regularly suffered from North African slave trading raids, when people living in coastal towns were seized and taken as slaves. (Linda Colley's book, *Captives*, is fascinating reading. It was not just Europeans and Americans who were guilty in the past of this despicable and evil practice.) Not until the Americans crossed the Atlantic in the early nineteenth century and rid the world of the Barbary Pirates were many European seaports safe from captive-hungry marauders.

A possible analogy?

But although fear of Islamic invasion is, in that sense, built into our historic psyches, that does not mean *theologically* that we as Evangelical Christians ought always to believe the very worst of *all* Muslims at every time and every place. Let us look first at a possible analogy, and then at some evangelistic reasons for discernment in how we approach our Muslim neighbours. (Remember, this is an analogy only. As I just wrote, we shouldn't read Christian differences into Islam.)

Is Billy Graham responsible for everything said by the pope? They are both professing Christians, after all! If, say, a Baptist minister denies the divinity of Christ, as one did in Britain a few years back, does that make *all* Baptist ministers equally guilty of that denial? (Or all Protestant ministers, for that matter, since all Baptists are also Protestants.) How often have we, especially those of us who are Evangelicals, been fed up with the stereotyping of Christians of which the press is so often guilty? How regularly do we groan when some newspaper or television programme finds some really way-out exponent of some view or another, and says, "Now this is what evangelistic [sic] Christians believe ..." Don't they even know that Evangelical and evangelistic are different terms?!

Here one can add that the 72 per cent of Arab Americans who are at least nominal *Christians* feel especially resentful. They both look like and actually are Arabs. But often the very reason why their family came to the United States in the first place is that they are *not* Muslims! Since some of them have fled Islamic-inspired persecution in their countries of origin, they have a much better reason to be suspicious of Islam than you have.

Alas, seeing only stereotypes is what we often do when we look at the Islamic world. A lot of that world *is* scary, but it is not all *necessarily* frightening. The only "all" is sad: How tragic that there are so many millions of people who have never recognized their urgent need of Christ as their personal Saviour and Lord. This, of course, brings us naturally to the imperative of evangelism, the other reason why always believing the worst is so unhelpful.

The evangelistic benefits
of rejecting stereotypes

Evangelistically too, we want to be good neighbours to those Muslims who live near us. While the core Islamic states seem closed to any kind of overt Gospel outreach, millions of Muslims now live in the West, whether in Europe or the United States. No law prevents us from evangelizing them! (For those who want more details on helpful evangelistic outreach to Muslim neighbours, *Muslims and Christians at the Table* by Bruce McDowell and Anees Zaka is one book that I have found helpful for US readers. British Christians can similarly read Chawkat Moucarry's book *Faith to Faith*.)

Those Muslims who are genuinely moderate will appreciate it if you do not visit them looking like a scared rabbit, terrified lest your hosts slay you as an infidel! If you meet a hard-line Muslim, he or she might be a fanatic, but not necessarily one who wants to blow up your local shopping mall. They might actually appreciate the fact that you, as a Christian, really do *believe something!* Both kinds of Muslim might be pleasantly surprised to find someone who not only practises their Christian faith but has strong views on moral issues as well. For many Muslims have stereotypes of *you!* They will discover that you are against drugs and premarital sex, for example, and share their sorrow at the moral vacuity of the MTV generation. They will discover that the words *Western* and *Christian* are not always coterminus! (We will see why this is so important later on in Chapter 8.)

Building this kind of relational bridge with our Muslim neighbours would indeed be a wonderful step. Christ tells us to love our enemies. Many in the West, especially after September 2001, have started to see the entire Muslim world as just that. As we will see later on, there are those who say that the Red Terror of Communism has been succeeded by the Green Terror of Islam! But if we as Christians, in obeying the command to love our neighbours as ourselves, reach out in Christian love and concern to those neighbours who are Muslim, such an initiative might be all the more appreciated by its recipients. *Well, at least the people who go to* that *church don't cross to the other side of the street when they see us*, a Muslim might think. Obviously, we must not hide our Christian faith and motivation when we reach out to our Muslim neighbours.

But at least Muslims, unlike so many of our vacuous, hang-loose, postmodern fellow Westerners, actually believe *something!* We were amazed in my Christian Union group at Oxford in 1976 when lots of the college Marxists became Christians through a university evangelistic outreach. But, as we reflected, perhaps this was because they already had real, active beliefs. In that sense, it was actually easier for believing Communists to become believing Christians, than it was for all the amiable woolly students around us, who were happy for *us* to be Christians as long as we didn't stop them from consuming their nightly pints of beer. Remember, it was Saul the persecutor of Christians who was converted on the road to Damascus. Once Muslims in the West see what Christians *really* believe, they might be more open to the Gospel than that self-centred, materialistic family next door who shares my own ethnic background.

Having said all this, there is nonetheless a real problem faced by moderate Muslims living in Western societies. Let us now see what that is and how we should respond.

The moral and religious dilemmas of nice moderate Western Muslims

Both in Britain and in the United States – and no doubt in other parts of the West with large Islamic populations – local Muslims feel very resentful of the way in which their neighbours view them after September 2001. From a human perspective, one can see this entirely and on both sides! Moderate Muslims did not kill anyone that day. But on the other hand, however much people on all sides proclaimed Islam *really* to be a religion of peace, it was inescapable that the perpetrators of the outrages did so very much *in the name of Islam*.

What fascinated me, as a Briton obliged to watch events from afar in Virginia, was the way in which in Britain many passionate British *liberals* were very clear indeed that Islam *was* a major reason for Al Qaeda terrorism. *The Guardian* newspaper, which many American readers will be astonished to know makes *The New York Times* positively conservative, was very clear indeed on this point.

Polly Toynbee, their pro-choice, anti-Christian columnist, lambasted the "limp liberals" who opposed American intervention in Afghanistan. As she put it on 10 October 2001, human rights are *universal* and are therefore applicable to all peoples everywhere. Here, surely, Evangelicals, a group she normally despises, can agree with her. The "fuzzy idea on the soft left" that she decries – Toynbee describes herself as a "hard-headed liberal" – is that cultures should be left to have their own practises. But that would mean there is "an Islamic cultural otherness that supersedes basic human rights." Here Evangelicals and atheists such as Toynbee can be at one. For the very same Islamic culture that a religiously neutral 2002 UN Human Development report says suppresses the rights of women forbids the free preaching of the Christian Gospel.

Furthermore, Hugo Young, *The Guardian*'s politically liberal and ancestrally Catholic commentator, wrote on 9 October 2001 an article entitled "It may not be PC to say this but Islam is at the heart of this." In it, he argued that while "political correctness allows no other analysis" than to say that Islam was not involved, this was in fact not true.

> Islam is at the heart of what is happening. When commentators muse about the evils of religious fundamentalism, in the modern context there's only one religion they can be talking about. That doesn't mean in any way that all Muslims are to blame. But the September terrorists who left messages and testaments described their actions as being in the name of Allah. They made this their explicit appeal and defense.

One of the things people said after 9/11 was that, strictly speaking, there is an element of unfairness in describing people as *Islamic* terrorists. No one called Timothy McVeigh a *Christian* terrorist, though his links with extremist, so-called Christian groups are well proven. I am sure none of us would recognize McVeigh as a Christian either. (Read Mark Juergensmeyer's fascinating and chilling *Terror in the Mind of God* to find out more.)

The difference is that after the Oklahoma bombing there were no Christian crowds in the streets of Britain and France applauding McVeigh and cheering on the group behind his actions. McVeigh might have believed in some warped version of Christian and white identity politics, but no one could really say he represented a major constituency in worldwide Christianity. On the other hand, large crowds in the Muslim world were to be found actively supporting bin Laden and Al Qaeda. Bin Laden became an overnight folk hero to many an angry young Muslim in a way that McVeigh did not for similar disaffected youth in the West. After the raid in January 2003 on the Finsbury Park mosque in London, it was found to contain many an alienated Muslim young man, captivated by the message of Islamic extremism preached there. But to be fair, equally large crowds in Iran charged through the streets shouting, "Death to terrorists!" There, the disaffected youth of Tehran and other places were making their support of the West very clear, in vocal rebellion against the hard-line Muslim leaders they felt had a stranglehold on the country.

So the real answer to the opening question of this chapter – Which is the *authentic* voice of Islam? – is an interesting one. *Both* are fully legitimate versions, depending upon the interpretation of Islam that you wish to follow.

How no single person speaks for Islam

Both King Abdullah of Jordan, a direct descendant of the Prophet Mohammed, and President Khatami of Iran have not hesitated, in the most vigorous language, to denounce terrorism and all its works. They are fulsome in their condemnation. There is a sense in which they are even harder in their attack on terror since they are devout Muslims who realize how badly such acts tarnish the name of Islam in the West.

But as we have seen, there is no single authority figure within Islam, such as the pope or the archbishop, to pronounce one way or another. Furthermore, there is, strictly speaking, no direct equivalent of the clergy in Sunni Islam either. Islam being in essence a religion of works-righteousness, there are only interpreters of the law, the *ulema*. But since no one interpretation is authoritative over another, even that does not help us. In addition, in countries that have powerful rulers the *ulema* often pronounce it in the way that the government wishes, and so are often ignored by anti-authority Muslims as stooges of the ruling classes.

This is all supposed to show the democratic nature of Islamic faith. In a way, it does. But it also means that if X interprets the Qu'ran in one particular way, and Y in another, it all depends on the school of Islamic thought that you follow as to which, if any, of them is speaking with authority.

So a nice, friendly follower of the Hanafi school of Islam says that Muslims should live in peace and tranquillity with the West because that is genuinely how he sees it. When such a person reads some blood-curdling *fatwa* from Osama bin Laden, who is from the Salafiyya branch of the Wahhabi interpretation of the Hanbali school of Islam, he will probably say that bin Laden has no right to hijack Islam for so evil a purpose. From *his* point of view, that is a true statement. But bin Laden could equally say that our friendly follower is quite wrong in saying that, and that only the Wahhabi version of Hanbali Islam is correct. All you then need is an Ismaili or Shia Muslim to come along and say that *both* of them are seriously deluded!

Moderate Islam

Why don't we hear more of the moderate versions of Islam? The reasons are twofold. First, how often do you read *good* news in your newspaper? "Mr. Smith wants the world to know that he had a great day today!" Often the very reason that we hear about something is because it is *bad* news: "Poor Mr. Smith was in a car wreck this morning and has a broken arm." Thus, some spine-chilling decree from an extremist Muslim that makes us afraid to go out shopping is more newsworthy than a sermon from a local imam telling everyone to get along with their Christian neighbours.

Not so long ago, I read a piece in the *International Herald Tribune* in which the writer bemoaned the fact that there were countless pro-Western demonstrations in Iran that were never mentioned in the press. The answer is that such nuggets of news can in fact be found, but in order to find them you have to do things such as checking out the BBC's website or making active Internet searches for Iranian pro-democracy pages in English. Most people obviously don't do this, and with many a newspaper you are in fact lucky if you find any news like that at all!

The other reason we don't hear more of moderate Islam is simply *money*. Moderate Muslims complain that the extremist view of Islam emanating from Saudi Arabia is just one version of Sunni Islam, and in that sense they are correct. But the Wahhabi-Hanbali school of interpretation has *lots* of money, all stemming from the very considerable coffers of the Saudi kingdom. Need a new mosque, complete with an imam? Your Saudi friends will pay!

This is having a serious global impact on the world of Islam. In Indonesia, for example, where different schools of interpretation have held sway and mingled with strong doses of local pagan religions as well, the austere Wahhabi version of Islam is steadily growing and is slowly superseding local viewpoints. While it is important to say that not all Wahhabi Muslims are necessarily terrorists, it is increasingly true that terrorists stem from the more extreme forms of Islam, such as the Salafiyya branch of Wahhabism.

To put it another way, a Muslim whose interpretation of the Qu'ran is that Islam is a religion of peace is hardly likely to go out and kill people! But if his understanding of Islamic teaching is that such an activity is all right, he will do one of two things. He will, if not violent himself, "understand" those who are. (Here one must in fairness say that something similar applied to terrorists in Northern Ireland. It was amazing how many otherwise nice Catholics "understood" IRA terrorism, while the most affable Protestants would profess to "understand" the equally violent Loyalist response.) Or, as we have seen increasingly in recent years, he might actually become violent himself.

How people do the unthinkable by thinking it's all right

Francis Schaeffer, the great Christian twentieth century thinker, once made a sad but significant observation about the prevalence of abortion and euthanasia in Western society. For him, it was not just a question of trying to prevent abortions from taking place. It was, as he so acutely put it, stopping the *abortion mentality*. As Christians, we know that thought precedes action. As Schaeffer realized, it is the fact that most people in the West today think that abortion is within the realm of the possible and permissible that causes it to be legitimized and take place. If you believe in a woman's sole right to choose, then abortion will follow!

In the same manner, in World War II many German soldiers denied that they had committed any atrocities. "We were only following orders!" they complained. Well, in a strictly literal sense they were: "Colonel Schmidt, shoot those fifty Jews we found hiding in the cellar!" But, one sincerely trusts, if we were asked to do something like that, we would refuse to obey and take the consequences. The very fact that such an order was given would also show to us that something had gone rotten in our society that we could be asked to commit so frightful a deed. This is precisely what had gone wrong in Nazi Germany. It was that such atrocities, whether against Jews, Russians, Gypsies, or other despised peoples, were within the realm of the possible and morally legitimate to commit.

Similar moral and mental contortions must have equally taken place in much more recent times. For example, in Bosnia, Serbian

Orthodox and Croatian Catholic soldiers were able to slaughter thousands of innocent and unarmed Bosnian Muslim men, women, and children, in cold blood, without blinking. (My book *Why the Nations Rage* goes into this in more detail.) This is what psychologists call *projection* and what we as Christians would describe as yet another version of original sin!

A truly scary experiment

A famous American psychologist carried out similar mind experiments that frighteningly show us the same thing (frightening because he shows what very ordinary people not unlike you or me could do!). He put the person whom he was testing in one room with an electric volt switch. Next door would be an actor – except the subject did *not* know this. Rather, they would be told some story, like the person next door had agreed to be experimented upon, or some other made-up tale. The psychologist would then ask the subject to flick the first electric voltage shock switch. A loud cry would come from the actor next door, who was pretending to be electrocuted! The voltage would then get higher and higher, and the screams from next door commensurately louder. Then they would arrive at a voltage so high that the nervous person flicking the switch would say something like, "Surely if I switch it to *that* level, the person next door will be killed!" Here we now come to the point of the experiment. The switcher was then told, "Oh, don't worry. You won't be held responsible if they do." What is truly scary is that most people still flicked the switch! What would often happen next is that the actor next door would make no sound at all – they were now supposedly dead.

What this, and other experiments of a similar nature, shows is that if humans feel they can legitimately pass the buck in doing something really atrocious – like flicking a switch and thereby killing someone – they will do so. It is, as we have just seen, within their perceived realm of the possible. Remember, the subjects of this experiment were ordinary, everyday Westerners, which in that sense we are ourselves.

In wartime we ask ordinary men to become soldiers and kill people, something that, one trusts, they would not normally want to do! But in the West, with sad exceptions such as the My Lai massacre in Vietnam, we have normally also taught the military that killing or targeting innocent civilians is wrong. It is said by experts that one of the reasons why Communism never gained legitimacy in Central Europe was that while the American and British soldiers liked local girls, they would never rape them, whereas the Russian soldiers frequently did. Iron Curtain Communism never fully recovered from the lack of legitimacy that stemmed from its barbaric origins.

How such things reflect in present-day Islam

It is the same with the different schools of thought within Islam. If violence is permissible, that is one step away from actually doing it, or at least "understanding" those who do. There are many suras within the Qu'ran that state plainly that violence against women and children – non-combatants – is entirely wrong. So when, after 9/11, many moderate Muslims pointed this out, they were doing so perfectly legitimately. The Qu'ran *does* say such things. In that interpretation, there would be complete unanimity between moderate Muslims and Christians who follow what the medieval sages such as St Thomas Aquinas called the Just War theory. (It is precisely on the basis of such early Christian thinking that President Bush felt legitimately able to launch the attack on Afghanistan, for example, or for Christians in the West to go to war against Hitler back in World War II.)

However, as we have seen, Islam also has the doctrine of *abrogation*. This means that some suras can supersede others. This is where things get messy. For it all depends on which suras supersede which. If you are on the moderate side, then what you might describe as the friendlier suras have superseded the more warlike ones, because the situation that necessitated them no longer applies. If, however, like most present-day Islamic terrorists or their rage-filled but not actually violent supporters, you take a different interpretation, then the violent suras *have superseded* the friendlier ones. And in this case actual large-scale physical violence against both total infidels (like us in the West) and fellow-Muslims who have gone soft (like President Anwar Sadat of Egypt) becomes entirely legitimate. In fact, it goes further than that: Such aggression actually becomes a *necessary holy act*. Violence becomes a duty, not even an option!

Jihad: just holy war or more than that?

It is here we must look at that widely known and often misunderstood term, jihad. As any moderate Muslim will tell you, the word derives from an Arabic verb meaning "to struggle." Jihad in that sense connotes *struggle*, and in whichever way you interpret it. So far so simple, but it gets complicated.

There are, as Muslims of all stripes will tell you, two distinct forms of jihad, one external and one internal. The one famous in the West – holy war – is the *external* meaning of the term, and is called by most Muslims the "lesser jihad." The other plain meaning is *internal*, or the struggle within yourself to be a better Muslim. This is commonly described as the "greater jihad." Let us start with the less controversial version – the internal struggle or the greater jihad.

Struggles within – the Muslim path to holiness

The greater jihad is, in many ways, at the heart of the works-righteousness system of Islam. It is, in a *very* rough sense, the Islamic equivalent of the Christian doctrine of sanctification, of becoming more Christlike in our thoughts and behaviour. However, as we have seen, Islam has no such thing as spiritual assurance. Your salvation comes from getting enough credits in the scales with Allah to get to heaven. Everything depends on what you do, not, as with Christian faith, in what (i.e., in whom) you believe and put your trust.

Here of course we must add the caution that faith without works is dead (cf. James 2:14–26). It is surely a strange "Christian" whose post-conversion behaviour is no different from what it was before. Christ is our Lord as well as our Saviour. (This being a book on Islamic rage, readers can do no better than reading either the authoritative series on Romans by D. Martyn Lloyd-Jones or John MacArthur's classic, *The Gospel According to Jesus.*)

But it is through our belief and trust in Christ's saving work on the Cross that we come into a real and living relationship with God. It is this personal relationship with God himself, and the presence of the Holy Spirit within us, that makes us want to grow more Christlike all the time. *This* is what Christian sanctification is all about, not some points that you nervously hope will add up enough to get you to heaven!

Such a concept of a personal relationship with God as Lord and heavenly Father is, as we have seen, entirely alien to Islam. God is more remote and *so* transcendent (as the theologians would put it) as to be *personally* inaccessible to us. As a consequence, it is works that save you and is thus this striving within – the greater jihad – that gets you to paradise. This is why it is *greater*, since for most people it is ultimately more important. (However, the lesser jihad does have a shortcut, guaranteed way to heaven – martyrdom.)

The greater jihad therefore is something that need be no threat to non-Muslims. In fact, if it is, as Muslims believe, good deeds that get you to heaven, it could be the opposite! Generous giving and kind hospitality are mandatory for all Muslims. This should mean that they *have* to be a good neighbour if you live near one!

So can you still kill the unbelievers where you find them?

Where Muslims differ today is not on the *internal* meaning, but on whether the *external* one still exists, in the sense of hordes of devout Muslim warriors going armed into battle and slaying their enemies. Here one must in fairness add that even those who do believe that the lesser jihad still exists are split upon its modern interpretation.

Some moderate Muslims would in effect take the view that external or lesser jihad simply no longer exists in the modern world. It describes situations in the past, and thus does not apply to Islam in the twenty-first century. You might call it the sublimated version, in which the violence of the past is sublimated into external struggles of a very different, and usually peaceful, kind. In Malaysia and Tunisia, to take two well-known moderate Islamic states, their respective rulers interpret the lesser jihad to mean the struggle to catch up economically with the West, for their countries to move out of underdevelopment into a more prosperous way of living. Jihad in this sense becomes an economic struggle rather than a military one.

However, as anyone who has read the decrees, or *fatwas*, of Osama bin Laden will know, there is also very much present in Islam a school of thought that says that jihad still carries its fullblown *military* meaning. It really is holy war. (For a helpful look at this in more detail, see Peter Bergen's fascinating best-seller *Holy War, Inc.*) Not only that, but as Anwar Sadat, the peacemaking president of Egypt, discovered when he was shot by Islamic radicals from his own country, the target of such rage fully includes Muslims who have, according to this interpretation, betrayed the faith.

Parenthetically, there is an interesting glitch in the works in Shiite Islam about whether they can still lawfully declare the military version of jihad. This is because, strictly speaking, only the true Imam can call one to holy war, and there has been no legitimate Imam to do this since AD 873! Needless to say, that did not prevent Ayatollah Khomeini from declaring all sorts of things when he was the ruler of Iran.

In the past, even those who felt that it was legitimate to have a holy war against the infidels differed among themselves. Most medieval Islamic scholars, such as Ibn Rushd (known in the West as Averröes), did not feel that you could lawfully slay non-combatant women and children. Furthermore, some parts of the Qu'ran say that if the infidels surrender, you should *not* kill them, but subjugate them and oblige them to pay the extra poll-tax that all non-Muslims citizens, or *dhimmi*, had to pay the Islamic authorities.

By even these standards, therefore, the slaughter of thousands of innocent civilians, whether in the United States in September 2001 or in Nigeria throughout the past few years, is quite wrong. However, as we saw at the beginning of this chapter in looking at just a small section from the infamous *Sword verse* of the Qu'ran, there are ways of interpreting that book that make such heinous acts entirely spiritually legitimate.

Though it may be spiritually legitimate, mass murder of any kind is thoroughly evil – and we as Christians would go further, holding that it is satanic. But does this mean that there is a unique degree of satanic force behind the Islamic threat to our world in the twenty-first century? We'll explore this issue in more detail in the next chapter.

CHAPTER 7

Is Islam Uniquely Satanic?

Christians often ask the question, "Is Islam satanic?" This is a quite natural question to ask, especially since this religion appears to be working against Christianity worldwide. But I do feel that to pose the question in this way is to make matters too simple. I would suggest posing the question like this: Is Islam *uniquely* satanic? Or, is Islam satanic to an extent that exceeds other entities? Is it especially a tool of Satan? We'll try to answer these questions by the end of the chapter.

Soldiers in a spiritual battle

We as Christians are involved, as the Bible continually reminds us, in a daily *spiritual* battle. Scripture shows that in this most important fight of all, neither our weapons or our enemies are physical (2 Corinthians 10:3–4; Ephesians 6:10–13). We are fighting unseen spiritual foes, whose basic identity is revealed to us in Scripture.

Here I should say that I would want Christians of all denominations to read this book, because we *all* need to be prepared in the struggle against Islam. This means that many of you will have particular views on spiritual warfare, demon possession, and a whole host of similar topics that godly Christians have disagreed upon for centuries! This issue is one that I fully appreciate as a minefield. So what I am trying to do here is to write along the lines of general, and I trust Scripture-inspired, principles that each reader can apply accordingly. As C.S. Lewis once said, there is a danger when it comes to the Devil that we either concentrate too much on what he can do or too little. I hope that this chapter carries with it a genuinely biblical perspective.

I therefore don't write about God's angels on the one hand, nor do I describe territorial demons on the other. Some of you will be mightily relieved while others will regard this as a serious omission. But I trust that we can all agree on the basic spiritual and scriptural teachings and proceed accordingly.

I think it safe to say, therefore, that *all* Bible-centred Christians would agree that *every* Christian is one of God's soldiers, regardless of our interpretation of the precise mechanics of how that works. We are *all* involved in spiritual warfare in one way or another, since that is more than clear from the teaching of the New Testament. We know that our armour is spiritual and that the Holy Spirit dwells in all God's people. It is also clear that our opponent is a spiritual one – the Devil and those fallen angels who rebelled with him.

Today we often forget that we live in an age of spiritual war. Militaristic language is increasingly unpopular – when did you last sing "Onward Christian Soldiers"? This is quite understandable. Human warfare is peculiarly horrible, and is thus a connotation that we have come to dislike. In addition, as we saw in Chapter 1, it reminds us of parts of our past – such as the Crusades – that we rightly want to forget. It also creates a doubtful imagery when it comes to evangelism and gives an impression that we are all firebrand-waving zealots determined to destroy our foes!

In the context of Islam, since we spend so much time apologizing for the Crusades and for twentieth century colonialism, it is even more an image that we wish to play down. Since the Crusades were a terrible mistake, this is a good reaction. But it is also a reaction that is unbiblical, since the New Testament is filled with warrior images. When we look at the Bible, we see that we are at war because Satan is at war with God. He began the battle! Whatever we might think of human warfare, the soldiers engage in a combat started by someone else. Sin and Satan's rebellion were the cause of the spiritual war that we as Christians now fight. It is as soldiers of Jesus that we are active in battle. The moment we become Christians, we become objects of hatred to the Evil One and in immediate need of the spiritual armour that Paul describes in Ephesians. Although invisible, this is surely a kind of warfare that any real Christian recognizes. If, as believers, we are aware of the daily struggles within, how much more should we be aware of the much larger scale battle without.

So the struggle between Christianity and Islam can be seen as part of this bigger picture, between the forces of God and his people on the one hand and those of Satan on the other. There really is a spiritual battle going on! Furthermore, as Christians we are automatically part of it, from the moment of our conversion onwards. There is no opt-out clause; in terms of the cosmic conflict, everyone is a soldier on one side or the other.

So is Islam satanic? Well, in this sense, yes. It is, from our point of view as believing Christians, something that is actively against the Gospel of salvation solely through Jesus Christ. But is it *uniquely* satanic? That is a much more difficult question!

A spiritual deception?

We know as Christians that ultimate revelation comes from God through Christ. Anything that contradicts that revelation cannot, by definition, be from God. An actively anti-Christian false religion such as Islam cannot be part of God's merciful common grace.

Penicillin is not mentioned in the Bible, but there is no doubt that many, possibly millions, of lives have been saved due to its discovery. So while you cannot say that penicillin is *directly* from God, surely God's general mercy towards our fallen race inspired the scientists who discovered and developed it. However, penicillin does not oppose or deny that Jesus Christ is the son of the living God. It does not abrogate his uniqueness as our Saviour. In that sense it is neutral. But that is not true of Islam. Likewise, if a Muslim scientist discovered a wonder drug today that also saved millions of lives, we should not refuse to take it simply because its discoverer is not a Christian. If God could use Pharaoh and a Babylonian emperor in the time of the Old Testament, today he can use people who reject his son, for good purposes as well as for bad.

Islam, as we saw when we examined its beliefs, has many *spiritual* teachings that are diametrically opposed to the Christian Gospel. So while many good things came out of Islam's Golden Age in terms of medical and technical advances, the religion *in and of itself* is part of Satan's lies and schemes to turn people away from the true worship of God. In the most important sense of all – the *spiritual* – Islam *is* a satanic deception.

Furthermore, we forget, because of the large Islamic conquests of the seventh and eighth centuries and the Ottoman and Mughal invasions of some centuries later, that much of Islam's expansion came by way of mission rather than by way of the sword. One can see this clearly in the enormous Muslim population of Indonesia today. Islam spread through traders and as a result of conversions that came from missionary rather than from military activity. The same is true of much of the Islamic growth in West Africa. It is a sad rebuke to the Christian church that these conversions came centuries after the massive Islamic conquests, and at a time when the church scarcely spoke beyond the European boundaries of Christendom. It was the Muslims who were active in evangelism while the Christians stayed at home.

The clash of universalisms revisited

But while no scimitars were involved, it was still a battle. Admittedly, it was people from one false religion evangelizing those from others, such as Hinduism and various other pagan cults. But Islam, like Christianity, is a *universal* religion. Hinduism, as the Indian-born Canon Vinay Samuel once told me, is a religion of *place*. In particular, it is the religion of the peoples of India, which is why today militant Hindus are killing Indian Christians and Muslims as traitors as much as followers of other faiths. Worship of local pagan deities is by definition not a global religion. Islam, however, says it is a *universal faith*, or, by its own evaluation, *the* true universal faith.

For when people become Muslims, it is not the same as if they are worshipping the gods of the trees and sky. Muslims are members of a specifically *global* religion, one that is in direct spiritual conflict, therefore, with Christianity, which is also a universally applicable faith. Both faiths are in direct competition *worldwide* for the souls of men and women. It is a clash of universalisms. In *that* real sense, Islam is perhaps an *especially* satanic deception, because it so closely mirrors the claims of Jesus Christ to be Saviour not just of the Jewish race but of the whole world. (For example, note Jesus' words in John 14:6: "I am the way and the truth and the life. No one comes to the Father except through me.") Islam may have begun as a supposed revelation to an Arab in Arabic, but it soon stretched far beyond Arabia's borders and now competes for converts with Christianity everywhere.

But is an especial threat a unique one?

Islam is so blatantly a threat to the Christian faith that Satan can hardly hide the fact from us; but on the other hand, there are plenty of things that deceive us Western Christians, which we all too sadly fail to notice.

Being in the United States in September 2001, I witnessed the massive increase in people going to church in the immediate aftermath of the attacks of 9/11. Since both the churches I attended (Anglican breakaway from the Episcopal Church and Southern Baptist) were theologically Evangelical, their respective ministers took full opportunity to be evangelistic. But, as across the rest of America, the initially high attendance numbers soon reverted to more normal numbers.

The Fall 2002 issue of *The Tie* had some fascinating insights into why this was. The authors said the United States saw a huge increase in *spirituality* but not actually in a genuine seeking after salvation in Christ.

Now, one hopes and prays that many people, and not just in the United States, were so shocked by the manifestation of sheer evil that they genuinely sought the answer in Jesus Christ. I am sure there were many real conversions. But in general I fear that the authors above were all too correct. In many instances it was, as they argued, a matter of people going to church merely to find comfort rather than an encounter with the living Christ. Whether or not the particular church people attended was an Evangelical one, the huge surge in church attendance proved all too fleeting. In fact it is possible that when many non-Christians heard the *real* Gospel, by default, as it were, they promptly left! For the *real* Gospel includes the ultimate in human *discomfort* – namely, that we are all fallen sinners in need of salvation.

In that sense, what we saw was a huge rise in a variant of New Age, touchy-feely spirituality, which makes you feel better but is certainly not challenging in the way that true Christian faith always is.

As I said elsewhere, it is surely far too early to say why disaster has hit in the West, in the Bali bomb, in the attack on Israeli tourists in Kenya, as well as in the events of 9/11. But what we can say about the whole of the West – Britain, Australia, and the many countries of continental Europe, every bit as much as the United States – is that it is profoundly materialistic. However religious many Westerners might be – and outside of the United States people don't usually even bother with that – it is materialism that they *really* worship. (I should insert a caveat here to say that it is the *love* of money that is the root of all kinds of evil, as Paul wrote in 1 Timothy 6:10, not money per se. And it is true that Osama bin Laden did not hesitate to use the fruits of his capitalist background to destroy thousands. It is a spiritual observation I am making here, not a political point.)

Few people could have been more excited than I when the Iron Curtain come down. But one of the sad statistics of that otherwise politically very happy period was that church attendance *decreased* in many of the newly liberated countries. But looking at it from a Christian perspective, one can see why such a tragedy occurred.

Christianity was for many of the people oppressed by Communism a kind of security blanket. Once the need for consolation had gone, so did attendance at church. Real Christians who were often persecuted continued as before. But their task was made more difficult by a new threat to Christianity: flagrant Western-style materialism. It is not surprising that the Bible warns us about the dangers of wealth (e.g., 1 Timothy 6:10). The temptations that a prosperous lifestyle brings are many, and they were now being discovered in abundance by millions of Europeans and Central Asians whose materialist desires had been suppressed by Communism.

Spiritually there is a hideous irony in all this. Communism is an entirely materialistic ideology – this world is all that there is. But in getting rid of Communism, the peoples of Central and Eastern Europe were merely substituting one kind of materialism for another. Greed and living for the moment is all there is, which is something the Bible speaks to often. How easily do we forget the commandment not to covet. How easily too do we condemn people for desiring things we do not particularly want, while forgetting to chide ourselves for desiring those things that *we* want. I may not fancy a sports car, but that wonderfully illustrated but rather expensive new book . . .

The danger of materialism is that, unlike Communism, it is not *explicitly* anti-Christian, which is why it is so insidious. It is all too easy for us to fall into its snare, including those of us who are Christian. Since Communism was, for all intents and purposes, explicitly atheistic, it did not tempt Christians in a way that materialism has been doing very successfully for many centuries.

There is also no doubt that materialism is a worldwide phenomenon. Greed and the desire to live only for material gain is something global in its appeal. Whether it is a state of the art ox for ploughing a field or the latest design of car, the motivation and desires behind such longings remain exactly the same, from Dallas to London to some remote hilltop in Papua New Guinea.

The lure of the Great Deceiver

Unfortunately for us as Christians, global materialism is seen in the Islamic world as being part and parcel of the Christian West. Bernard Lewis was right on PBS and in his books to say how clever Ayatollah Khomeini was in describing the West as "the Great Satan." There is, of course, an element of hate in that phrase. But in picking that up correctly, Lewis reminds us in explaining that expression in more depth, we forget Satan's other danger – that he is a great *tempter.* The point about temptations is that they are attractive, otherwise we would not be tempted to succumb. Khomeini knew full well the many and manifold temptations of the West to people in Iran, since that country had long been one of the most developed and technologically advanced in the Islamic world. The lures of the West were ensnaring many a young (and probably also not so young) Iranian away from the true and purer path of Islam.

However, where we would disagree with Khomeini is that Christianity, properly understood, is *not* part of the temptation of the West. Where we *would* agree with his diagnosis is that it is a universal snare into which it is all too easy to fall. Furthermore, we can agree that Satan *is* a great deceiver, since he deceives many people, Christians included, into believing that there is nothing wrong with greed, materialism, and all that goes with that way of thinking. He is, as Jesus described him, "the father of lies" (John 8:44).

Where we would of course entirely part company with Khomeini is in our contention that Islam is another one of the Great Deceiver's lies! It too, like materialism, is universal in its scope and global in its aspirations. But where we must be especially careful as Christians is not to get so blinded to the profound dangers of an active, proselytizing Islam that we forget to be aware of the equally insidious tempter lurking on our own doorstep. Prosperity of a kind that makes people oblivious of their need for salvation is every bit as impervious to the Gospel as resurgent Islam. Satan, "the god of this age" (2 Corinthians 4:4), blinds eyes in many different ways. Evangelizing the complacent, postmodern, MTV generation is as hard in many ways as spreading the Gospel in the streets of Tehran.

Nationalism – another great danger

I have written in other books about another great universal danger – the force of nationalism. I am not going to duplicate here what I have said elsewhere, but there is little doubt that in the twentieth century nationalism was responsible for the deaths of literally millions of people, fifty-five million in World War II alone. This too is very insidious since, if we love our country, we automatically presume that God is on *our* side! German Christians prayed as assiduously for victory in World War I as did Christians fighting for Britain or the United States. Furthermore, nationalism is dangerous as it too deceives Christians.

During the Balkan wars of the 1990s, many Serbs and Croats fought against the usually innocent Bosnian Muslims in the name of revenging themselves against earlier centuries of Islamic rule. It always puzzled me why Osama bin Laden, in his pronouncements from 1998 onwards, mentioned the Crusades but didn't mention the horrific massacres by Serb forces (who would identify themselves as Christian) against entirely innocent Bosnian Muslim men. We must not forget that the Srebrenica massacre, of seven thousand unarmed civilians, was by Serb Orthodox against Bosnian Muslims. The Serbian Orthodox Church eventually turned against their country's leader, Slobodan Milosevic. But for much of the war, they were a classic example of *religious nationalism*. Prince Lazar, the fourteenth century Serb leader who lost his life at the Battle of Kosovo in 1389, was frequently likened to Christ in sacrificing his life in combat and has, alas, been so seen by many a Serb nationalist ever since.

Nationalism is in one way an entirely local, not global, phenomenon. If *my* nation is right, then others are often, by definition, wrong. But after the fall of Communism between 1989 and 1991, nationalist wars and movements sprung up all over the world. Because the Cold War was over, local wars were no longer in danger of triggering an Armageddon (used in the secular sense of that term). Many Christians became swept up in the nationalist tide. Rwanda is a place that is said to have seen enormous revivals in decades gone by. But it has also seen some of the most vile and large-scale ethnic massacres of recent years, with hundreds of thousands of innocent Tutsi being murdered by their Hutu compatriots. This is not to say that there were thousands of Hutu Christians wielding machetes to slaughter their neighbours, but it is legitimate to ask where the church was when all this was going on.

Srebrenica, Rwanda, and 9/11 – three hideous faces of evil

Although we will deal with Islam as a possible nationalist phenomenon shortly, the massacres at Srebrenica and in Rwanda do have a relevance regardless of nationalism to the main *spiritual* theme of this chapter, namely is Islam *uniquely* satanic? There is a tendency to say, "Look at the horrors of 9/11! The perpetrators were Muslims! Nothing like that has ever happened in Britain or America, so therefore Islam is evil!"

As I write this, the King of Jordan, himself a direct and proven descendant of Mohammed, has just had written for him in British and American newspapers, condemnation of what he regards as extremist Islam and praise of what he calls its moderate version. We saw when we looked at the many variants of Islam that such a statement could be true and false at the same time. But it is certainly true that moderate Muslims would decry such evil as much as we would, if we allow the words *moderate* and *Muslim* to co-exist.

The problem, though, is that we are *all* selective in what we describe as being evil. This is true of Christians as well as Muslims, and is therefore pertinent to the wider question of whether Islam is *uniquely* evil. For what, other than totally evil, were the massacres of Muslims in Bosnia – hundreds of thousands if you add up the total numbers of individual massacres, of which Srebrenica was only the worst? What too was the near genocide of the Tutsi of Rwanda by their Hutu neighbours? (Both these conflicts show all too clearly – as do the historical English, French, and American experiences – that *civil* wars have a peculiar horror of their own.) If three thousand killed on one day is evil, what is seven thousand? What are hundreds of thousands?

Yet where were the Evangelical leaders then who write so eloquently about the evils of 9/11? Is anything less evil simply because it does not affect the country in which we live? *Everyone* on God's earth is a human being made in the image of God, whether a Bosnian Muslim car mechanic, a Tutsi peasant, or one of the many Britons and Americans killed in the World Trade Center. *All* of the violent events under discussion are abominable to God!

Obviously, something closer to home is bound to affect us more than something thousands of miles away, or in a country of which we know little. So from a human point of view, such a reaction is understandable. But is that the *Christian* response?

In particular, how much better a witness we would have had to the Muslim world if thousands of Christians worldwide, and especially in the West, had led global protests at the atrocious mass murder of innocent Muslim civilians by Serb soldiers who claimed to be Christians? Or if Evangelicals, who had read about the Rwanda revivals of past years, had been in the forefront of agitating for Western countries to get involved in order to prevent the massacres there from taking place. (It is a sad fact that we *did* have notice that they would happen, as BBC correspondent Fergal Keane showed clearly from his books and broadcasts.) Then perhaps it would be much more difficult for extremist Muslims to get away with confusing *the West* and *Christianity* as they do at present. For if, as Christians, we love our neighbours as ourselves, then a Bosnian Muslim mechanic or a Tutsi farmer is our neighbour too!

The Muslim nation

Nationalism, so far as the matters of this book are concerned, is tangential to our main theme. Islamic groups are said to dislike it and, in the sense taken above, one can see why. As both Bernard Lewis and a look at an old map demonstrate, the present-day boundaries of the Middle East are entirely modern and equally artificial. Only Iran can be said to have existed for thousands of years in roughly its twenty-first century position, but even its current borders are different from where they were hundreds of years ago. As for North Africa and the Middle East, the present-day state boundaries are very different, because most of those states simply did not exist as presently constituted until the twentieth century. Their borders were delimited by European colonial powers, in the case of the Middle East especially after the fall of the Ottoman Empire in 1918. These nations are to a considerable extent what the sociologist Benedict Anderson calls "imagined communities."

The reason for this is that they have been, in some form or another, part of much larger units. The great Ummayad and Abbasid caliphates extended over thousands of miles – in theory, for a while, from Iran to Spain. The successor Ottoman Empire was similarly large in scope. Loyalty was to the caliph, an Islamic office, not to your nation.

Historians disagree passionately as to when nationalism began. Some, like the well-known writer Conor Cruise O'Brien, have it beginning as early as King David. Modernists and Marxists of different hues have it all starting with the French Revolution in 1789, which to me is far too late a date for so powerful a phenomenon. Others, Evangelical readers will be interested to know, posit nationalism's early stirrings with the Reformation in England and what we now call Germany. People can take their pick. But thankfully in this book, the great debate on nationalism's origins do not really concern us, because the key point here is that everyone agrees it was in full flow in the twentieth century.

As often mentioned in news articles related to Iraq, that country is totally artificial, a post–Ottoman Empire merging together of three totally disparate peoples (Kurdish Sunni Muslims, Arab Sunni Muslims, and Shiite "Marsh Arab" Muslims) by the British in the 1920s. In that sense, being an Iraqi nationalist is rather a contradiction in terms, as the British and American governments are currently finding. Likewise, Nigeria, which is entirely a twentieth century British invention, also finds it difficult to stay together, especially now that the northern states are turning increasingly to Sharia Islamic law, to the horror of their pagan or Christian southern neighbours.

From the failure of Arab nationalism to the Islamic nation of Al Qaeda

What post-independence leaders such as Nasser tried to do was to give people a loyalty to a wider entity. This, as Chapter 5 showed, was Arab *nationalism* and to Nasser's own ideological version of it, Arab *socialism*. But as we have seen, this failed. Being Arab increasingly meant being beaten by the Israelis! So now Islamic ideologues, from Sayyid Qutb onwards, have been resurrecting the ancient two worlds *Islamic* identity – the *Dar al-Islam* and the *Dar al-Harb*, the House of Islam and the House of War. It is this identity to which Osama bin Laden, Qutb's disciple, refers when he says that the nation of Islam has been suffering for over eighty years (since the abolition of the caliphate).

This is obviously a religious identity rather than a geographical or genetic identity. Anyone can be a Muslim, regardless of where they live or from whom they descend. It is also true that when we think of the word *nationalist* we primarily think in terms of Serb nationalist, or Nazi, or some similar ethnic/political/geographical configuration. This would also have been true of Arab nationalists, since they were ethnically Arab and lived in a defined geographical area (the Middle East and North Africa). But since

Muslims can and do come from everywhere, many reject the notion for which I argued in *Why the Nations Rage* that there can be such a thing as a religious nationalist. A Serbian Orthodox religious nationalist makes sense to them: Serbia is a place, the Serbs are a defined ethnic people in the Balkans. But an *Islamic religious nationalist* – can such an entity exist?

Bin Laden the nationalist?

Maybe such a creature is impossible by Western academically defined criteria, but as I have said many times, it is vital to remember to define people also by how they see themselves. (For more cerebral readers, this statement has the full imprimatur of the great early twentieth century thinker, Max Weber. He is mainly known for the interesting and much discussed theory that Protestantism led to the rise of capitalism in the West, something that many Catholics, agnostics, and atheists argue for as well.) But if that is indeed the case, then you really could call Osama bin Laden and other types of Muslim extremists *Islamic nationalists.* If that is also true – and I am being controversial in saying so – then you have to understand nationalism in order to understand twenty-first century Islamic rage.

This is why the statements in December 2002 by Yasser Arafat, the Palestinian nationalist leader, are so interesting. He has in effect told Al Qaeda to get off his turf. He correctly pointed out that Al Qaeda's conversion to the Palestinian cause is a recent one, and an opportunistic one at that.

In terms of the war against terror as taken generically, many Palestinians *are* terrorists. (I should also add that many are not, especially the Evangelical Christian Arab minority.) But the point is that they are *Palestinian* terrorists. Their struggle is a very local and specific one. Al Qaeda, by contrast, is operating on a global scale. There have never been PLO attacks on Australians in Indonesia. On Israel, yes, and often! On Israelis outside of the Middle East, as in Munich in 1972, again, yes. But although the PLO are still terrorists and Al Qaeda are also terrorists, they are each very different kinds of terrorists, something the generic term "War on Terror" sometimes fails to distinguish.

Many Muslims wrongly support the Palestinian cause because they see it as part of the *Muslim* struggle against the West. With the diaspora of many Palestinian Christians to the West, the United States, Australia, and elsewhere, this is increasingly true *in practice*. But there have been and still are many Palestinian "Christian" nationalists and terrorists, because theirs is the *Palestinian* cause and not a specifically Muslim one as such.

Bin Laden and his like, however, represent by equal definition a global cause, fighting in the name of Islam literally all over the world. Palestinian terrorists operate against the interests of a particular state, Israel. Al Qaeda sees itself as against Jews, but also as against Christians, and, for that matter, against corrupt Muslim regimes they deem to be insufficiently anti-Western. So when we talk about terrorism, we always need to define the kind of terror in question. Bin Laden is clearly keen to hijack the popular Palestinian cause for his own nefarious ends, and Arafat intends to stop him. The *intifada*, or rebellion, is, to the horror of the predominantly nationalist PLO, in danger of being used as a pawn in a much bigger, global struggle.

In the sense of religious nationalism, Osama bin Laden is a nationalist, even though it is for a religion that claims global reach. What we as Christians need to be very careful about is that our patriotism does not become nationalistic – my country right or wrong. For the current war against terrorism has been used as the excuse by many Islamic extremists to portray a struggle of the West against Islam, and we as Christians must be especially careful not to give them any ammunition for their claim!

"Nuke Tehran" and other human reactions to Islamic rage

"Nuke Tehran!" "Bomb Afghanistan back into the Stone Age!" These were the understandable but sadly misguided reactions of many of my American friends to the Iran hostage crisis in 1980 and to 9/11 respectively. (Here I had to explain to people that, thanks to the devastation wreaked by the Taliban, much of Afghanistan was bombed back into the Stone Age already!) From a purely human, gut-response level, I could see fully why my friends felt as they did. We tend to react viscerally at moments of extreme provocation or crisis. But is this a *Christian* response? The answer has to be no.

The people who live in these countries are made in the image of God in the same way in which God made us. They are individuals with souls. Anger against the West is very much of a reaction of the Islamic basement rather than the Muslim street, to use Thomas Friedman's phrase. As I write this, thousands of people have demonstrated in Tehran chanting "Death to dictators!" not "Death to America!" or "Death to Britain!" The same *New York Times* columnist I just quoted has also written of like groups in Egypt, who similarly long for democracy, and of a kind that is not necessarily anti-Western. We might, in other words, be nuking people who are on our side!

But geopolitics aside, surely we should be praying for the inhabitants of the House of Islam to discover Christ as Saviour, rather than simply wanting to destroy them out of a visceral sense of revenge. Christians whose loved ones have been evilly butchered by IRA terrorist bombs in Britain have been the best imaginable witnesses for the love and forgiveness of Jesus when they publicly forgave their murdered relatives' attackers on prime-time television. Some of my own family, who lived in Beirut as tentmaker missionaries during the worst of the Lebanese civil war, were able to give similar testimonies as they were airlifted off the beach while bombs and shells rained all around them. Jesus told us to love our enemies and we should do the same.

Unfortunately, a lot of the revenge language gives powerful ammunition against the West to those who would perpetuate the violence. I saw this for myself in Lebanon. When Maronite Phalangist "Christian" militiamen would carry out some atrocity, the hard-line Muslim leaders would say to the Lebanese Christians and to the other villagers: "See what you Christians are doing?"

The fact that the Maronite killers, who were often also high on hashish as they murdered, were completely *unchristian* in what they were doing was neither here nor there – *all* of us were deemed equally guilty.

Fighting a truly Just War

We must as Christians, therefore, distinguish between *Western policy* and *Christian response*. One trusts that our own countries will never do anything unchristian. But in war, mistakes are made and the wrong people sadly end up being killed accidentally. Afghanistan is now a liberated country, but not a few innocent Afghan civilians unwittingly were killed in the process. Christian Just War theory says that civilian casualties are always wrong, and the *deliberate* taking of such lives certainly must be. But as we saw in the Kosovo conflict when a US Air Force plane accidentally bombed a civilian convoy, thinking it was one of Serb soldiers, such things are tragically unavoidable in what soldiers call the fog of war.

(This is not a book to go into the Just War theory in great depth. Good articles have been written about it in *First Things* and Professor Larry Adams' tapes, available through Mars Hill recordings, are especially helpful for those wanting to explore in more depth whether war can be deemed right from a Christian point of view.)

But if we echo the bellicose language of those around us, we give credence to the promoters of Islamic rage, namely that this *is* a war between Christianity and Islam. As we have seen, the *real* war between the Muslim religion and Christian faith is ultimately a *spiritual* one, not one fought with tanks, bombers, and other military means. Afghanistan may be free from Taliban rule, but its people will still go to hell if they remain as Muslims and reject the Gospel, just as the worshippers of Mammon (see Matthew 6:24) down our street will if they too spurn salvation. Islam, Mammon – they are both weapons of Satan to lead people away from reconciliation to God the Father through the finished work of Christ.

So is Islam *uniquely* evil?

We return to the question: Is Islam *uniquely* evil? From a spiritual point of view, the answer must be yes. Islam is a false religion that has deceived people for well over a thousand years. As we saw when we looked at what Muslims believe, one could go so far as to say that it is especially the *good* things in Islam that are the worst deception, because they are what makes it so attractive to many. We must remember that, while the early conquests of Islam were through the sword, most of its recent expansion has been through missionary growth. It is thus a very subtle deception, and perhaps none more so than at the present, when people in the West are taking an interest in it often now for the first time.

But while we in the West might not be tempted to convert to such a religion, there are plenty of other false gods to whom our neighbours bow down and worship on a daily basis. Furthermore, through globalization, we are actively exporting just such Mammon worship worldwide. Since I enjoy eating at McDonald's – at least you can guarantee the menu whatever country you are in – I hope I am not being blinded myself in saying that there are many parts of globalization that are *in themselves* morally neutral. But as the Ayatollahs in Iran have realized, and as we should too, the problem is often not the goods themselves but the *values* that come with them.

Western commentators such as Malise Ruthven in *A Fury for God* have pointed out the reference of Islamic writers to *westoxification*, or similar phrases, depending on your literal translation from the Arabic or Persian originals. Here it is all the more important for us as Christians to make the firm distinction between *Western* and *Christian*. For in many ways, as we will see in the next chapter, the Islamicists are right, even though for completely the wrong reasons. There *is* a lot wrong with our "live for the present," often mindless, money-worshipping culture. Of course, where we part company from Muslim extremists is on the solution: It is not massacring three thousand capitalists on a single day, but new life in Jesus.

Likewise, the kind of false religions that lead people to slaughter others – the Serb Orthodox soldiers killing Bosnian Muslims at Srebrenica, the VHP-inspired Hindu mobs massacring thousands of Muslims in Gujarat – are profoundly evil. (Note that Muslims were the innocent victims, not the perpetrators, in both sets of massacres.) As Christians, we should be as much against *them* as we are against Al Qaeda or the groups linked to them killing innocent people from Bali to Kenya.

Trying to strike a biblical balance

In conclusion, we need to strike a biblical balance. On the one hand, saying gooey things like, "Well, Islam is a religion of peace; and, hey, let's all love each other anyway," does not do much good. Yes, there are moderate Muslims doing their best, people as diverse as King Abdullah of Jordan, Pakistani-born Professor Akbar Ahmed in Britain and now in the United States, and the brave reformers in Iran, risking their lives for their views. But then there are those such as Al Qaeda, extremist anti-Semitic imams in the Middle East, and Indonesian leaders such as Abu Bakr Bashir, each one of whose views are very much the opposite.

Islam contains both moderates and fanatics, and no one group can claim to speak for *all* of Islam. Further, while there are sincere people who do good things in Islam, as there are in most religions, as a *religion* Islam is false. Whatever its finer points, and whatever agreement Muslims and Christians have on many moral issues, you still cannot get away from the basic *spiritual* issue that Islam is a false religion that therefore deceives many.

On the other hand, if we single out Islam as *uniquely* evil, we risk turning our eyes away from many other evil things that spiritually have the same result. Many Christians today fear for their lives, and it is not Islam that endangers them. In atheist China, in Hindu Nepal and India, Christians are *still* being actively persecuted, and many have been put to death in India for their beliefs. In the West many millions of young people either reject any kind of overt religion altogether, while unconsciously worshipping

Mammon in the process, or turn to the New Age commitment-free mysticism so prevalent in our culture. The Great Deceiver has them too!

Surely the biblical answer is that *all* these things are manifestations of the Evil One. With some it is Islam, with others Hinduism, or the unfortunate and completely inaccurate way in which "Protestant" and "Catholic" sectarian violence has been linked with supposed spiritual differences in Northern Ireland. With others, increasingly in the developing world as in the West, it is secular materialism. The temptations may be different, but the Tempter remains the same. It is our duty and privilege as Christians to reach *all* these groups with the Gospel of Jesus Christ. Islam is evil, but if the Devil can't get people that way, he has plenty of other ways to try. Thankfully, as we will see later, he is on the losing side!

CHAPTER 8

A Clash of Values: Islam, Christianity, and Western Civilization

One of the most influential theories in recent years leaped from the ivory towers of academia to the everyday discussion of ordinary people and their daily newspapers after 9/11. This theory, developed by Harvard professor Samuel Huntington, is called the "clash of civilizations." He originally propounded it in an important article in the journal *Foreign Affairs* in 1993, which he then expanded into a book called *The Clash of Civilizations and the Remaking of World Order* in 1996. Many secular commentators and not a few Christians feel that his controversial theory was validated by the perpetrators of 9/11, and by the fact that it was Muslims deliberately killing innocent people in the United States in particular. Since his theory predated those events by eight years, he is seen as prophetic by his supporters in both the academic world and Christian community alike.

I mentioned in the Introduction that this is not yet another post-9/11 book. But I began the book by referring to that event since that tragedy woke most people up to this powerful theory that has been the cause of passionate discussion in universities around the world. (I thought I would get lynched when I lectured about it to an international audience of postgraduate students in 1995.) It has even been the subject of major United Nations summits held before September 2001 designed to prevent so dreaded an event from ever happening.

So what is this theory, and why has it caused such heat? As we will soon see, it is that the entire world is divided up into what Huntington calls civilizations. These are not like the old Cold War divisions – Capitalist, Communist, Unaligned. They are primarily cultural and within that, to a very large extent religious. This is because Huntington often uses religious descriptions – Western (Catholic/Protestant), Orthodox, Buddhist, Islamic, Sinic (Confucian), and so on. To him cultural differences will, in particular, be the source of future wars, and not old-fashioned concepts such as ideology, economics, or sheer territorial aggrandizement. This is a slight simplification of a very complex theory. (My book *Why the Nations Rage* goes into this in much more depth.)

We will see more of this theory as the chapter unfolds. Suffice it to mention here that, because it gives a major role to religion in the explanation it gives of world affairs, it is one that many Evangelicals have found attractive. However, the current global environment is actually not quite so simple. If we look at it from a specifically Evangelical point of view, we also need to examine the equally well-written, and to Evangelicals no less fascinating, writings of the Classics (Roman and Greek history) scholar Victor Davis Hanson. Also a university professor, he has gained a considerable following among thoughtful Christian political conservatives in the aftermath of September 2001.

We will look at whether our responses to events are specifically Christian, or whether they are patriotic first and Christian second. For if they are truly *Christian*, then a fellow believer in Nigeria, Brazil, or Singapore (all places where God's church is expanding with amazing growth), should have exactly the same response as us. But if it is essentially a British or American response, we need to ask ourselves whether our patriotism is fully compatible with our biblical understanding. There is no necessary incompatibility between my being a loyal European and a fervent Evangelical. But the issue in this book is that of *religious* loyalty. As we have seen, Islam is very much a multinational faith as well, not just an Arab phenomenon.

So it is important that we distinguish *as Christians*, as part of God's family worldwide, what our response should be in a way that secular writers, by definition, do not. It is the Christian faith to which we are ultimately loyal, not the right of Western multinationals such as McDonald's to be able to sell burgers – however tasty – in every part of the globe. (Note that I say *Western* rather than *American*. Other Western countries have their multinationals, for instance, until 2002 Burger King was actually British owned!)

A civilization, says Huntington, is a broad cultural identity that all people living within it share in common. Most of you reading this will, according to him, be part of *Western civilization*, which, roughly speaking, is Western Europe, North America, Australia, and New Zealand. Clearly we don't all have English as a common language – the French would most certainly object! But what we do have in common is what Huntington regards as the vital cultural glue: our Western Christian heritage. Why don't we form part of the same civilization as Orthodox countries such as Russia or Greece, and why are we different from, say, Catholic Brazil?

The key here is that Huntington's civilizations are essentially religious based – Islam is one, for example – and that civilizations will replace the Communist/Capitalist divide of the Cold War as the new basis for twenty-first century conflicts. Since recent terrorism has been in the name of Islam, and since he defines Islam as a unified civilization, we need to see if he has come up with the key to understanding the new forms of conflict that have re-erupted in recent years.

So who is clashing with whom and why?

Huntington's theory aims to explain the present. But in order to do so, he goes back to the end of the Cold War. We must do the same. Between, roughly, 1948 and 1989–91, the world was a scary but very simple place. We spent a lot of that time in danger of a nuclear war. But, as we know, this never happened because, for all intents and purposes, we lived in what specialists call a *bipolar* world. After World War II, only two nations emerged strong enough to be called superpowers: the US and the USSR. They were the two poles around which everyone else revolved – hence *bi*polar. Every conflict everywhere sooner or later had a superpower dimension to it. While this allowed individual wars to happen – as in Korea, Vietnam, and several smaller wars in Africa, for instance – the *big* war never happened. The Cold War never turned into a hot World War III.

The reason that the Cold War never erupted into World War III, as I recall Cambridge professor Sir Harry Hinsley arguing, was precisely because both sets of superpowers had so many nuclear weapons that they could each destroy the world many times over. (You don't have to be a political conservative to believe this, as do many Americans and Europeans of all persuasions.) The destructive potential of the NATO and Warsaw Pact nuclear arsenals was so great that, if they were ever used, they would for sure cause what defense planners called *mutually assured destruction.* (Is it any coincidence that the initials are M.A.D.?) Both sides knew this. Although we now also know, from several British spies such as Oleg Gordievsky, the Secret Intelligence Service's most successful agent, that there were times when the Soviets were crazy enough to think that they could win a nuclear war.

Here in Cambridge, England, we are very near many of the top US Air Force bases that date back to World War II. During the Cold War, these bases were fully equipped with the very latest nuclear missile technology. While my father cheerfully felt that we could survive a nuclear attack by living in the family's medieval cellars – with a centuries-old private well thrown in – my feeling was always that I would be dead of radiation poisoning by the time I got to their village. Many teenagers were lured by the false promise of the Campaign for Nuclear Disarmament, which sadly would have made no difference had such a war begun, since we would probably all have been killed in a nuclear exchange anyway. If most of the missiles had flown and duly landed, the atmospheric pollution from the fallout would have been so great that the *entire* earth would have lost direct sunlight contact with the sun, so that no place on earth would have been exempt.

This is why I believed Sir Harry's thesis to be true. He basically argued that the more complex and devastating the weapons of mass destruction, the *less* likely you are to have war, because all combatants know that the damage done to *everyone* will be so great as to make victory impossible. This is a variation of what is called the *deterrence* theory: Weapons are designed not so much to attack people as to stop them from attacking you.

Although leading fellow Evangelicals on both sides of the Atlantic, such as John Stott in Britain and Ronald Sider in the United States, decried nuclear weaponry, I tended to agree with thinkers such as the writer Jerram Barrs, a member of the Francis Schaeffer founded movement, L'Abri. He argued that such weapons actually stopped war, and it appears that view is turning out to be right. We haven't had World War III, the Iron Curtain came down peacefully in 1989, and the Soviet Union disintegrated from within in 1991. All this happened without the carnage and total destruction that so many people had dreaded for so long.

But what about the thousands of war deaths since then?

But since 1991 hundreds of thousands of people have been slaughtered in wars worldwide. What is worse, as Robert S. McNamara and James G. Blight showed in their book *Wilson's Ghost*, casualties are now *mainly civilian* rather than military. You don't even need twenty-first century weapons to slaughter on a large scale, either. Hundreds of thousands of people were butchered in an orgy of genocidal murder in Rwanda, and the weapon of choice was a machete, which is similar to the sword of biblical times. Similarly, much of the carnage in the former Yugoslavia was caused by rifles and machine guns, which were no more advanced than the weapons used in World War II or even the American Civil War.

Why is this? What happened to the great post–Cold War dreams of a New World Order? Since I had spent much time with persecuted Christians behind the Iron Curtain, who are now wonderfully free, I was probably as guilty of euphoria as former president George Bush Sr. and millions of others around the world. But there can be no doubt that our hopes were devastated by the harsh reality of the global mayhem that has taken place since that all too brief interlude of hope and freedom.

It is here that the Hinsley thesis shows its continuing relevance. For once the Cold War was over, local wars were exactly that – local. There was no superpower rivalry involved any more, no danger that a dispute in one obscure part of the world could act as trigger for a superpower war leading to nuclear Armageddon. There was a way in which this was a good thing. Unsavoury and profoundly corrupt despots could no longer claim Western aid in the name of keeping their poor, oppressed, and benighted subjects free from Communism. Democracy has increased considerably since 1991, almost certainly as a direct result of the end of the Cold War. Countries such as Nigeria and Guatemala, for example, have also seen dramatic church growth, with the Evangelicals growing the most rapidly. On the other hand, now that local wars have little danger of escalating into global conflicts, they happen far more frequently than before. Since the combatants are not nuclear weapon superpowers, but much smaller countries with normal arsenals, the doctrine of deterrence effectively ceases to apply. In places such as Rwanda and the former Yugoslavia (Bosnia, Croatia, Kosovo), hundreds of thousands of deaths, mainly civilian, followed as a result.

This has tended to mean that while we in the West are now much safer – the threat of nuclear war has gone – for most people the world has suddenly become much more dangerous and far more violent. War has now entered the world of the possible again, just as before the Cold War. As a consequence, writers are now talking about the New World *Disorder*, because the stability that bipolar superpower M.A.D. brought has vanished.

The other big change is that we now live in what experts call a *unipolar* world (literally, one pole). There is now only one kid on the block – the United States. (The French say that the United States is now a *hyperpower*.) Quite simply, no other power on earth even remotely approaches that held today by the United States. American defense spending in 2002 was *well* over ten times that of her NATO allies combined – and that includes major nations such as Britain, France, Germany, Italy, and Spain. (It will probably be even higher still by the time that you read this.) Never before in history has *one* such power held such global predominance, not even the British Empire at its height in the nineteenth century.

Living in a very complicated post-1991 world

So what does America being a super-superpower mean? And what has that to do with Islam and clashing civilizations? What repercussions does this have for us as Christians? (By now you will not be surprised to learn that I am optimistic about the spiritual side while uncertain about the geopolitical ramifications.)

During the Cold War, all of us in the West knew who our enemies were: the Russians and the Soviet bloc. Christians knew, of course, that that applied to the governments and not to the oppressed citizens, many of whom were fellow believers who were themselves persecuted. But the world was essentially simple: There were the good guys in the West, led by the US, and the bad guys in the Communist world, led by the USSR. With the fall of the Soviet Union in 1991 things became much more complex. Look today at Russia, for instance. Many Russians retain their old anti-Americanism, and the events of 9/11 led many visceral anti-US Europeans, many of whom have never forgiven the United States for the Vietnam War, to crawl out of the woodwork. But in the War on Terror, President Putin is doing everything possible to help the United States. There is now a Russian delegation to NATO, hitherto the Soviet Union's sworn enemy. Post-9/11, many

passionate left-wing feminists found themselves zealously *pro–*
George Bush! This was because the Americans, in liberating
Afghanistan from Taliban rule, also freed the women of that country from years of oppression. Many of the Russian students I have
taught at Cambridge, coming as they would from middle-class
homes, are pro-capitalist and so pro-Western.

In the Gulf War in 1991, Saudi Arabia and the United States
fought side by side. But fifteen of the nineteen 9/11 Al Qaeda terrorist hijackers were Saudi citizens, and many Americans have
woken up to the fact that much of the most violent Islamic
extremist and anti-American propaganda has been paid for by
Saudi money. By contrast, Iran saw *pro*-American demonstrations
after 9/11. Iranians chanted, "Marg bar terrorist!" (or "Death to
terrorists!") in the streets, and Iranian women at aerobics classes
in Tehran, the capital, deliberately played the "Stars and Stripes"
to the astonishment of visiting American and British journalists.
Strange forces were clearly at work.

In other words, the world has changed considerably. Some
Russians are pro-American, others are not; most British people
still love the United States, but some loathe her. Germans loved
the United States during the Cold War, but many now feel
ambivalent towards her. Many of the Saudis whom the United
States saved from Iraqi destruction and conquest are supporting
the murderers who slaughtered thousands of US citizens. The sim-
plicity of the Cold War era is truly gone.

During the Cold War, people sought explanations for what
was happening. It was, in many ways, an ideological conflict
between capitalism and freedom on the one hand and Marxism
and party dictatorship on the other. (That is a rather simple
statement, but since this is a book on Islam, it will do for now, for
certainly that is how many people perceived it.) Now that
ideological clash is over and a far more complex, nebulous, and
uncertain world has come in its place. This is where writers such
as Samuel Huntington and Victor Hanson come in, and where
the relevance of these ideas to the present situation will soon
become clear.

What thinkers such as Huntington are trying to do is to explain the world in which we now live. As Colin Powell said in 2001, we don't just live in the post–Cold War world anymore, but in the *post*-post–Cold War world. This is certainly true for the United States, but, as I noted in the Introduction, there is a good case for saying that most other parts of the world were hurled into the post-post–Cold War world of violence and ethnic and religious conflict much earlier on. (My book *Why the Nations Rage* goes into this in considerably more detail, in looking at the innately *religious* nature of conflicts in places such as Bosnia and Kosovo.) This is something that Huntington can, with some merit, be said to have predicted.

For what the clash of civilizations theory does is to explain where conflicts will come now that the Cold War is over. His thesis, which I outlined briefly earlier, is that religion and religious differences will play a major role in future conflicts. Or as he puts it, "religion is a central defining characteristic" of what wars may be in the coming century – if his theory proves correct.

In this Huntington is not alone. You do not have to agree in full with his thesis to argue that *religion* is going to be a major cause of massive conflict in the twenty-first century. I argued the same in the original 1997 edition of *Why the Nations Rage*. More well-known books than mine are those by University of California professor Mark Juergensmeyer: *The New Cold War* and his more recent *Terror in the Mind of God*, both of which considerably predate the events of late 2001. Likewise, another influential book, which we shall look at in more detail later, is *Jihad vs. McWorld*, also written by an American professor, Benjamin R. Barber, again long before 2001.

But where Huntington differs from these books is that he splits the world up into the cultural/religious identities that we alluded to earlier: *civilizations*. The civilizations Huntington names are Western, Orthodox, Islamic, Sinic (i.e., China and Chinese-influenced countries), Japanese, Buddhist, Hindu, Latin American, and African. Everyone lives in one of these civilizational groupings. Huntington doesn't recognize Judaism as a distinct

civilization, but rather aligns Jews civilizationally with the countries in which they live – a New York Jew is part of the West, for
example.

This division in itself has been highly controversial. When I
have lectured on this in Britain and the United States, for example, to an audience containing Russians, Serbs, or Pakistanis, I have
had a very rowdy reception. I have also kept changing my mind
on my own response to Huntington and his case. In the original
1997 edition of *Why the Nations Rage* I tended to favour Huntington's theory, but by the 2002 edition I found myself agreeing
with it in parts but rejecting it as what sociologists call an overarching metanarrative theory – or in plain English, as an idea that
seeks to explain everything! (Professor David Little at Harvard
Divinity School was very helpful in enabling me to reorganize my
thoughts on these complex issues.) To put it another way, while
it explains *some* things, it does not explain *everything;* and to be
fair, Huntington himself admits this, even though he still feels that
his theory is basically right.

The "bloody borders" of Islam and the religious resurgence of the twentieth century

What has really set the cat among the pigeons, to use a famous
British phrase, is Samuel Huntington's phrase that Islam has
"bloody borders." Specifically, this means that Islam is involved in
many conflicts on its borders, but it has been interpreted as saying that current-day Islam is innately prone to violence. Needless
to say, this is very controversial. Some argue that Huntington is
demonizing Islam in a most unfair way, while others, as we saw
earlier, feel that he is a prophet of our time fully vindicated by
the Islamic nature of the attacks of 9/11.

So is Huntington right? Are we at war with Islam? Specifically, how should we as Christians view so powerful a thesis?
When British people want to say that something is partially right

and partially nonsense, they call it a "curate's egg." There is an extent to which we can say the same about the Huntington thesis from a Christian point of view, as well as from an academic perspective.

On the one hand, it does not work as an explanation of *all* that is going on. For instance, oil and other natural resources will surely, as many pundits have argued, continue to be a major source of twenty-first century conflict. It is also significant that the Shiite Muslim Ayatollahs of Iran, in the war between Eastern Orthodox Armenia and Shiite Muslim Azerbaijan (the only other majority Shiite state other than Iran itself), supported not their fellow Shiites but predominantly Christian Armenia. Both Britain and the United States supported the Kosovar Albanian Muslims of Kosovo in 1999, not the Serbs who would claim to be our fellow Christians. Much of the power struggle in Central Asia, often known as the "Stans" (Uzbekistan, Tajikistan, etc.), is one of influence between Muslim Turkey and Muslim Iran. There are numerous other examples that I could give.

On the other hand, Huntington is surely right to talk about the massive resurgence in religion in recent years and the dramatic political effects that this has had. In this he is not alone; the eminent French writer Gilles Kepel, in his now famous work *The Revenge of God*, has also highlighted this fascinating phenomenon. (You know if respectable secular sociologists say it is happening that it must be true.) However, as Kepel has shown, this resurgence is by no means limited to Islam. Religious parties are growing in Israel as well, and, tragically, the man who assassinated Yitzhak Rabin, the Israeli Prime Minister, was not a Palestinian Arab but an ultra-Orthodox Jew.

People such as Mark Juergensmeyer, whom I have referred to earlier, have accurately documented the frightening rise of rabid Hindu ultra-nationalism. Recent Indian governments have been dominated by the BJP, a Hindu nationalist party that has its origins in the same movement (i.e., the RSS) from whom Mahatma Gandhi's murderer came. The groups that slaughtered Western Christian missionaries in the past year or so were Hindu extremists rather than Muslims and indeed, in places such as the Indian state of Gujerat, Muslims have been massacred in large numbers by extremist Hindu mobs. In India, Christians and Muslims alike have been the victims and not the protagonists. Hindu scriptures are now taught as literal truth in Indian schools that hitherto kept to the adage of Jawaharlal Nehru, the first prime minister, that India should be a secular country in which no faith had the predominance. Many in the BJP argue for *Hinduvta* – that all Indians should be Hindus, something with grave consequences for the millions of Christians in the subcontinent, Jains, Parsees, Sikhs, and Buddhists, let alone the 130 million Indian Muslims and the tiny Jewish minority in southern India.

All this is part of what American commentator George Weigel has called the "unsecularization of the world," a trend that goes against everything the secular pundits were saying when they predicted the demise of religious belief. Like it or not, religion is a major player once again in world affairs. Not all of this is harmful, however, as Christians are now taking their political obligations as citizens seriously. Britain has a devout Anglo-Catholic prime minister (Tony Blair) and the United States the first Evangelical president in over twenty years (George W. Bush). Since Blair is a Labour politician and Bush a Republican, they clearly don't agree with each other on every issue; but they do, it seems, agree on matters such as the War on Terror. When I worked for the British government briefly in 2002 on the issues involved in this chapter, even secular friends of mine told me to emphasize my Christian faith as it would help me to be heard in the top political circles. The person I saw in No. 10 Downing Street, the prime minister's official residence, was a keen Evangelical Christian.

So while Evangelical Christians differ on the best way in which to implement the Sermon on the Mount politically, and probably always will, at least the return to political engagement is encouraging. The man whose action led to the British abolition of the slave trade (William Wilberforce) and the politician whose action ended British child labour (the Earl of Shaftesbury) were both nineteenth century Evangelicals. One can hope that the twenty-first century will see those who really do know God playing such pivotal roles once again.

How Osama bin Laden looks at clashing civilizations

Before discussing how Christians ought to judge Samuel Huntington's theory, we should look at how some Muslims see it, and then go on to formulate our own response. We do know how Osama bin Laden sees it all, since he has helpfully made his views explicit in many of his recent statements. As the BBC put it:

> Classic Islamic theology divided the world, as he [bin Laden] has, into two realms – the House of Islam and the House of War. Osama bin Laden made this clear in his statements on November 1, 2001: "The world has been divided into two camps: one under the banner of the cross, as Bush, the head of infidelity said, and another under the banner of Islam."

George Bush might be amazed to know that *he* is the head of Western Christianity! But as we have seen, Muslims do not always make the same distinction as we do between state and religion. Bush, in the mind-set that bin Laden represents – and it is important to remember that bin Laden speaks for many and not just for himself – is the leader of what is seen as a Christian coalition against Islam. As bin Laden was quoted in *The Guardian* as saying on 7 October 2001:

> These events have divided the whole world into two sides. The side of believers and the side of infidels, may God keep you away from them. Every Muslim has to rush to make his religion victorious. The winds of faith have come. The winds of change have come to eradicate oppression from the land of Mohammed, peace be upon him.

This is the clear divide between the *Dar al-Islam* (House of Islam) and the *Dar al-Harb* (House of War) that we have mentioned before, with the non-believers in the West being in the realm of war. We see this again in the *fatwa*, or religious pronouncement, that Al Qaeda and bin Laden issued on 10 October 2001 denouncing the decision of the United States and its allies to bomb Afghanistan:

> I address this message to the entire Muslim nation, to tell them that the confederates [i.e., the US and its allies] have joined forces against the Islamic nation . . . We now live under this Crusader [i.e., Western] bombardment that targets the entire nation. The Islamic nation should know that we defend a just cause.

This statement is interesting for many reasons. First, as we have seen elsewhere, bin Laden refers to Westerners as "Crusaders," which, as we stated previously, is unfortunate from a biblical Christian perspective because that is not what we are.

Second, bin Laden refers to the whole Muslim world, from Morocco in the west to Indonesia in the east, as a single Muslim entity, the Islamic nation. The whole world, as his 1 November statement quoted above shows, is divided into two. Bin Laden reiterates this in his 3 November 2001 diatribe against the United Nations:

> This war is fundamentally religious. The peoples of the East are Muslims. They sympathise with Muslims against the people of the West, who are the Crusaders. Those who try to cover this crystal clear fact, which the entire world has admitted, are deceiving the Islamic nation. They are trying to deflect the attention of the Islamic world from the truth of this conflict . . . Under no circumstances should we forget this enmity between us and the infidels. For the enmity is based on creed.

We must remember that getting rid of Osama bin Laden (something that has so far eluded the United States and its allies as I write this) will not purge the world of this point of view. We should not forget that there are, fortunately, millions of Muslims who completely reject this standpoint, but there are also millions who *do* agree with bin Laden. In that sense, winning the War on Terror is not as simple as military victory, and we, as Christians, especially should not delude ourselves on this point. As the last chapter of this book will argue, what is needed is a *spiritual* victory in the *real* battle, and that is something that we know God can and will ultimately provide.

So is Islam a single entity?

Specialists would say that Samuel Huntington *essentializes* Islam – he sees it, in effect, as a monolithic whole, a single civilization. On this perspective of viewing Islam as a single religious entity, Osama bin Laden is in agreement with the normally secular supporters of Huntington and his thesis.

Huntington and bin Laden do, I must add, come to the same conclusion about Islamic unity from radically differing perspectives – Huntington is a profoundly patriotic, upstanding, loyal American citizen. But the fact that his theory, post-9/11, asserts that there *is* a clash between Islam and the West profoundly scares many Western leaders, George W. Bush included. As we saw, he went to a mosque almost immediately after the attacks of 9/11 precisely to deny that there is such an Islamic/Western clash and to say that Islam is a religion of peace, not war. In Britain, Tony Blair said the same thing. Christians such as Franklin Graham who said otherwise were denounced from all sides.

While there were good *political* reasons for George W. Bush to say what he did – the West needs allies in the so-called moderate Islamic world in order to better fight terror – there was a legitimate *religious* basis for what he said as well. Moderate Muslims really don't want to go to war with the West. Some, like Professor Akbar Ahmed in the United States and Sheikh Badawi in Britain, are devout Muslims living happily in Western countries.

But as Harvard Divinity School professor David Little has correctly pointed out, it is perhaps more accurate to describe events as a *confusion* of civilizations rather than a *clash* of civilizations. Similarly, Yale professor and missionary historian Lamin Sanneh, a West African convert to Christianity from an Islamic background, has said the "bland consensus," or woolly secularist, as we might put it, of the West is not an effective response to the surging worlds of religious extremism. We need to ask two questions: First, is Islam as monolithic as people say? Second, is the West *really* all that Christian? England and Scotland are technically Christian countries (Wales is not) and the United States has, according to many, actively Christian roots. But if we are truly Evangelical Christians, how *genuinely* Christian can we call the lands in which we live? How do we compare, in terms of conversion growth, with countries on the Islamic/Christian frontier, such as Nigeria? Or in relation to a Buddhist/Christian country that also has remarkable church growth, such as Korea? We shall now be bold and try to answer these complex questions in an understandable way!

As I showed at the beginning of this chapter, Samuel Huntington's theory has had an impact like few have in recent years. His 1993 *Foreign Affairs* article has been called, probably correctly, the most influential think piece since the article by George Kennan ("Mr X") set the tone for the Cold War back in the late 1940s. Many people, like the Russian, Serbian, and Pakistani students I lectured to back in the mid-1990s, felt that Huntington was trying to create a new group for the West to hate now that we had won the great ideological battle against the Soviet Union. The "Red Menace" of Communism was gone; the "Green (the Muslim colour) Menace" of Islam had taken its place in Western demonology.

Historically speaking, Huntington's critics were inaccurate. As we saw in Chapters 2 and 3, there has been a confrontation of some sort or another between the Islamic world and those of other faiths ever since the seventh century. Militant Islam is therefore not an enemy conjured up in 1991. On the other hand, one does need to ask why we need to find enemies, now that the global Soviet threat has disappeared. Huntington, in his writing, dismisses the views of people such as Senator Daniel Patrick Moynihan, the author of *Pandaemonium*, who say that what we really have after the end of the Cold War is not one overarching struggle but a chaotic world with a whole multitude of new threats.

This latter view seems more accurate to me. The leading BBC journalist, John Simpson, has written that a downside of the War on Terror is that it makes us forget other vital conflicts, such as the need to eradicate drugs, and the chaos that narco-terrorism creates. (It is true that much of the West's illegal drugs came from Taliban-ruled Afghanistan. But places like the Golden Triangle of Southeast Asia or the massive drug-growing areas of Central and Latin America are causing devastation among the millions of addicts in the West, and have nothing at all to do with Islam.) The wars in the former Yugoslavia or Rwanda had nothing to do with extremist Islam, and in places such as Bosnia and Kosovo, the Muslim inhabitants were the victims not the perpetrators.

The Iranian president and the "dialogue of civilizations"

But what worried the United Nations and other leading international bodies was Huntington's notion that religious differences could once again lead to war. After all, in the West, such ideas were supposed to have vanished after the Protestant-Catholic wars of the sixteenth and seventeenth centuries, and the Peace of Westphalia in 1648 in particular. (Foreign policy specialists, like Henry Kissinger, often refer to the "Westphalian System." This so-called *realist* doctrine teaches that since 1648, it has been the interests of individual states that cause wars, rather than old-fashioned things such as religious differences.) Now one of the most eminent American academics at Harvard was arguing that this might not any longer be the case.

All sorts of learned international gatherings consequently took place, before the disasters of late 2001, with leaders from both Western and Islamic countries getting together to profess love, not civilizational hatred, for one another. As with many of these grand affairs, it was very much a question of the élites from one nation meeting their counterparts from another. But in the case of Iran, one could say that the Iranian president said something that not only he actually believed himself, but many of his people did too.

Iran is a complex country over which Britain and the United States have lovingly agreed to differ. Britain's foreign secretary, Jack Straw, has visited Iran and said that Britain wishes to actively engage with the moderates in Iran, such as President Khatami, so that eventually a genuinely pro-Western Iran will once again emerge. In the United States, not merely did President Bush ally Iran with Iraq and North Korea as part of the "axis of evil" in early 2002, but people close to the administration to whom I spoke argued that even Khatami himself will soon be toast. Whether he will lead his people away from the violently anti-Western theocracy of Ayatollah Khomeini, as the British hope, or whether he will be an Islamic equivalent of President Gorbachev, the final and ultimately unsuccessful ruler of the Soviet Union, we may know by the time you read this book. Even an issue of *The Economist* magazine in early 2003 was unable to come to a clear prognosis, and if they could not, who am I to pronounce?

Regardless of what happens in the near future in Iran, the theological and political implications of what is happening there long-term are both interesting and, from both a Western and Christian point of view, very encouraging since Iran was the one really major predominantly Muslim power in which the hard-line radicals actually succeeded in seizing power. (Afghanistan was too much of a mess to count as a major power, and if you think that Saudi Arabia is extreme, which it is *theologically*, it is still under royal rule and nominally friendly to the West.)

However, the key with Iran is that the radicals failed to deliver what they promised the people when they seized power from the Shah. Unlike most of the West's notional allies (except for Bahrain, which in 2002 allowed democratic elections in which women could vote), Iran is a functioning democracy. Everyone – women included – can vote, and the parliament and president are both anxious to see reform. But what stops such increased democratization and friendship with the West taking place are the vestiges of the old Khomeini regime, the clericalist establishment that can still exercise the power of veto on any progress. To ordinary people this latter group is seen as oppressive and corrupt. Since your enemy's enemy is your friend in much of the Middle East, that means that since the repressive part of the regime is seen as anti-American, the ordinary Iranian is often pro-American. Reform-minded democrats in Iran are often accused by the reactionaries of being pro-American stooges, which makes the pro-reform popular majority (around 75 per cent of voters) support the United States, their oppressor's enemy, all the more.

In addition, we saw in looking at Islamic history that there was a split in Islam very early on, between the followers of Ali, now called the Shiites, and the majority Sunni, who represent over 80 per cent of today's total Muslim population worldwide. Iran is a Shiite country.

An Islamic Luther: Will Shiite Islam produce its own reformation?

Many experts say that the actual doctrinal differences between Sunni and Shia Islam are more cosmetic than real, and go more to a seventh century dispute over political power than the more profound doctrinal differences between, say, Protestant, Catholic, and Orthodox Christianity. Ayatollah Khomeini, while very much a Shiite clergyman, always liked to think that he spoke for Islam generally rather than just for his particular, mainly Iranian, version.

However, while that view has merit, it is a bit simple, especially in relation to the more recent developments in Shiite Islam. Sunni Muslims say that they, unlike Christianity, have no clergy. In a strict sense this is true. There is no Sunni equivalent of the pope, or even of an outstanding Christian leader with no formal leadership position, such as Billy Graham. Technically speaking this is also true: Sunni Islam is a religion of theoretical equals (if you are a man). Clerics – the imam of the local mosque, the *ulema* in a Muslim country – are, by the nature of Islam, the Islamic equivalent of ecclesiastical law experts. But since Islam is very much a religion of law, they have a critical role to play in the life of the Islamic community. Their job is to interpret and expound the law, and that is what the imams do on Fridays, or the *ulema* to the local Muslim ruler.

In strict theory, this is also true of Shiite Islam. But in practise, they have leaders, especially at the exalted rank of Ayatollah, who are for all intents and purposes the same as leading clerics, such as bishops, in the West. However, Khomeini was only one of their rank, albeit an especially revered member, and not all of the present Ayatollahs in Iran agree with the continuation of theocratic rule.

But there are even more important theological distinctions than this that relate to the key Islamic doctrine of *ijtihad*, or private interpretation. The overwhelming consensus among the legal scholars of the Sunni Islamic world is, as they put it, that "the gate of *ijtihad* is closed." Not only that, but it was closed hundreds of years ago. There might be the famous four schools of Islam we saw in Chapter 5, but all four of them would not say that interpretation could change. This is however *not* true of Shiite Islam; for them the gate remains very much open. This allows for the possibility of change that does not exist in the more ossified Sunni versions of Islam.

If one takes a speech by former President Ali Akbar Hashemi Rafsanjani as an example, the non-immutability of the Shiite version can be seen (quoted from Bruce B. Lawrence's book *Shattering the Myth: Islam Beyond Violence*):

> The important point here is that the Islam which developed 1400 years ago on the Arabian peninsula – a settlement where the people were fundamentally nomads – was a legal code specific to that society [*my note: see the emphasis on law*]. And even that code was promulgated slowly over a period of seven or eight years. Now the legal code,

which was executed in those days for that particular nation, aspires to become the code for a world in which humanity has plunged the depths of the earth . . . competed in space to conquer Mars . . . At this very moment millions of people are engaged in legal research to better human society. The Islam which was revealed some 1400 years ago for the limited society of that time, now desires to become the fulcrum of [modern] social administration.

Rafsanjani, when president of Iran, was no friend of the West! Nor was he any friend of Israel. But my point here is theological: The Shiite version of Islam allows for change in a way that Sunni does not. As Milton Viorst says in his book *In the Shadow of the Prophet*, Shiite Muslims are both conceptually able to cope with changing times and, because *ijtihad* remains open for them, adapt theologically as well.

Finally, one of the main things said by secular commentators is that Islam never had a reformation. Here one can easily agree. But it would seem that with *ijtihad* being firmly shut, it would be virtually impossible for one to emerge from Sunni Islam unless there comes someone brave enough to demand its opening. But in Shiite Islam, as the gate never shuts, there are thinkers such as Abdolkarim Soroush, who argue for theological as well as political reform in present day Iran. He was interviewed by American journalist Judith Miller in her fascinating book *God Has Ninety-Nine Names*. He has sometimes been hailed as a potential Islamic Martin Luther. He told her that he wanted to

open up Muslim societies and the Islamic faith to original interpretation. In the process he founded a foundation for a pluralist and tolerant society . . . "We've abandoned the export of the revolution and now we're thinking about the export of Islamic democracy," he said . . . "We still need to do a lot of thinking about democracy, freedom and human rights before these ideas are complete. But now we're heading in the right direction."

Reacting to possible Shiite reformations

How should we react to all this? As Christians we should of course be sad that however moderate they are becoming, they remain Muslims. We should want them not merely to reform but to repent and be saved. However, a half-empty glass is also half-full. Judith Miller, in the book quoted above, shows that while Saudi Arabia funds mosques all over the world, there is absolutely no reciprocity at all. No church may be built on sacred Saudi soil. This is, however, different from Egypt, where churches can – under massive restrictions – be built with government permission. There is a small Christian population in Iran, one of whose leaders was martyred during Ayatollah Khomeini's oppressive rule. Freedom and human rights in Iran would make all the difference to our Iranian brothers and sisters in Christ, and for that we can be thankful! At least some kind of evangelism might become possible, albeit clandestinely, in a way hitherto so dangerous that brave Christians lost their lives.

Politically, the fact that such changes would be coming about from *within* (as is happening slowly in terms of the extension of democracy in tiny Sunni Bahrain) would make an enormous difference. While democratic activists are glad of American support, the possibility that democracy can be seen as something imposed from *outside* by heavy US pressure makes it look alien and therefore undesirable in the eyes of many. A truly democratic-cum-theological reformation in Iran would be wholly *internal* and much more likely to succeed.

What will be significant is whether, as Islamic thinkers such as Soroush hope, Iran becomes pluralistic, tolerance extends religiously as well as politically. In the West, the appearance of a spiritual rivalry to Catholicism in the form of Protestant Christianity led to the eventual rise of spiritual tolerance in Western countries. It will be fascinating to see if that will happen in a country such as Iran. Here I should say that expert friends of mine such as Professor Larry Adams, who is both a specialist academic and a keen

Evangelical, retain an open mind. What will also be interesting is if, as in the West, tolerance of any *religion* leads to tolerance *of no religion at all*. That might be a development that will take even longer still. As Christians, our main hope and prayer must of course be for a major turning to Christ in areas where the Gospel was once clearly preached, but where open proclamation of the truth has been severely restricted for a very long time.

CHAPTER 9

Christians and
the Arab Street

We are always reading in the papers about what the "Arab street" will and will not do. We see pictures of Islamic mobs raging against the West – one of the best of these being on the cover of this book! But what is the much vaunted Arab street, and how afraid of it should we be? This chapter aims to explore the reality behind the book's cover and the headlines we see each day.

One of the main reasons for Islamic rage and for much of the present wave of terror is the hatred many Muslims have for their *own* oppressive governments. A genuinely democratic and pluralistic Iran, whose existence we saw is on a knife edge – for which human rights for Christians would be our version of icing on the cake – would be most effective in what pundits and politicians refer to as draining the swamp. If a *legitimate* means of dissent is present, which can include voting out one government and democratically installing another, then the breeding ground for terrorism is considerably lessened.

Further, as the distinguished Evangelical preacher John F. MacArthur Jr. showed in a sermon of his, non-violent protest has other ramifications as well. Pro-life Christians in the United States, as he argued, have no need to resort to violence, even if such action were theologically justifiable, because they are free citizens of a genuine democracy. They can, through the elective process, vote for people in favour of Christian morality. The same is true in any democracy. But in a dictatorship, all such avenues of independent thinking and dissent are firmly closed. In such repressive circumstances, ordinary people may not go along with violent opposition to the government themselves. But since there exists no legitimate mechanism for free expression, many, while not themselves violent, understand those who are, which therein lies the extremists' opportunity.

If states in the Middle East such as Iran and Bahrain succeed in their democratic experiments, others may follow. Since much Islamic anti-Western feeling is, in a sense, displaced hatred of the local dictatorship, then in the future not as many states may be hotbeds of Islamic rage as is now the case. Countries could still be predominantly Muslim but, like Turkey, a NATO ally of the United States and an aspirant European Union member, not at all anti-Western. This would therefore considerably alter the current gloomy climate, in which many fear the clash of civilizations between Islam and the West is all too likely to take place – if it hasn't already begun!

In terms of the Huntington thesis discussed in the previous chapter, I agree with critics such as David Little, who is a religion specialist as opposed to a political scientist. They say that although the theory is based on a religious understanding of civilization, it fails to grasp that there is as much a clash within Islam itself as between *some* Muslims and the West. Furthermore, the Islamic radicals hate many of their fellow Muslims as much as they do us in the supposedly Christian West. A democratic Iran or Bahrain is not going to be on the same side as a repressive Saudi Arabia, and there are going to be Islamic countries that are *pro*-Western as well as those that remain against the West.

The Arab street and the Arab basement

The point about the benefits of democracy cannot be emphasized too strongly, whether the moderate Islamic majority gain *full* power in, say, Iran, or whether, as many in the United States hope, a successor regime will come to power that is both non-Islamic and secular and also pro-Western.

For, as we have seen in the last chapter, the *real* issue for many of the Islamic extremists is their profound hatred for their *own* regimes rather than for the United States as such. America is hated not just because it is the No. 1 superpower, or because they think it is Christian. To many Islamic extremists, it is hated because it is seen as the ally of the oppressive regimes in the radicals' *own* countries, such as Egypt or Saudi Arabia. While it is true to say that in November 2002 Osama bin Laden made Al Qaeda as much against Israel as against the United States, I don't think it is equally the case that such radical extremist groups principally hate the United States because of America's support for Israel.

Where *that* issue is important is in the key distinction made by *New York Times* journalist Thomas Friedman between the "Arab street" and the "Arab basement." The ordinary Arab in the so-called street probably hates his government and feels sympathy for the Palestinian cause, but would never dream of carrying out acts of extreme violence on anyone. It is also interesting, for example, that none of the 9/11 killers was a Palestinian. As I mention elsewhere, Palestinian terror against Israeli citizens has been truly awful, whether suicide bombers in pizza parlours or attacks on Israeli athletes abroad, as in 1972. But Palestinians have *not* targeted the United States in the way that the Saudi and Egyptian terrorists have done – and likewise the massacre of German tourists in Egypt was by local Egyptian extremists. The terrorists are what Friedman calls the "basement," not the street.

Where US involvement in the peace process might help is in preventing pro-Palestinians from the street descending one floor and being recruited to the basement. It might possibly reduce sympathy in the street for basement acts of terrorism. But what will really hurt the terrorists in the basement will be democratic regimes in Arab countries who will not need to spew forth vile anti-Semitic articles in government-controlled newspapers so their citizens will hate Israel and not their own government. For some of the worst anti-Semitic garbage comes from Egypt, an effectively non-democratic dictatorship, in which all dissent is repressed, but which receives billions in aid from the West, especially the United States, every year.

As many journalists pointed out after 9/11, the terrorist team was largely Egyptian brains and Saudi muscle. The inspiration for present-day Islamic terrorism was the Egyptian thinker Sayyid Qutb, who was put to death by the Arab socialist nationalist leader Nasser in the 1960s. His relevance here is profound. He regarded regimes such as Nasser's as being in *jahiliyya*, in unbelief, an apostasy that was all the worse because such leaders, in theory, were supposed to be proper Muslims. So while Qutb supported jihad against the West, his *main* desire was to see holy war against apostate *Arab* regimes, such as his own. It was for this view that he was executed.

The problem with countries such as Egypt or Saudi Arabia is that, because they are not democracies, popular dissent is like a pressure cooker boiling steadily but inexorably from below! By definition, dictatorships lack the legitimacy enjoyed by democratic governments voted in by the people's own choice. (In the West, your side may lose, but you can work for victory next time.) In such oppressive societies, most inhabitants simply keep their heads down and try to cope the best they can without attracting the attention of the secret police. They do their jobs as best and unobtrusively as possible, and enjoy the company of those close friends and family who they feel sure enough not to be informers for state security. Most people, therefore, dislike the regime, but regard it as too dangerous to do anything about – a decision which is probably very wise!

From Roman bread and circuses to the Islamic terrorists of today

Since Roman times, governments in such places try to think of diversions, or what the Romans called "bread and circuses." Bread keeps the masses basically fed and prevents food riots. Circuses act as safety valves for the pressure cooker and divert people's attention from the fact that they are politically oppressed.

Over the centuries, one of the best means of ensuring a docile population was to get the repressed citizenry to hate other groups or countries. Called *projection* by psychologists, this has taken many different forms over time. Serbs in the 1990s were encouraged to hate, and often kill, innocent Bosnian Muslims or Kosovar Albanians, with frequently horrific results. Perhaps the best-known and most hideous example of this phenomenon was the Holocaust – the destruction of over six million innocent Jews by the Third Reich. Any glimpse at many a Palestinian, Saudi, or Egyptian textbook will demonstrate that anti-Semitism remains a powerful tool of projection to this very day, even if not at the full-scale level of the Nazi period.

Recently, I attended a seminar by a leading Israeli specialist. He showed us current, authentic Palestinian textbooks that seriously argued the case for the infamous and entirely fake *Protocols of the Elders of Zion*, a late nineteenth century Russian secret police forgery designed to whip up anti-Semitic hysteria in czarist times. Similarly, the lie that four thousand Jews were warned not to turn up for work in New York on 9/11 because the Israelis and CIA were behind the Twin Towers attacks, was something firmly believed by otherwise sane and normal people throughout the Middle East.

As Professor Christopher Andrew of Cambridge told us at the seminar (and London *Times* readers later on), many Western analysts and commentators have severe difficulty believing that successful plotters such as Hitler and Stalin in the past (both of whom were very anti-Semitic) and Osama bin Laden today can carry out major operations in an entirely rational way and yet sincerely believe such paranoid rubbish. Yet Professor Andrew is right – they *can* believe such obscenities, and, in the case of Hitler and Stalin, have managed to lead major countries at the same time. Sanity has never been a requirement of dictatorship! But, as I have just shown, even otherwise sane and normal people believe such lies, especially if, in the context of a dictatorship, that is the only viewpoint they have ever heard since childhood, day after day after day, all their lives.

How hating the United States can harm receptivity to the Gospel

The Jews are not the only victims of projection in the Middle East, however. The other major victim is the West. Because the biggest Western power – indeed the most powerful nation anywhere – is the United States, followed by its usually faithful British ally, America is the cause of much projectionist hatred throughout the non-Iranian Islamic world. Here again, the nature of the projection is obvious. But for Christians, it is also dangerous, since there is a very real sense in which anti-American hatred hinders the spread of the Gospel.

Muslims have massive conceptual and theological difficulty in separating church and state, since in a proper Muslim state this is not supposed to happen. To many Muslims, America and Britain must be Christian countries. The downside is that when men such as Sayyid Qutb go there, they become horrified at what they see as the decadence and immorality all around them. We saw before that it is often in going to the West that they start to hate us, so seeing how people in the West live can often have the precise opposite effect from the one we would like. As Christians, we can sympathize with their moral outrage! However, as Bernard Lewis points out in *What Went Wrong*, as does the BBC/PBS series "Empires of Faith," Muslims often have a much wider view of immorality than we do. The very fact that Western women can walk around freely, unchaperoned by male relatives, is often enough to condemn them in many Islamic eyes, even if such women are modestly dressed and thoroughly moral in their behaviour.

Nonetheless, *everything* that is wrong in the West, from easy divorce to drug abuse and much else besides, is blamed upon Christianity and its supposed weaknesses. Christian faith is therefore often judged on behaviour patterns abhorrent to most practising Christians, who are held responsible for them. The fact that for us Christianity is a *personal* relationship with Jesus Christ, and not a consequence of our having been born British or American, is lost on an Islamic mind-set whereby if you are born in a Muslim country you are and must remain a loyal Muslim.

Consequently, everything that Western countries do, whether right or wrong, is also linked to Christianity and is seen through Islamic theological eyes. This is, as I said earlier, not just therefore a question of American support for the state of Israel. It is equally because of the hatred for American global power and, as we saw, for the comparative lack of a similar Islamic power since the fall of the Ottoman Empire after World War I.

Osama bin Laden and the presence of US troops on Saudi soil

The thing that initially infuriated Osama bin Laden was *not* the oppression of the Palestinians – something of concern to the Arab "street" no doubt – but the *continuing* presence of American troops on the sacred soil of Saudi Arabia following the Gulf War in 1991.

Bernard Lewis has once again come to our aid with helpful explanations, as he did in a *Foreign Affairs* article, prophetically named "Licence to Kill," on the subject of the *fatwa* that bin Laden issued back in February 1998. In it (following the Lewis translation), bin Laden said:

> Since God laid down the Arabian peninsula, created its desert and surrounded it with its seas, no calamity has befallen it like the Crusader hosts that have spread in it like locusts, crowding its soil and destroying its verdure; and this at a time when nations contend against the Muslims like diners jostling around a bowl of food . . . For more than seven years [i.e. 1991–97] the United States is occupying the land of Islam in the holiest of its territories, Arabia, plundering its riches, overwhelming its neighbours, and using its bases in the peninsula as a spearhead to fight against the neighbouring Islamic peoples.

Looked at rationally, all this is nonsense! How could a small base of US troops possibly be accused of taking over Saudi Arabia? So worried was the US government about offending Saudi Islamic susceptibilities that it insisted that US servicewomen conform to Islamic dress codes and chaperone rules off base. (Needless to say, one of these women then sued the American government for infringing her rights as a US citizen!) In addition, except for the massive presence of forces from America, Britain, and many other countries in 1990–91, there is every reason to suppose that Saudi Arabia could well have been overrun by Saddam Hussein. It was largely American forces who kept Saudi independence!

Furthermore, statements like this remind me forcibly of anti-Semitic diatribes in a country such as Rumania back in the 1930s. There, Corneliu Codreanu, leader of the Iron Guard, wrote similar rubbish about the tiny Rumanian Jewish minority polluting the whole country simply by their very physical presence. (We get this in the West too, alas, when a mere handful of refugees are said to "swamp" a nation with a population tens of millions strong.)

However, to the extremist mind-set, whether 1930s Rumanian anti-Semitic or 1990s Islamic radical, such arguments make entire sense – *if* you hold to their basic point of view! The external sense might be entirely lacking, but the *internal* logic is sadly entirely consistent, however crazy the basic premise might be. In Nazi ideology, Germany had to be *judenrein* – free of all Jews. Similarly, to the extremist Islamic mind-set, the infidels are a part of the *Dar al-Harb*, the House of War. Since Islam began in present-day Saudi Arabia, its soil is, as Bernard Lewis reminds us, especially sacred. Mecca and Medina are the two most holy Islamic sites. Consequently, the land is the ultimate *Dar al-Islam*, or House of Islam. Yet protecting it against its external foes are American soldiers – not merely infidels but in many cases *female* infidels, which is deemed to be even worse. Their very physical presence is thus an insult to Islam and a major humiliation. The mind-set, from Nazi to Al Qaeda, is thus alarmingly the same.

We saw earlier, that in the Golden Age of Islam and the caliphates that Jews and Christians lived perfectly peacefully, albeit with diminished rights, throughout the Islamic empires. So as well as being ungrateful to the American forces who rescued Saudi Arabia from Saddam Hussein, there is a real sense in which bin Laden is forgetting the actual history of the Islamic Golden Age to which he supposedly harks back so fondly. But as we also saw, there is a major difference between the great caliphates of Cordoba and Baghdad and the Saudi Arabia of the present. In those days, the Islamic world was the superpower and European Christendom was under a permanent sense of siege. Now, the very heartland of Islam depends on infidel outsiders for its own protection, and supposedly Christian America, whom bin Laden sees as the spiritual descendants of the Crusaders, is the superpower. The sense of humiliation is total.

As we can see, bin Laden links the West with Christianity and with its most unfortunate and destructive era, the Crusades. For us as Christians, perhaps the two key questions to ask here are: Is that fair, and is it the West or our faith that we are defending?

Greek philosophers and Galilean fishermen: The roots of the West

One of the areas in which I do agree with Samuel Huntington is that religion is what the international relations experts call a major *player* in global politics today. With the carnage of supposed Christians massacring Muslims in Serbia, to Hindus butchering Christians and Muslims alike in India, to Islamic terrorists murdering Christians worldwide, the rise of religious extremism as a powerful force is hard to deny.

However, as we have seen, Islam is not at all monolithic. So while Huntington is unquestionably right to say that *some* forms of Islam are very much as he describes, others not. I also think that, to some degree, Huntington's divide between the Orthodox Christian world and the predominantly Catholic/Protestant West is a helpful distinction. In Greece, it is *still* illegal to try to convert a Greek Orthodox Christian to Protestant or Catholic Christianity. In Russia, it is often quite difficult to establish a church that isn't Russian Orthodox, even though that country is no longer Communist.

But when we look at the West, how Christian is it? What are we defending? Are we defending a civilization defined by *Christian* values? This is where the great interest shown by many thoughtful American Evangelicals in the works and newspaper articles of Victor Davis Hanson is relevant. (In Britain you can read his book *An Autumn of War.*) It was over thirty years ago that I read in the original classical Greek the thrilling true tales of Xenophon, the writer-warrior, and the stories of how his Greek soldiers managed to escape the far larger forces of the Iranian emperors. But I have no reason to doubt Hanson's thesis that because the Greek troops were soldier-citizens, they had a built-in advantage over conscripted Persian armies. They were fighting for themselves, for their ideals, and for freedom, and not at the command of a distant emperor. To Hanson, that has given the forces of the West an innate advantage over soldiers under tyranny ever since.

However, from a *Christian* perspective, there are some flaws in what is otherwise a very convincing thesis. First of all, Islamic armies, such as the phenomenally successful invaders of the seventh century, were also fighting for a cause in which they believed profoundly, and with results that gave them over a thousand years of victory over the Christian West. Second, much of the Greek ideology we have actually comes to us via Islam – from great early Muslim thinkers such as Avicenna (Ibn Sina). He and others translated much of Greek philosophy and medicine into Arabic. It was thus often from the Arabic translations, rather than from their Greek originals, that much ancient Greek wisdom came down to us in the West. (We usually forget that Western Europe had a mini-renaissance in the twelfth century, during which time many of these ideas re-emerged in the West.)

But finally, and from an entirely theological perspective, although it is entirely true to say that enormous amounts of what we call "Western civilization" came to us from ancient Greece, that wisdom was not at all Christian. That is not to say that God, in his love and common grace, could not have inspired much of the better Greek notions, such as mathematics, medicine, and democracy. We can surely thank God for all those things! We drive cars and take drugs to cure diseases, all of which had non-Christian inventors but which have great benefit to the way we live. Nevertheless, although we in the West use such things and they may be part of Western civilization, they are not *directly* Christian.

A typical American or British Christian has, in a *spiritual* sense, far more in common with an Andean peasant who travels on a donkey and uses herbal medicine than he has with his next-door neighbour who is also white, drives a car, and uses modern medicine—but isn't a Christian. The Andean peasant is his brother or sister in Christ – and you cannot get more in common than that! As Jesus taught us, we are in this world but not of it. Paul, when visiting Corinth, Athens, and other Greek cities, knew that, while their inhabitants had much, they lacked true knowledge of God's salvation in Christ. Modern medicine has a gigantic debt to Hippocrates, as do British and American soldiers to Xenophon. It is far better in every way to live in a democracy (which is, after all, a Greek term) than in a dictatorship. There is no question but that our Greek heritage has improved all our lives in the West for the better. But as *Christians* we have more in common with our fellow believers in countries both democratic and non-democratic, such as Nigeria, Guatemala, China, India, or Iran than we do with the non-Christian Westerners among whom most of us live.

Huntington, for example, is worried about the effect that large-scale immigration from Latin America will have on the specifically Western values of the United States. While I tend to think that the melting-pot aspects of Britain and the United States are what make them such dynamic countries, theologically what he is saying is irrelevant. As John MacArthur says, if a church really preaches the Gospel, it will have all possible races in it. This is very much the case with the large church that he himself pastors in California, and was also true of my late grandfather

D. Martyn Lloyd-Jones's Westminster Chapel in London, which had regular members from all over the world.

If one looks at the phenomenal church growth in countries such as Korea, Nigeria, Brazil, Singapore, and Guatemala, to take just a few, the fact that the churches in these places are now sending missionaries to convert the increasingly post-Christian West is spiritually very exciting! Ours is the true *global* faith, not just a product of Judaeo-Christian Greek interaction. Nigerian and Afro-Caribbean Christians have made a very positive impact in Britain, and lively Latin American Christians have had similar effects in the United States. If the immigrants are Christian, may more of them come! If they aren't, then what difference, in a spiritual sense, does their arrival make?

As the Roman Empire discovered, a small band of fishermen from Galilee turned the world upside down. Peter, an unlearned and unschooled fisherman, has had more impact on the world than Plato, Aristotle, and many of the greatest Greek thinkers and sages put together. That is not to despise the West's Greek heritage – far from it! Few things could be of greater benefit than Greek political philosophy and the democratic ideals that stem from it. But as Jesus taught us, what good does it do to gain the entire world and lose one's soul (Mark 8:36)?

Jihad versus McWorld: Religious values and the impact of globalization

One of the things that makes the new twenty-first century so exciting is that Christianity really is now reaching *all* parts of the globe. So when it comes to *spiritual* globalization, the results for the church are wholly positive! In addition, what makes *this* globalization so interesting – and perhaps unique – is that it is *not* a Western-led phenomenon. In many cases, such as in much of Africa and all of China, the dramatic surge in conversion growth took place *after* the missionaries had either dwindled in number or been expelled altogether. No one can any longer say, for example, of the Chinese church that it is full of "rice Christians," nominal converts pretending to profess faith in order to get more material benefits. Becoming a Christian in China can get you locked up, and, as we have seen in the past few years, in Indonesia and Nigeria it can get you killed. Christianity is therefore a genuinely global faith that belongs to *all* its adherents, rather than being a product of a particular culture or part of the world. Even secular sociologists are realizing that Christianity is now predominantly a faith of the "South" – the world south of the Equator – rather than the tribal faith of the white man.

On other kinds of globalization, there is much heated debate, at the Global Summits in places such as Seattle or Genoa, that often turns to violence when the anti-capitalist demonstrations sometimes get out of hand. This area is a political and economic minefield into which it is often dangerous to tread. For me to come down on one side or the other in this debate is something that could turn people against the rest of the book! So with the permission of my readers (and maybe to the relief of my publisher), I shall declare here that globalization *as such* is not a theme relevant to this book. (Those seeking a specifically Christian approach to this thorny topic can turn to my father Fred Catherwood's recent book, *The Creation of Wealth*, written in the aftermath of many of the big financial scandals in Britain and the United States.) However, some parts of the globalization debate *are* relevant, whether one agrees that globalization is a good thing or not.

Writers such as Samuel Huntington are dubious about whether the West should insist on *its* values being *universal* values. One can see his point. For example, before the economic collapse in Asia in the 1990s many leaders in that part of the world denounced the West's insistence on human rights and democracy as incompatible with *Asian values*. To some, both in the West and out of it, to insist on democracy smacks of white imperialism and neo-colonialism. This creates antagonism to the West in many countries; and if you want to ensure that your part of the world has as few enemies as possible, then not insisting on democracy everywhere will help in that process. In addition, the argument goes, the freedoms we have and take for granted in the West are to a large extent a product of our peculiar history. Not only did they take centuries to evolve to what they are now, but it is ridiculous to insist that civilizations whose history and traditions are quite different from ours should embrace all the values prevalent in Western culture.

The other problem – and this is where the advocates of this view can be said to have a case – is that often people outside the West put everything they observe in the West together into a stereotyped package. Many outside of the United States, for example, have developed a particular hatred for McDonald's. The theories of American academic Benjamin Barber in his best-seller *Jihad vs. McWorld* are relevant here. (McWorld is the modern version of "coca-colanization.")

For some reason, McDonald's has become the new symbol for America's global capitalist domination of the world (no country even begins to have the international reach of the United States). In France, a local villager became a hero after destroying his local McDonald's. In India, even though the company goes out of its way to sell veggie burgers, instead of beef burgers – since they would be offensive to vegetarian Hindus – McDonald's restaurants have been destroyed by irate Hindu mobs, especially in high technology modern enclaves such as Bangalore, the Indian equivalent of Silicon Valley. "McWorld" is therefore used by writers such as Barber to symbolize the public face of international American capitalism – and beyond that the forces of globalization that it has spawned.

You don't have to agree on whether globalization is a good thing to see beyond dispute what its effects are in terms of local and religious reaction. Barber's book sold well after September 2001 because of the Islamic word jihad in its title. But he is careful not to use it in the Muslim sense of that word alone – he gives it a far wider meaning. To him, and to writers such as Mark Juergensmeyer, *all* religious reaction to the effects of globalization are jihad. Hindu mobs, enraged traditional Catholic French farmers, extremist so-called Christian survivalist fanatics – all of them are part of this kind of anti-capitalist jihad. Barber tends to be rather anti-capitalist himself, but you don't have to agree with that part of his conclusion to see that globalization has provoked a major reaction worldwide, much of it being profoundly religious. On *that* score, we could all say that he is right, whether or not you eat at McDonald's wherever you go!

We use your tools but we hate your values

The use of some of the latest technology by Osama bin Laden shows that many who reject the *values* of the modern Western world certainly don't reject its tools. Similarly the anarchist, anti-capitalist demonstrators, who protest against globalization in London every year on the first day of May, all use websites and email messages to tell their fellow protestors where to turn up.

Where Samuel P. Huntington and his disciples have a good point is that they make clear that it is the *values* of Western technology and the package that goes with them that are so rejected by millions outside of the West. (He calls globalization "Davos culture" after the Swiss town in which the world's leading politicians and businessmen congregate for an annual conference.) But regardless of our own views on big business, it is this *package* element that is and should be worrying for us as Christians.

Without question one of the most successful Western exports into the rest of the world has been media culture – Hollywood, rock music, MTV, and all that goes with it. Few things have shown the reach of globalization as cinema, television, and music recordings. I remember visiting a Muslim family some twenty years ago in Bahrain. The American soap opera *Dallas*, which was also popular in Britain, was dubbed into Arabic on Bahraini television. As the dutiful guest, I had to watch the soap opera I usually avoided in the middle of the Persian Gulf!

As L'Abri-linked British culture critic David Porter put it, there was something particularly symbolic about this series. Hollywood and the media seldom give any representation to real Christianity or to Christian values – one only need read American

Jewish commentator Michael Medved to know this. But *Dallas* was supposedly set in the middle of the Bible Belt, and yet there was not a single Christian portrayed in the whole programme! (The fictional Ewings were said to be indirectly inspired by a real-life Texan family, some of whom *are* Christians.) So what was so offensive was not merely the casual immorality, which is endemic to a lot of television soaps, but also the deliberate decision to ignore one of the most important elements of real-life Dallas: the large number of practising Christians who live there.

Christians in both Britain and the United States have been protesting for years about the way in which Christianity is either ignored or caricatured in the media – this is not a new problem! But what is relevant to this book is that it is the absence of Christianity, or its false portrayal, that people in the Muslim worlds see on their televisions, through their satellite stations, and in the many other forms of Western media available in their part of the world. This pertains not just to Muslims living in the predominantly Islamic world, but also to the members of the large Muslim diaspora in the West itself, in Europe and the United States. As we saw earlier, it was his horror at things he saw when living in America that so alienated the main inspirer of recent Islamic terrorism, Sayyid Qutb.

This is where Barber is a better interpreter of the modern world than Huntington. For what we are talking about here is what the Western Muslim writer Bassam Tibi correctly calls "a clash of universals." (His book *The Challenge of Fundamentalism* is a very interesting work from his specially informed perspective.) It is not that the issue of globalization is the same in Seattle as in Kabul. What we are seeing now is not even what Huntington once called "the West versus the Rest." What we are seeing here is a conflict in *values* – secular global materialism, radical Islam, Hindu nationalism, European particularism, all competing against one another. Global materialism is not just a Western thing any more; there are millions world over who worship its values. It is, in that sense, a universal value. But whereas you could say that the Hindu or French responses are local to their particular areas, Islam claims to be a universal truth, and so too, of course, does Christianity. And ours, we know, really is the truth!

Fighting for Christian values

The problem we have as Christians is that, while Hollywood and MTV don't portray *our* lifestyles and aspirations, they *do* present a horribly accurate picture of the thoughts, hopes, and worldviews of many in the West. Divorce is rising, drug abuse is getting out of control, crime is rampant in many areas – we hate all these things, but we know the statistics to be sadly all too true.

Unfortunately for us as Christians, even though there are many things, such as democracy, human rights for women, and medical discoveries, that *are* good about the West, there are plenty of other things that are not. Furthermore, some good things can be used to bad ends as well. The same freedom that exists in proclaiming the Gospel is used in the United States by pornographers, who claim the right to publish their wares as being protected by the Constitution. When it comes to the issue of Western values, we have to concede that there are many of them that have profoundly harmful side effects that do the West no good in the eyes of the Islamic and other non-Western cultures outside it.

We have to do two things in response. First, we must make clear again and again that the West and Christian faith are *not* part and parcel of the same thing. America, for example, is not so much a *Christian* country but a country which, thank God, has a live and dynamic church and many millions of active Christians living in it. (Although Britain *legally* is a Christian country, it is sadly all too easy for British Christians to point out how few people there actually do go to church or practise any kind of Christian faith.) This is a vital distinction that is surely in the interests of the Gospel to make. If we fail to do so, then Christianity will continue to be seen in the Muslim world as the home of high divorce, drugs, *Dallas* lifestyles and values, and all the kinds of things that we as Christians are as aghast about as our non-Western critics.

However patriotic we may be – and there is nothing necessarily wrong with that – we cannot ever defend those things that are commonplace in our country but which are contrary to the Word of God: freedom yes, immorality and secularism no!

Second, we must aid the rest of the worldwide body of believers that makes up the Christian church, God's people spread across the globe. For there are things that they can say or do that we as Westerners cannot. To give a more mundane example, I always had difficulties when I studied at Oxford University in the 1970s convincing people that the university, while undoubtedly intellectually élitist, was not *socially* élitist as well. Unfortunately for me, I have a very socially élitist accent. (One of the reasons why a preacher such as Billy Graham is so popular in England is because, as an American, he does not have an English class or regional accent that would alienate half his audience!) So as a consequence, no one believed me! But when friends of mine from rough Welsh working-class backgrounds related how socially inclusive Oxford was, to their happy astonishment, people believed them straight away! In other words, I was the wrong person saying the right thing.

So while Osama bin Laden and his ilk might continue to portray the West as a latter day embodiment of the Crusaders and Western civilization as soft and decadent, the reality of the global spread of Christianity is going to make this increasingly difficult to do. Terrorist groups such as Al Qaeda, and their allies in places such as Kenya and Indonesia, are very much at the core of what Friedman calls the Islamic "basement." But as we saw, one of the ways in which to drain the swamp is to reach out successfully to the "street," from which the basement derives its recruits.

How only the Gospel brings true liberation

Here I really do think that the Gospel is going to be far more effective, with far greater world-changing, earth-shattering, long-term results than any weapons technology dreamed of in the Pentagon or Whitehall. Drones may kill individual terrorists, as in Yemen in late 2002 and possibly, by the time you read this, in Iraq and other places later. But as many commentators have warned, British and American soldiers liberating much of the Middle East is not *necessarily* going to make for a permanent change in the hearts and minds of the liberated. From a Christian perspective, such action in and of itself will sadly make no change at all. What *will* make all the difference is the eternally liberating power of the Good News of Jesus Christ.

Korea, Brazil, Nigeria, Indonesia – our brothers and sisters in Christ from countries such as these are not part of the "package" that comes, in the eyes of the Muslim world, with the West. There may be a sad but real extent to which *Western* Christians trying to persuade the Muslim world of the universal truth of the Christian message may not be heard, in the same way that I was ignored for my accent when I defended Oxford's social inclusiveness. (Not that I would equate these two things when it comes to absolute truth!) But if we as Western Christians get together with our fellow believers in the "South" and support them actively in prayer and logistics, then there is much that could happen. For while the sociologists and political scientists divide the world up, whether into civilizations or pro- or anti-McWorld, all Christians everywhere are united in the saving power, truth, and values of the Gospel. Islam claims to be a universal truth and values system, but *ours* is the one sent from God in Jesus Christ. However much we may love our country, it is *God's* values that we proclaim.

CHAPTER 10

Oil and America: The Political and Religious Consequences of Everyday Decisions

The famous late twentieth century chaos theory claims that a butterfly flapping its wings in one part of the world can cause a tornado in another. Not being a scientific expert, I have no idea if that theory is true. But it *is* often true that small decisions made by enough people can have massive consequences. We are now clearly living in an era of explosive Islamic rage, an anger that has global ramifications. What we are going to look at in this chapter, among other things, are the ways in which Muslim countries see economic decisions and the global effects of personal decisions that we make as private individuals. In the West we distinguish sharply, as we previously noted, between church and state, while the Islamic world does not. This means we are dealing with people whose very mind-set is completely different from our own.

We must, therefore, begin to see Muslims as *they see us*, so that we can respond to them properly. This is not to engage in the woolly navel-gazing, breast-beating attitude that led many Americans to blame solely themselves after 9/11. Nor is it to confuse Western civilization and Christianity, the politically opposite response in which many patriotic Americans indulged. Seeing ourselves as others see us is not to concede that the other side is right in looking at us the way they do. It might be, of course, that they see us as mistaken in some areas but do so for the wrong reasons. As we saw in Chapter 8, we as Christians are as concerned about the effects of MTV culture, drugs, and sexual licence as are our Muslim critics at home and abroad.

But, as I argued there, the problem is that the Muslim world sees the West as a package. As Christians we can and do decry increasing moral decadence. In Britain, Evangelical parents have sometimes gotten together with Muslim parents to stand up for family values in our increasingly secularized schools. Moral issues, therefore, are often clear. But when we look at Bassam Tibi's helpful term, "clash of universalisms," some specific thoughts about Christianity come to mind. The issue goes beyond Christianity as *the* universal truth versus Islam as a false but equally self-proclaimed universal truth. What worries me is that there is much about the West that enrages the Muslim world *but that we don't see about ourselves.*

Athens and Jerusalem?

In the Fall 2002 issue of *The Tie*, the journal of the Southern Baptist Theological Seminary, I read a significant phrase that refers to what secular writers call the triumph of Athens over Jerusalem. This would, in particular, mean the so-called prevalence, since the Enlightenment, of rational over religious values. Now it is true, as we would readily admit, that something like democracy is an Athenian value for which we can all be grateful. But as Christians who read in the book of Acts about Paul's visit there (Acts 17:16–34), we know that there was a lot profoundly wrong with Athens!

I am writing this the very week in which seventy-five million new citizens from applicant countries such as Poland, Hungary, and the Baltic States were voted into the European Union, to join in May 2004. For those of us who spent time behind the pre-1989 Iron Curtain, this is a deeply emotional moment. As the British press has put it, a lot of countries that enjoyed freedom between 1919–39 and then lost it, first to the Nazis and then to the Communists, are now coming home. They are part of the democratic community of nations – you must be a democracy to be in the EU – in a way that they could never have been under Soviet domination. If you had seen what it was like to be a Czech, Pole, or Hungarian prior to 1989, you would fully understand how the citizens of those countries feel!

So the authors in *The Tie* are right to say that as Christians we can be glad we live in a country with democratic values. But if we want to export *that* part of the West, we have to remember that that is not all the Muslim world sees. They also see the massive economic domination and globalization of Western countries – themes we explored in Chapters 8 and 9. But there is a real sense in which we in the West have made ourselves very dependent on the same Islamic nations whose citizens feel such anger against Western civilization and all it stands for. This is in the area of oil.

Can Christians drive an SUV?

One of the pleasures of visiting friends and relatives in the United States is that the cars are often far more comfortable than the much smaller vehicles that we are used to in Britain. One of the most popular vehicles in America is an SUV, a lifesaver for those with large families, especially of teenage children. Yet there is one very perturbing statistic, which relates to the petrol ("gas" to Americans) cost of keeping such a large vehicle on the road. According to the experts, SUVs get nine miles to the gallon, while ordinary automobiles in the United States twenty miles to the gallon. The more fuel-conscious cars in Britain (and some brands in the United States) get thirty-five miles to the gallon, or over three times the amount guzzled by an SUV.

In addition, although the United States is one of the biggest oil producers in the world, its population, which is only 5 per cent of the total number of global inhabitants, *consumes*, according to Middle East pundit Malise Ruthven, no less than 65 per cent of the world's energy supplies. Much of that is industrial, but a lot of it is personal, with SUV drivers firmly taking the lead. This is not to toot a British horn but to point out the increasingly scary statistics relating to the sheer volume of energy that even ordinary US citizens consume each year, Evangelicals fully included! According to newspaper reports in both Britain and the United States early in 2003, it seems that an interesting collection of some Evangelical leaders and political conservatives have joined together with environmentalists and road safety experts in making noises of concern. But it is not a politically partisan, environmental, or safety point I am making here, since I am no fuel expert.

Because of its incredibly high energy consumption, the United States, despite being a major oil producer, has to import around 7 per cent of the world's *total* production of oil each year, and does so mainly from the Middle East. This in particular means Saudi Arabia and other Gulf countries. Even if much US oil is imported from a tyranny-freed Iraq by the time you read this, that is still a scarily high amount of petroleum to be importing from the Islamic world.

As we know from the press, much of the Saudi petrodollar millions have gone into subsidizing the particularly extreme Wahhabi form of the Hanbali interpretation of Sunni Islam. When moderate Muslims protest that most of Islam is *not* of the kind propagated from Saudi Arabia they are, as we saw elsewhere, technically right. Most Muslims, in so far as they are aware of what system they follow, practise one of the other three ancient Legal Schools of Islam, or, in the case of around 15 per cent of all Muslims, the Shia interpretation observed mainly in Iran. But as the television news is reminding us daily, the sheer financial power of Saudi Wahhabi Hanbali Sunni Islam is growing globally almost by the hour, mainly financed from the massive oil revenues streaming into that kingdom.

It is not at all surprising that some neo-conservative publications, such as *The National Interest*, have started to ask pertinent questions along the lines of, "Well, isn't our *real* main enemy Saudi Arabia itself?" Even more liberal authors and newspapers are asking the same questions. But it goes without saying that politically this is *very* complicated. The West needs the Saudi regime in its fight against terror – and it also needs the kingdom's considerable oil supplies. To alienate the Saudi royal family would be an enormously high-risk strategy!

Furthermore, so isolated have ordinary Saudis become from the world outside, and so indoctrinated for decades have they been from the Wahhabi hard-line educational establishment, that, if Saudi Arabia were to move overnight to full democracy, most Saudis might well vote for people whose views are not at all dissimilar from Osama bin Laden and his followers. In other words, democracy, while being a Western value, might yield results profoundly inimical to the West. (This is the concept of *illiberal democracy* invented by Evangelical political scientist John Owen IV and his fellow student Fareed Zakaria, who went on to make it famous.)

So it could be argued that if you have a high-energy-using car, and even if you regard it as a necessity for a large family not as a luxury, you are, in a sense, helping to support a hard-line Islamic regime in the Middle East! Of course, it is thankfully not that simple. But it is true that, for example, a lifestyle in which most people drive everywhere rather than using public transportation does create a level of energy consumption that puts countries such as the United States enormously at risk. Were America or Britain to restrict petrol use, citizens of such countries would have to change their lifestyles quite drastically.

Exporting terror to a gentler world

How wise is it for our Western nations to be so reliant on energy sources from countries that do not hesitate to use that money to propagate not just a non-Christian faith but a variant of it that is overtly and zealously hostile to Christianity? This is something that we need to ask as Christians as well as patriots. In the West, the petroleum giants' money goes to private shareholders as well as to general taxation. Furthermore, BP or ExxonMobil do not use large chunks of their profits for Christian mission. (Would we want to take it if they did?) But in places like Saudi Arabia, such

Western distinctions do not exist. Saudi petrodollars can and have funded mosques of the Wahhabi persuasion all over the world, even in the United States.

I recently saw a chilling documentary on the BBC showing how extremist Wahhabi Islam is actively penetrating Indonesia, financed by money and emigrants from the Arabian Peninsula. Until recently, Indonesian Islam was what one might call *syncretistic*, a mish-mash of genuine Islam, what missiologists call "folk Islam" and original, pre-Islamic Indonesian folk paganism. Academics such as Clifford Geertz and other writers all attested in the past to the fact that Indonesian Islam was a much nicer, milder, gentler version of Islam than the more austere and often violent version one would encounter in the Arab world.

As another example, Bruce Lawrence in his book *Shattering the Myth* tells how Muslims in Malaysia often interpret jihad as the struggle to transform that country into a more modern, technologically advanced nation rather than as a form of violence against unbelievers. (Evangelicals, however, will note that even Malaysia, despite being a parliamentary democracy, does not allow its Muslim citizens to be evangelized by Christians.) In Indonesia, the situation under the longtime military dictator General Suharto was that *all* religious extremism was banned and that the state was secular. Since Indonesia has considerable numbers of Hindus, Christians, and followers of smaller, often pagan, religions, this kept the lid on any possible expressions of dissent, but also, as a by-product, made local Christians safer as well.

The tragedy of the Bali bombings in late 2002 alerted the rest of the world to the facts that the new, post-Suharto regime had tried to suppress. This was that large numbers of Al Qaeda-supporting terrorists were now both at large and very active in that country. (It is interesting that the post-bombing Al Qaeda statement linked both the Australians as well as the British together with the United States as part of the enemies of Islam. Australian troops had been active, under UN auspices, in helping predominantly Christian East Timor to gain independence and to protect that new nation's fragile democracy. Needless to say, this did not go down well with extremist Muslims in Indonesia, who realized that the East Timorese were now lost to potential Islamic rule.)

Christians and the democracy/licence dilemma

But what is also very tragic, as the BBC documentary referred to above made clear, is that in Indonesia democracy has brought Islamic extremism to the fore in its wake. From a Christian point of view – and also, it must be said, from that of people such as feminists as well – this creates a hideous dilemma for Western Christians wanting to protect the well-being of fellow believers worldwide. For there is no doubt that democracy often unleashes profound evil, when the restrictions of dictatorship are removed. With the freedoms that democracy brings frequently comes licence and an easier time for wicked people.

My Hungarian Christian friends, in the pre-1989 Iron Curtain days, would come up with what was an interesting and very telling observation. Sometimes they and their Jewish dissident friends, who were also heavily restricted under Communism, would make the joke: "What is the difference in freedom of speech between Hungary and England? Well, in both countries, you are free to speak. The difference is that in England you are still free *after* your speech . . ." Christians, political dissidents, creative artists, and many others suffered under terrible restrictions in Communist dictatorships.

But as my Hungarian Christian friends would point out, there was a silver lining. A young Hungarian woman going at night to a clandestine Christian student meeting was in danger of arrest *at the meeting*, which was certainly not the case in politically and religiously free Britain. However, she could walk by herself to that meeting and, more important perhaps, walk home from it, even late at night, completely without the fear of being mugged or assaulted. The same State Security Police apparatus that caused believers such problems also ensured that crime was kept under far more effective control than in the capitalist West. By contrast, a young woman returning home from a similar meeting in Britain, during which she was in no fear of arrest, would often have to have some kindly men walk her home, lest something bad happen.

This was also true of Baptists in Franco's Spain in the 1970s, when the fascist dictator was still alive. He persecuted Protestants, but female students going to clandestine Bible studies were quite safe. But when *political* freedom came to Spain in Western Europe, and to the post-Communist countries in Central Europe, female students swapped one kind of freedom for another. Now Spanish Protestants, Hungarian Evangelicals, Czech Brethren, and many other groups could meet with an openness hitherto impossible. At the same time, however, the crime rate in those countries soared. Even now the Albanian mafia control large parts of organized crime in the United Kingdom, and the Russian *mafiyya* similarly have large tentacles out in Florida and other parts of the United States.

In other words, with political and religious freedom has come crime, corruption, physical danger to innocent people, an exponentially growing illegal drugs problem, widespread and open immorality, and a whole host of other equally unsavoury things besides. In Indonesia it has brought not only these things but also the rise of militant, Saudi-funded Wahhabi Islam. Dictators do not like their subjects to have alternative sources of loyalty other than to themselves. They want, by definition, *total* loyalty, or, if comparatively more benign – Suharto was no Hitler – no focus of active competition. Hitler did not merely persecute the church because he was evil, though that was surely the case, but because Christians had a higher loyalty than to him, the Führer. Similarly, under Suharto, Christians were not likely to come out in open rebellion against his regime. But radical Muslims were willing to rebel openly, so the specifically Islamic identity of most of Indonesia's citizens was actively suppressed. (Likewise, the former Yugoslav dictator, Tito, disliked Catholics since they were associated *politically* with the old World War II fascist regime in Croatia. But Protestants living there had no such *political* loyalties, so could more or less do as they wished.)

Once Suharto's regime started to unravel, rather like Tito's in Yugoslavia in the earlier part of the 1990s, the glue that held that enormous and geographically diverse nation together came massively unstuck as well. Everything that the corrupt crony-capitalist regime had suppressed came into the open. From one point of view all this was a splendid thing – one of the world's largest and most heavily populated countries was now a democracy! But once again with freedom also came licence, and in the case of Indonesia this meant that all the millions in that land who thought of themselves primarily as Muslims were now able to proclaim that identity with complete freedom.

Where does a Christian's ultimate loyalty lie?

Pre-1989, Central European Christian friends of mine said that they would rather be arrested for producing their *own* illegal Christian literature than accept smuggled literature from well-meaning Christians in the West. The reason was simple: Christianity, they knew, was *absolutely* true! This meant it is as true for, say, a Czech Christian as for one in England or Virginia. So if an Evangelical Czech student was arrested for attending a clandestine Bible study, or for having an unauthorized printing press, it was important that they be arrested *for being a Christian*. That may sound obvious to us, but it was actually *spiritually* more important than that. Many felt that if they had Western imported smuggled Bibles, however excellent the godly intentions of the smugglers, they would, if caught, not be arrested for being a Christian, *but for being in league with the West*. Since, during the Cold War, a link with the West was like committing treason, the reason that the non-Christian Communist government would give for jailing Christians *would therefore be political and not spiritual.*

Christians in such countries, like their fellow believers in majority Muslim countries today, took very seriously the teaching of Jesus: render to Caesar what is Caesar's and to God what is God's. If the government asked you to pay taxes or obey the speed limit, you obeyed them. But if they asked you to stop going to church, reading the Bible, or praying, then you ignored them and, as Peter said to the Sanhedrin, obeyed God rather than men (Acts 5:29). But if a particular law caused no conflict of interest between your obedience as a Christian and the one you owed as a citizen, you obeyed the law.

What the Christians felt was vitally important, both in their witness to fellow nationals and in the way in which Christianity was portrayed generally, was to do everything possible to avoid giving the state the excuse to say that Christians were the stooges of the wicked West. For the reasons why my Czech, Croatian, Polish, Russian, and other friends had faith in Jesus Christ as their personal Saviour and Lord had nothing whatsoever to do with the fact that millions of people in the West were Christians as well! They knew Christianity was true because it *is* true! Christianity is true in all places and at all times because it is the message of eternal salvation in Jesus Christ. It would still be true even if all Britons and Americans in fifty years' time were all New Age pagans and the only Christians left were Czechs, Nigerians, Brazilians, and Chinese.

One could say that the real reason, as was often the case, that the Christians behind the Iron Curtain were persecuted was because they had a source of *ultimate* loyalty other than that of their regime. To put it another way, their *complete* loyalty was to Jesus not to Karl Marx. Obviously, an atheistic, materialistic belief system like Communism disliked Christian faith on principle as well as in practise. Clearly as well, any anti-Christian belief system, from atheistic Communism to theistic Islam, wants in some form or another to do harm to Christ's people – as we discussed elsewhere in this book. But from an *Evangelical* perspective, it is interesting, for example, that in Communist Poland, because the Catholic Church was seen as a major source of opposition to the regime, *Protestant* Christians sometimes got freedom in that country not open to other Protestants in similar Communist regimes. The reasons Baptists in Warsaw and elsewhere in Poland had more freedom than those in Prague or Budapest is that, by definition,

Protestant Christians are not Catholics! From the point of view of an atheist Communist commissar, if people were going to be Christians, which he would rather they did not, how much better they followed Catholicism's rival than the politically active anti-Communist Catholic version instead!

So under a dictator like Suharto, what mattered was that everyone was *Indonesian*. Because the regime did not place many restrictions on Christians or on their evangelism since they were unlikely to support anti-government guerrilla groups, Christians in Indonesia did not have much of a conflict of interest between being good Indonesian citizens and active Christians at the same time. That is not to say that being a Christian was problem free – it is not at all easy being an honest person in a profoundly corrupt state! But so long as Christians kept out of politics, the state, which was officially non-religious, left them alone. Christians were Indonesians, Hindus in Bali were Indonesians, and so was that country's large Muslim minority.

In a democracy, however, that changes. Under a dictatorship there are, in effect, no politics. This, as we see in countries such as Algeria and Saudi Arabia and probably Egypt, is a major problem.

The Great Game in Central Asia

There are petroleum and gas sources apart from the Middle East, notably in Central Asia. But as former US National Security Adviser Zbigniew Brzezinski says in his fascinating book *The Grand Chessboard*, tapping into those sources is not so simple. This is because, as Brzezinski and many other writers have made clear, there is a new "Great Game" being played in the former Soviet states in Central Asia. It is not insignificant that Pakistani journalist Ahmed Rashid's post-9/11 best-seller *Taliban* was subtitled *Militant Islam, Oil, and Fundamentalism in Central Asia.*

Rudyard Kipling, author of the *Jungle Book*, wrote a wonderful, thrilling story entitled *Kim*. Kim is a child of the British Empire, or *Raj*, in India and soon becomes involved in what historians refer to as the "Great Game." This was the nearly century-long battle to control the key points of Central Asia between the British, on the one hand, who ruled present-day India, Pakistan, and Bangladesh, and the Russians, who ruled what is now known as the "Stans": Kazakhstan, Uzbekistan, Turkmenistan, Tajikistan, and Krygyzstan.

The buffer state between the two competing empires was the kingdom of Afghanistan, a country that the British tried to invade – and failed to keep – in the nineteenth century and the Russians the same in the twentieth century. If you look at a map of that sad war-torn land, you will see a thin sliver of land that prevents the "Stans" from having a direct border with India and Pakistan and that also gives Afghanistan a tiny but direct border with the People's Republic of China. This odd shape goes back to the Russo-British rivalry, and was designed to ensure that the British and Russian Empires did not have a direct border between them.

The Great Game (about which Peter Hopkirk's many books are invaluable) was mainly played up in the Himalayas and Hindu Kush mountains, and was the attempt by the respective empires to gain predominance over each other. One of the great Russian goals – acquiring a warm water port on the Indian Ocean – was defeated when the British were able to conquer what is now the Pakistani side of Baluchistan, on the border with Iran. By the early twentieth century the rival empires effectively made up, but the Russian Revolution in 1917 gave a new impetus to the Great Game, when Lenin decided to "set the East ablaze." Two major changes then happened: in 1947 the British quit the Raj and in 1949 Communists also took power in China. So for a long time we forgot about a part of the world that had been at the centre of a major global rivalry for nigh on a century.

Three dramatic developments changed everything. The first was the Soviet attempt to seize permanent power through a puppet regime in Afghanistan in late 1979. The second was their failure to do so and the disintegration of the Soviet Union itself in 1991. The third was the discovery of large-scale reserves of oil and petrol in the "Stans" in recent years. Suddenly a new version of the Great Game began, but this time with Russia the only one of the original players still left. Many of the chilling scenarios that pundits such as Brzezinski and others describe in their books might be coming true in the next few years.

The Great Game revisited

But as Ahmed Rashid and Zbigniew Brzezinski show in their books, the stakes in the Great Game are now higher. As Al Qaeda's presence in Afghanistan showed, the nefarious plotting in obscure bazaars in the Hindu Kush have had global ramifications of which Kipling could never have dreamed when he wrote his exciting children's stories. For as we know, many of those behind the 9/11 attacks were trained in exactly this region. The Taliban extremists received their theological training in Islamic madrassas in Pakistan, in the same alley-ways in which Kim and other Kipling characters once played. Rivalry over oil is now international in scope, and the decision where to put pipelines for the oil coming from this region has massive geopolitical implications. For the shortest and cheapest route carries a price – it is through Iran. The longer way is through war-torn parts of the Caucasus and then on through Turkey to the Mediterranean. Another possible route also has a political price: it would be through the People's Republic of China.

Many people regard the oil from this region – and from the potentially large oil fields of Russian Siberia, beneath the permafrost – as strategically vital. This is because, if the oil there really proves as big as experts say that it is, then the West's (and Japan's) current over-reliance on the Middle East will be greatly reduced. However, all this in turn depends on the "Stans" remaining open to the West, if not actually sympathetic. But all the countries in that region are notoriously brittle, and none of them could exactly be described as stable democracies. Iran is spreading one kind of Islamic influence, Turkey another. Meanwhile, Russia does not like the fact that she has lost her old sway over the region and the Chinese want to gain power in what is their Central Asian backyard.

But most important is the fact that all of these countries have enormous Muslim populations or outright majorities, as Ahmed Rashid demonstrates in his best-sellers on the area. The problem in Uzbekistan is as potentially lethal as it is in Egypt, with an American-friendly strong-man ruler and the Islamic extremist opposition seen as the only way in which to get rid of him.

The first nuclear war – on the roof of the world?

Perhaps the most dangerous "Stan" is the one that has been independent since 1947 and which, during the Cold War and the war in Afghanistan, was seen as an active ally of the United States. This is Pakistan. (India was seen as pro-Soviet, because the Chinese conquered part of India's territory. So Pakistan was pro-American and pro-Chinese. Poor Britain regularly gets in trouble by trying to be amicably neutral and friendly to both these Commonwealth countries.)

This nation, which has existed in its present form since the 1970s when Bangladesh or East Pakistan broke away, is lethally dangerous in many ways. The first is because both Pakistan and India possess nuclear arsenals. The Indian nukes are named after Hindu deities and the Pakistani missiles after Muslim saints. A nuclear war between the two countries could, I learned from private and well-informed sources, cause up to *fifty-two million deaths.* That is a lot of people – possibly up to thirty-five million dead in India and maybe as many as seventeen million dead in Pakistan. Those are only the direct casualties in those two countries. If the wind blows one way, nuclear radiation fallout could get as far as Iran and maybe even reach Israel, in the same way that fallout from the Chernobyl reactor failure in the Ukraine affected sheep in Wales hundreds of miles to the West. Wind blowing the other way would reach China, and possibly Japan and Taiwan. Radiation sickness mortality could thus take the total casualties much higher still. It is hardly surprising, therefore, that the United States, with more international muscle than my fellow Britons, has done everything possible to stop war from breaking out!

Islamic terrorists have a big stake in this conflict. All this goes back to the dissolution of the British Raj in 1947 and its splitting into two states, India and Pakistan. As the film *Gandhi* portrays, Mohammed Ali Jinnah, the Muslim League leader, realized that in an independent India the Muslim minority would be massively outnumbered by the enormous Hindu majority. (Christians, Buddhists, Jains, and those of other faiths were too small a percentage and too geographically diverse to have a state of their own.) As a result, Pakistan, meaning "land of the pure," was formed, initially in two very distant halves, West Pakistan and East Pakistan. The thing to remember here is that although Jinnah did not want an *Islamic* state in terms of political ideology, as his biographer Akbar Ahmed has made clear, he nonetheless created a *Muslim* state in terms of population makeup, so that Indian Muslims would thereby be protected from what he feared might be the results of majority Hindu rule.

Pakistan, one should add here, is simply that part of Muslim-majority Central Asia conquered by the British as opposed to the Russians. Afghanistan, likewise, is also ethnically an entirely artificial state. Many of the Taliban were ethnic Pashtun (formerly known as "Pathan" under the Raj), which is exactly the same ethnic race as that of large swathes of western Pakistan. In the 2002 elections in Pakistan, these regions voted into power people of strongly Islamicist views. This, as we will see, makes controlling Islamic terrorism in the region much more difficult, because they have a natural religious and ethnic sympathy for their fellow Pashtun and Taliban kinsmen over the border. Likewise, many of those in the Northern Alliance, which supported the British and American troops in 2001, were ethnic Tajiks, who are from the same people group as the former Soviet state of Tajikistan.

At independence in 1947, the hereditary rulers, or *maharajahs*, who had had considerable local power under the British, had to opt which state to choose. In most cases this was no problem, since the ruler and his subjects were of the same faith. Hindu maharajahs chose India and Muslim maharajahs chose Pakistan. But two states created a major problem. In the case of Hyderabad, where the *nizam* (the local word for ruler or maharajah) was a Muslim ruler of a mainly Hindu people, the Indians simply invaded the area and incorporated it into India. The Indians took the simple view that the people's wishes prevailed over that of one man. But Hyderabad had no border with Pakistan. Conversely, in the beautiful mountain kingdom of Jammu and Kashmir (one state not two), there was a Hindu ruler of a mainly Muslim people. Under Indian pressure he opted for India, and in this case the Indians took the ruler's side. But Kashmir and Jammu had a border with the new Pakistan, so India and Pakistan thus went to war, as they have done again several times since. To make a *very* long and complex story short, Kashmir is divided along the "line of control" with one part of the former territory in India, another in Pakistan, and a much smaller part now ruled by the People's Republic of China.

Many a Muslim radical has fought alongside those Muslim Kashmiri separatists who want to be a part of Pakistan. (Hindu Kashmiris like being part of India, while many Kashmiri Muslims switch between wanting more autonomy within India or outright independence. Not all Kashmiri Muslims want union with Pakistan.) So while it would be wrong to say that the Islamic extremists in Kashmir, fighting the Indians, are automatically members of Al Qaeda, many of the guerillas fighting in that region have also fought in Afghanistan.

From General Zia to the Twin Towers

What makes the potential for war in this area so serious is thus twofold. First, there is now a profound danger that a conventional war over Kashmir could go nuclear, with the first strike being launched by the country that thinks it is losing a ground war. With the potential casualties mentioned above – fifty-two million is not much less than the entire population of Britain or some large US states – the results would be catastrophic. Further, if a Muslim nation like Pakistan were to lose millions in such an exchange, it is hard to see how other Muslim countries could stand aside and fail to come to her aid.

Second, the big problem is that while Nehru in India and Jinnah in Pakistan wanted essentially secular states, albeit predominantly Hindu and Muslim respectively, that is increasingly no longer the case today. For a long time, the rulers of Pakistan could be summed up as clean living but military dictators, or oligarchic but democratically elected. Pakistan has oscillated since independence between military rule and notional parliamentary democracy. But until the 1970s they basically maintained the essentially secularist orientation of the state, not unlike Turkey after 1924.

However, in the 1970s my Oxford contemporary Benazir Bhutto's father, the corrupt but democratically elected Prime Minister Bhutto, was overthrown in a military coup. His replacement was another general, Zia al-Haq. General Zia was not personally corrupt. But he was a more than strict Muslim, and under his rule Islamic schools (madrassas) and much Islamic Sharia law was introduced to Pakistan. Because the Taliban learned their extremist version of Islam – heavily funded from Saudi Arabia – in Pakistan, you can draw a line leading from Zia's coup all the way to the Twin Towers and Pentagon attacks. Pakistan became the base – *al Qaeda* in Arabic – of all sorts of Islamic groups designed after 1979 to overthrow Communist rule in Afghanistan. The border town of Peshawar, another familiar place to readers of Rudyard Kipling, became probably the most heavily armed place on earth!

After 9/11 a book entitled *Blowback*, written some while earlier by former American government official Chalmers Johnson, became an accidental megaseller. While I would not agree with all of Johnson's conclusions, he nevertheless showed very effectively that American policy in the 1980s, during the war against the Soviets in Afghanistan, had quite hideous consequences for that poor country during the 1990s and, as we now know, for the United States itself in 2001. The West supported anyone who was anti-Soviet, and many of the *mujahadin*, fighters against the

Russian occupation, were exactly the same Islamic extremists who were against the West after the Soviets left defeated. One of these was Osama bin Laden, and whether bin Laden was, as some allege, actually funded by the United States during the 1980s is irrelevant, because *in general* there is no doubt that the United States *was* supporting anti-Soviet forces, without looking too closely at what the long-term consequences would be. It is precisely those unforeseen long-term results that Johnson calls *blowback* – how one set of decisions in your favour can lead to a whole host of unpleasant by-products years down the line.

While much of the funding came from the United States, much also came from Saudi Arabia, which was later to be one of the *very* few nations, along with Pakistan, to recognize the legitimacy of the barbaric Taliban regime in Afghanistan. Much of the actual recruiting and donkey-work was done by the pro-Islamicist Pakistani military intelligence agency, the ISI, which still wields enormous power even to this day. The current Pakistani ruler, General Musharraf, thus faces a nightmarish scenario, as an indirect but no less powerful result of all these earlier activities. Pakistan is therefore a tinderbox, like all the other "Stans," but it is one with nuclear weapons. And radical Islamic groups did surprisingly well in the 2002 regional elections, adding to the tension.

The specifically *Islamic* identity of Pakistan is stronger than ever before, and at a very dangerous time. Moderate Pakistani Muslim voices, like Akbar Ahmed, do exist, but the pro–Al Qaeda demonstrations in 2001 were worrying. Worse still from our point of view have been the massacres of *Pakistani* Christians – thus not Western expatriates – by Islamic extremists in the past few years. At one time Pakistan had a female prime minister, Benazir Bhutto, which the extremists would never tolerate. (Benazir is now in exile.) Jinnah might be turning in his grave, but Pakistan is not really any longer the country he envisioned. The prospect of an Islamic extremist Pakistan, which indisputably has weapons of mass destruction, without the need of UN inspectors to tell us, is one that should worry all of us.

Ram Ram India

Nehru, as we saw, like Gandhi before him, wanted India to be an *officially* secular country. As I said elsewhere, this is in no small part because, despite the massive transfer of millions of people at partition in 1947, there are still *130 million* Muslims living in India. Under the great Mughal emperors, they had much respect and often held high positions. But that was now a very long time ago and their descendants often live nervously today, especially in places such as Gujarat, where thousands of Muslims were massacred in 2001–2.

Theoretically speaking, India still is a secular state, or rather, a state in which no one of the many religions on the subcontinent has a predominant role. (One tiny regional state near the border with Myanmar is the one predominantly Baptist state in the world!) The new president of India is from the Muslim minority – 130 million people in India is a minority. There will probably be in the neighbourhood of a *billion* Indians by the time you read this. That makes India the biggest democracy in the world by far in terms of sheer population size and geographical extent.

But as we have seen, there is now a very strong Hindu nationalist party, the BJP, that currently shares power in India. They are trying to make India as Hindu as the hard-line mullahs are doing with Shiite Islam in Iran. Christians – both Indian and missionary – have been killed in recent years, often in gruesome circumstances, like being burned to death. Lord Ram is the main Hindu deity followed by such fanatical activists, and they want to create an all-Hindu "Ram Ram India" in which all true patriotic Indians will also be devout Hindus.

From a Christian point of view, this is worrying in and of itself. If India actually does or soon will have a billion citizens, then the Christian-professing population of just 2.5 per cent will still come to around twenty-five million people. That is a lot of fellow believers being in danger of persecution!

But Hindu fanaticism is also perturbing from the particular angle of this book, that of the dangers of Islamic rage. Here the consequences could reach into many cities in Britain and the United States, as well as the Indian subcontinent and the Muslim world. For at the moment, the Indian Muslim population is remarkably quiescent. Many of them are simply keeping their heads down, and others still regard themselves as happy patriotic citizens. But if something were to go wrong, then that 130 million or more people could set off a firestorm with international repercussions.

We tend, quite wrongly, to associate Islam with Arabs – to the cost of Arab Americans, over two-thirds of whom are professing *Christians!* In Britain, most inhabitants of South Asian ancestry are Hindu or Sikh – again, not Muslim. But in both Britain and the United States, many of the immigrants are nonetheless some form of Muslim. If a major war erupted between a predominantly Hindu India and an overwhelmingly Muslim Pakistan, that would be certain to have very major law and order implications in Britain and America. You can hardly feel relaxed living next door to someone whose ethno-religious kin have just killed millions of your own ethno-religious kindred in a nuclear exchange! More worrying is that many of the most dynamic, entrepreneurial emigrants to the West come from the region of Gujarat, on the Indo-Pakistani border, which is thus likely to suffer from a quite disproportionate number of casualties in a nuclear war.

It is also the case that, with modern information technology, we hear about things from all over the world, and often react accordingly. Take the "Salman Rushdie affair," when liberal Indian-born writer Salman Rushdie wrote a novel called the *Satanic Verses* that religious Muslims thought blasphemed the Prophet. While there were comparatively mild demonstrations by the Muslim community in Britain, where Rushdie then lived, there were major riots in India in which people were actually killed. The death, in the event of a Pakistani-Indian war, of even thousands of people in Pakistan would lead to huge pro-Islamic demonstrations in all parts of the world, out of Muslim solidarity. Were *millions* to die in a nuclear weapons exchange, it would be worse still! Furthermore, while most Indians are, thankfully, still moderate, the sad truth is that extremist Hindus are getting more and more powerful all the time. For many such people, a war with Pakistan *would* be a religious war, and a specifically anti-Islamic one at that. It would be revenge on present-day Muslims for decades of Mughal rule centuries ago. Neither Britain nor the United States would be exempt from the ripple effects of a South Asian conflagration.

So can Christians drive an SUV?

So is having an SUV or similar high-energy-consuming car a prudent thing to do? Perhaps more to the point, is the dependence of the West on unstable regimes at all a wise thing to continue? From the Christian standpoint, to what extent is our endless need for traditional sources of energy playing into the hands of those who oppose the Gospel?

One of the things this book is keen to avoid is party political controversy! In Britain, since abortion is always a vote across party lines, there is no one single party for which Christians, and especially Evangelicals, vote for overwhelmingly. There is a real sense in which this is healthier. First, Evangelical Christians can have a major influence whoever is in power – they don't have to wait for a sympathetic regime. Second, the truths of the Gospel are not seen as being linked to a particular *political* point of view, which is often the danger if most Evangelicals only ever vote for one party at election time. However, I do know that in the United States the situation is very different! So to say something about the use of fossil fuels in this book would have very different results in America than in Britain, Australia, or elsewhere. In Britain, New Zealand, and other Western nations, Evangelicals probably have as many political opinions as there are different denominations. Most of my fellow Evangelicals I have met in the United States do not! (It could of course be true that my friends are exceptional.)

In other words, what follows is *not* designed to be part of the debate between Republicans and Democrats in the United States on whether or not to drill in Alaska or sign the Kyoto Protocols or on other environmentally contentious issues. But regardless of your politics, we do, as Evangelicals, have to think very hard about the geophysical realities, namely, that most of the world's oil is to be found in predominantly Muslim countries. Some, like Saudi Arabia, persecute and sometimes even execute Christians. What might happen in Iran is anyone's guess! Brave men such as Sam Ericsson of Advocates International and my father, former European Parliament Vice-President Sir Fred Catherwood, have gone to Central Asia to argue for Christian religious human rights, and in some places have been successful. Some nations, like Kazakhstan, are slowly allowing the Gospel to be preached. But such countries are near nations without oil but on the edge of the precipice, such as Pakistan and Uzbekistan, semi-totalitarian and mainly Muslim states where the extremists would like to push those countries over the edge.

Learning to see how others see us

As I argued earlier, the problem is the way in which the West and the Western need for oil are linked inexorably in the Muslim mind with Crusader Christianity and the Western desire to control the world's natural resource markets. The need for fuel for an SUV and the need for the eternal truth of salvation in Jesus Christ are of course completely separate and incomparable! Most Christians worldwide are probably still using means of transportation our Lord himself would have recognized. But perhaps the really important thing that needs to happen is for people in the West to realize that others see us quite differently from the way we see ourselves. Clearly, large swathes of Christians in the West see no link between, say, Kyoto and global warming and Islamic feelings of rage against the Western world. But according to an interview with Lindsay Brown, the General Secretary of the International Fellowship of Evangelical Students, for most Christian students in the developing world, global warming and consequent climate change is one of *the* big life-threatening concerns today.

In other words, there is nothing wrong with having different political opinions, so long as we are sure that the ones that we hold are biblically thought through. But we have to check *all* our views this way! Parents with teenage children can often make a very convincing case for their gas-guzzling SUV. It can be that the ability to pick up all your kids in one vehicle ends up being cheaper than everyone having to take public transportation. But quite simple things like our choice of vehicle can have global ramifications if made by enough of us. *My* car is not going to change the world. But when millions make the same decision, it certainly does.

When it comes to cars, those consequences are not merely environmental. The fact that many in Western Europe are convinced that America's policy on Iraq is not based upon principle but on naked economic greed might be irksome, but it does not affect the Gospel. There are not millions of Germans who reject Christ because of US interest in Middle Eastern oil! In a *direct* sense, that rejection is not true of the Arab and wider Islamic worlds either. But as I mentioned earlier, the Muslim world looks at us as part of a package. We can actively preach the Gospel at home regardless of how we vote. Our view on drilling in Alaska or on where to dump disused oil platforms in the North Sea does not alter the way in which our neighbours hear an evangelistic sermon. But the key thing is this: *the lands of Islamic rage do not make that distinction.*

An American president once said, "But we're Americans – of course our motives are honorable!" As often as not, Europeans end up agreeing with the United States, albeit *possibly* less and less as the Cold War becomes an increasingly long time ago. On the other hand, many in Britain and the rest of Europe might say that they love *Americans* but strongly dislike US policy – usually if a president of the wrong persuasion is in power! But if all this is true, how much *more* true is it for the Islamic world and the way in which they see the West, though it is unfair if others completely misinterpret our genuinely good motives, as we all too often discover at an individual level in everyday life.

God does not have
a passport

Being married to an American, and spending a lot of time there every year, I am perhaps more naturally sympathetic to US perspectives than many of my fellow Britons. But one of the things I swiftly discovered is that a driving force in America is the emigration to it over many centuries of people wanting to create an optimistic new world. Many of these immigrants to the New World were Christians. (My book *Whose Side Is God On* goes into this in more detail.) Americans therefore tend to give a moral basis for their decisions that they naturally think will be obvious to everyone. I am inclined to find this US sense of optimism refreshing in relation to European cynicism (or *realism* as people on this side of the Big Pond would say!). But it is vital to realize that most people in the rest of the world do not take the United States at its own valuation.

One of the main themes of this book is that God does not have a passport. He is, for example, neither British nor American. He has his people in every nation under earth. But that has a profound *theological* implication. It means, as we saw in Chapter 8, that defending the West and defending Christian truth are by no means necessarily the same thing. There may be excellent reasons for a lot that we do as Westerners, but they are not necessarily inspired by or encouraged by God! The issue of the world's natural resources may be a neutral one and there may even be a perfectly legitimate defense of our levels of oil consumption. A political defense of Western energy consumption may be entirely merited. But it does not have the same level of absolute truth behind the claims it makes as we as Christians do when we proclaim Jesus as the whole world's only possible Saviour and Lord.

Yet a lot of the specifically *Islamic* rage against the West is very much on the basis of economics. The need for oil, globalization, climate change – all these things are seen as part and parcel of the *Christian* West.

Running out of oil
and Islamic rage

It is fascinating to note that it is the UN-linked, Arab academic written *Human Development Report* that shows why so many Muslim countries have enormous natural resources and at the same time have millions of people on the breadline. Arab states should be among the richest per head of population in the world. But one only has to look at the increasing poverty of ordinary inhabitants of these countries to show that this is very far indeed from being the case.

On the other hand, a small nation such as Singapore, a tiny offshore island with no natural resources to speak of, is one of the world's most prosperous countries! One can even say that it is because it has no *natural* resources that it is so wealthy. This is because it has the best and longest lasting resource of all – its own people! It is Singaporeans that make that nation rich, not anything drilled from its soil. By contrast, most of the Arabian Peninsula was very poor before the discovery of oil. Such resources not being infinite, and the international price of oil not being constant, the wealth of the average Saudi citizen is in fact going down, not up.

This is, as many commentators have pointed out, a major source of Islamic rage. For as Bernard Lewis shows so clearly in his excellent and invaluable *What Went Wrong*, the tendency in much of the Muslim world is not to ask, What could we do better? but, Whose fault is it that things have gone wrong for us? The big problem Lewis shows is that there is usually a total failure to look *within* for what has gone wrong. Jews, Israel, America, Western oil companies, globalization – all these are what one can best describe as *scapegoat* solutions.

What is therefore so significant about the UN-sponsored report is that it was written *by* Arabs *about* Arabs. Things that Westerners have talked about for years – the treatment of women, the levels of corruption under such despotic regimes – were all now mentioned as clear reasons why Arab states have failed so badly in developing the full human potential of their own people. While it is true that many from the countries of the Arabian

Peninsula have been Western educated, the mind-set seems to have remained resolutely the same. One can say that the abundant riches of oil have been as much a curse for the relevant countries as a blessing. For oil is simply just there! In Arabia, as opposed to permafrost deep oil fields in places like Siberia, it is also exceptionally easy to extract.

But now the good times are ending, and a place such as Saudi Arabia has millions of people inadequately educated at Islamic schools who no longer have the remotest prospects of a decent job. While men such as Osama bin Laden were wealthy, and Egyptians such as Mohammed Atta were internationally trained professionals, many of the 9/11 Saudi terrorists were from just such parts of the Saudi kingdom. It is among these people that what Thomas Friedman calls the "Arab basement" is doing its best recruiting.

Now that Arab *natural* resources cannot always command the highest prices, the very considerable lack of *human* resources is coming home to roost. Since nothing can ever be your own fault, it must always be the fault of others. Thus when a heroic figure comes along, someone who has fought bravely for Islam against the infidels in Afghanistan, and says, "It is all the fault of Jews and Crusaders," he gets a rapturous hearing!

How Christians living in the West should respond

So while it is unfair to blame Christianity for the wrongdoings of the West, there is, in this sense, a very real connection between oil and Islamic rage. It is, of course, an *internal* one, a failure *within* Islam – as Fareed Zakaria, for example, pointed out in his article "Why They Hate Us" in *Newsweek* in late 2001. Modernization was, as we saw earlier, something associated with Western colonization after 1918. The ideology of Al Qaeda and similar points of view originated very much as a debate not just within Islam but inside specific Muslim countries, such as Egypt and Saudi Arabia.

As we have seen, Arab governments are very good at scapegoating: If our oppressed subjects hate Israel and the Jews, they won't hate their own despotic governments! But this just makes matters worse, of course, since such oppressed citizens soon find their own scapegoats. The fact I do not have a job is not the fault of my government in not having a proper economic and human resources policy. It has nothing to do with the fact that the ruling family siphons off millions of dollars to play with each year. Rather, it is because, such people come to believe, the Crusader powers such as Britain, Australia, and America are plotting new deeds of evil against the Islamic peoples.

All this, objectively speaking, is severely mistaken. But sensible Western logic is not always very applicable, even though ancient Greek logic was actively pursued and discussed in the days of the great Arab caliphates in the Middle Ages.

So whether or not we have an SUV, or support a particular angle on environmental policy, we must, as Evangelicals, remember that we are Christians first and foremost. There is too much in the Western world that we take for granted. It really is a *very* different world out there. Even the most educated hate America and, in the case of the founder of present-day Islamic rage, Sayyid Qutb, they do so *because* they have lived in the United States. Likewise, living in Germany did not turn Mohammed Atta into a supporter of the West.

Evangelical Christians, of all people, should be those who think *biblically* and *globally.* In the area of life that counts most, we have more in common with a llama-riding Peruvian Evangelical Christian than with an SUV-driving non-Christian next door. It is *Jesus* we proclaim. In many parts of the world, such as in Africa, Christians are in direct competition for the souls of ordinary people. Muslims are now active in evangelism in the West, as the large presence in the United States of the African American nation of Islam bears witness. Whatever country is on our passport, the Bible tells us that our citizenship is in heaven. Whether or not you keep your SUV or switch to solar power, we must remember that as *Christians* who live in the West, we must not give ammunition to the growing global forces of Islamic rage.

Conclusion

Maybe reading this book has made you slightly depressed. But as I mentioned in the Introduction, I am finishing this book on what can be regarded as a highly optimistic note. Why is this? The Bible has very good reasons for making us cheerful, not in a false, human way but in a profound and thoroughly Christian sense.

It comes down to asking this question: How big is your God? Is he big enough to transform the world, to overthrow evildoers, and to bring the many peoples of the Middle East *back* to Christian faith? Although admittedly rather daunting, I trust you will be able to respond to this question with a hearty yes!

For hundreds of years, effectively from 711 to 1689, Christians lived in an era in which militant Islam posed a major threat to the very survival of Christian Europe. Once again, Muslims of similar persuasion attacked what they perceive to be the Christian West, or the Christian Jewish Crusader coalition, as they call it. This is therefore, as I wrote at the beginning of the book, *not* something new that suddenly erupted without apparent warning on the world in late 2001. It is in many ways a conflict that has been going on ever since the seventh century, or for nearly fourteen hundred years. For most of that time, Islam, not Christianity, was winning the battle. Thus, there is a very real sense in which the predominance of the West over the rest of the world is a comparatively recent phenomenon, and not one that we should take for granted.

I, therefore, hope and pray that all Christians reading this can agree on the necessity of spreading the Gospel of salvation through Jesus Christ. I also pray that what I wrote about Islam and Muslim rage is *in and of itself* an accurate picture of what is going on in our world today. I have done my best to give what I believe is a true interpretation of both the Islamic past and present.

God is in charge

Thankfully, as Christians, we can know one thing for absolute certainty: *God is in charge*. This is, to my relief as an author of a book like this, a sure biblical fact that *all* Christians can agree upon without any degree of disparity. God knows the past, present, and future, and it is in his hands. Whatever the mechanisms and timing of the end of history, God has determined it and is in absolute control of how it all works out.

New Testament passages emphasize that while God knows what the future holds, we *don't*. For instance, most of Matthew 24 concerns the Second Coming, and, as Jesus says in verse 36, "No one knows about that day or hour, not even the angels in heaven, nor the Son, but only the Father." And as Jesus reminded the disciples just before the Ascension: "It is not for you to know the times or dates the Father has set by his own authority" (Acts 1:7). This is a good yardstick for us – not least because it is one that Jesus himself asserts! Jesus' next words – "But you will receive power when the Holy Spirit comes on you; and you will be my witnesses" (Acts 1:8) – charges us, instead of speculating, to get on with being obedient Christians, actively doing our best to be faithful followers of Christ and fulfillers of the call in the Great Commission.

Several times in this book I have written that some of my more optimistic forecasts might be proved wrong, which they may. However, since I am the one who has made them, they are by definition merely human. Some things could get far worse, rather than better. If the past twenty years are a good guide, almost anything could happen at any time!

For example, failure to predict the fall of Communism in Central Europe in 1989 was an inability to see that in fact things for people in that part of the world were about to get dramatically better. Tyranny was overthrown! Countries that were stuck behind the Iron Curtain under Soviet control are now in NATO and about to join the European Union. By contrast, the complacency of many that life was improving and would continue to do so was sharply jolted not just by the tragedy of 9/11 but also, in 2000, by the end of one of the longest financial bull runs in world history. Not merely are many people living in fear of terrorism, but many more have now discovered to their horror that their large savings accounts are now worth a fraction of their former value. That early retirement has disappeared. Here, then, the failure was to foresee bad news, not good.

However, for God there are no surprises. He cannot be caught off-guard. As Christians, this should be a source of never-ending joy and thankfulness to us. Nothing, however bad it might seem to us at the time, is outside of the power of God. As the old saying goes, "It's Friday, but Sunday's coming!" On Friday Christ was crucified; on Sunday he rose from the dead.

An amazing testimony from a persecuted Christian

One of the greatest privileges of my life was to spend time in Beijing, China, in 1980, with a Chinese Christian leader who had survived the full horrors of Mao's Great Proletarian Cultural Revolution. One thing this brave Christian said to me then was that however bad the persecution got – and *millions* died during that time, whether Christian or not – that he and his fellow believers had an overwhelmingly powerful sense of God's presence with them regardless of what was happening. When one considers what God's people suffered during those dreadful years, his is quite a testimony.

Not only that, but what he told me reflects Paul's words to Timothy, when the great apostle was imprisoned for the faith:

"But the Lord stood at my side and gave me strength, so that through me the message might be fully proclaimed and all the Gentiles might hear it. And I was delivered from the lion's mouth" (2 Timothy 4:17).

If we remember that the Chinese believers were totally isolated from the rest of the world, often having no idea of what was happening outside their own village, let alone globally, that is even more of a remarkable testimony still. We now know that in fact the church in China during that time was seeing exponential growth, increasing yearly by *millions*, in a way of which we can only dream in nations such as Britain or the United States.

In other words, God was mightily at work, despite the very best efforts of Mao and the Red Guards to destroy Christianity from the face of China. Some experts even think that there might now be as many as ninety *million* practising Chinese Christians today! One should say that exact figures are hard to verify, since much of the church in China is both unregistered and therefore illegal. But even a figure of half that amount would be an enormous increase on the two million or so Christians the missionaries thought they were leaving behind when all Westerners were expelled in the 1950s. Since evangelism is very hard in China – if not actually against the law in some areas – that growth is all the more remarkable still.

It is, one can say, a present-day fulfilment of Christ's words to Peter: "I will build my church, and the gates of Hades will not overcome it" (Matthew 16:18). How easily we in the West can be discouraged! We forget whose church it is and the power through whom it was created.

So what has the growth of God's church in China have to do with Islamic rage? I think that in fact all these things are closely interrelated.

God is with us

First of all, God is with us, whatever befalls. Not far from where I am writing this, a tragic murder of some young schoolchildren took place last year. The entire country was shocked by the suddenness and brutality of the murders, all the more so when it was discovered that the prime suspect was a local school caretaker whom the children would have known and therefore tragically trusted.

However, if you read accounts of what happens to children of the same age in many other countries around the world, you cannot help but be struck by how privileged in comparison Britain is that so few murders like that take place. In some lands children are sold wholesale into slavery, and in others homeless street children are massacred in large numbers by gangs often made up of off-duty policemen. So when people asked where God was when those British children were murdered, local Christians were able to use tragedy to preach the Good News of a God whose own Son, our Saviour Jesus Christ, was murdered by cruel and wicked men. But tragedy also connects us to those of our brothers and sisters who are suffering worldwide, and motivates us to pray for those faithful Christian missionaries in places like Peru or Ghana where so many children without a home are being brutally murdered every day.

I imagine that the same is true in the United States as it is for Britain. As Christians we have suddenly started to wake up and realize what it is like for most people "out there," especially since "out there" is now coming closer to home!

We live in a terrible and violent world. If terrorism has awakened us in the West from complacency, then good has already started to come from evil. Often it takes things like the stillbirth of a child, a premature death in the family, the fatal injury of a colleague in a car wreck, to make us realize that things are not always as we would wish them to be.

At least for British and American Christians, our faith does not usually land us in jail or forced exile to a remote part of the countryside. Yet those two things were usually the fate of Chinese Christians during the Cultural Revolution of 1966–76. But as we saw, God's church grew greater during that period than we could ever imagine!

Some encouraging biblical perspectives

This truth is what we see time and time again in the Scriptures. Whatever hideous things Satan hurls against the church, it is God who prevails, not the Devil.

As we read in Revelation 12:10–11: "For the accuser of our brothers, who accuses them before our God day and night, has been hurled down. They overcame him by the blood of the Lamb and by the word of their testimony." This is encouraging to us, therefore, regardless of what happens in light of the current global resurgence of militant Islam. However strong the Muslim world looks like it is becoming, however scary the threat of worldwide terrorism might be, *God is still in charge*. Our lives are in God's good and safe hands. As the apostle Paul writes in Romans:

> If God is for us, who can be against us? He who did not spare his own Son, but gave him up for us all – how will he not also, along with him, graciously give us all things? Who will bring any charge against those whom God has chosen? It is God who justifies. Who is he that condemns? Christ Jesus, who died – more than that, who was raised to life – is at the right hand of God and is also interceding for us. Who shall separate us from the love of Christ? Shall trouble or hardship or persecution or famine or nakedness or danger or sword? . . . No, in all these things we are more than conquerors through him who loved us. For I am convinced that neither death nor life, neither angels nor demons, neither the present nor the future, nor any powers, neither height nor depth, nor anything else in all creation, will be able to separate us from the love of God that is in Christ Jesus our Lord (Romans 8:31–39).

This is not to say that it is somehow immoral or un-Christian to be somewhat scared! The prospect of violent injury is not a pleasant one, as I know from the two that I have suffered accidentally in my lifetime. The idea that one of our loved ones will be blown up, leaving us behind and grieving, is not something about which to be cheerful either. On the other hand, I do think that, as Christians, our faith can and should liberate us from the sheer terror of the unknown that can so overwhelm those living around us. We *can* make that plane trip, in the knowledge that our life *is* in God's hands.

As we read in Matthew, in our Lord's own words:

> Therefore I tell you, do not worry about your life, what you will eat or drink; or about your body, what you will wear. Is not life more important than food, and the body more important than clothes? Look at the birds of the air; they do not sow or reap or store away in barns, and yet your heavenly Father feeds them. Are you not much more valuable than they? Who of you by worrying can add a single hour to his life? (Matthew 6:25–27).

I will always remember this passage – it just "happened" to be the Bible passage for the day when I was leaving a country in which many tens of thousands have been put to death by despotic governments. I had to wake up the man who was guarding my flea-ridden hotel with a submachine gun in order to get out through the metal bars and get a taxi to take me to the airport. The people at the security check-in weren't worried if I was carrying explosives – they wanted to be bribed! Following Christian practise in such countries, I refused – and that led me to being taken to a little room for persuasion. The memory of that Scripture was a great help! Providentially, they obviously thought I was not worth the trouble, as they eventually let me on the plane. Never was I more glad to reach the security of the West when my flight took off and landed me safely at my destination. However, one thought stayed with me: I was not a native of the country I had just left – I could leave it. Many Christians living there could not, and have paid the price with their lives.

Also, if we in the West do not know what might befall us, how much truer was that the case with, say, the Chinese Christians to whom I referred earlier? It was, many have commented, the wonderful witness in horrific times of these faithful Christians that brought so many of their fellow Chinese to conversion during the very worst of persecution. Not only that, but we are not talking about supermen and superwomen. These Chinese believers were ordinary human beings like you or me. So if we are inclined to panic, remember that our trust in God in globally uncertain times can and surely will be a powerful evangelistic testimony to those living around us.

God is in charge of history

The next key thing to recall is that God is in charge of history. We see this with Pharaoh, with Nebuchadnezzar, and in many other instances throughout the Old Testament. In 2 Chronicles 36:22 we read that God "moved the heart of Cyrus king of Persia." God can work through people whether they believe in him or not.

Not only that, but he is *really* in charge. One of the things we noticed is that Muslims tended in their good times to believe that the seventh century world conquests were a sign that they were right, that Allah was *with them* and not with the Christian peoples being conquered. But this is why the contrast made by non-Christian historians as well as by me about the different origins of both Christianity and Islam is such an important one. For the history of the Christian church, from the book of Acts onwards, is that *God does not need political or military victories for his church to grow.*

The importance of this cannot be overestimated! This is the critical point about which historians as divergent as Bernard Lewis and Malise Ruthven have written. For its first two hundred years, Christianity was an underground, persecuted religion. Yet it eventually turned the world upside down! The Roman Empire is long gone, but the Christian faith is with us still.

On the other hand, we saw that Muslims in the seventeenth and eighteenth centuries had doubts about sending Ottoman embassies abroad as it would result in Muslims needing to live in a non-Islamic country. The millions of Muslims living in Western countries face this very dilemma today. How can you be a good Muslim living in the *Dar al-Harb?*

Christians, however, do not have this problem. Nor do we need sympathetic governments – although no one actually wants to be persecuted! Rampaging mobs and death threats are clearly not hindering the wonderful God-given growth of the Gospel in Nigeria, Indonesia, and in many other parts of the world. In fact, the old saying is proving true once more: the blood of the martyrs is the seed of the church!

So when we look at what we *do* know about the future, it is that God's purposes have never been defeated, nor can they be either. *He* commands the course of history! God's plans cannot suddenly go unexpectedly awry. Satan *will* be defeated.

What does all this tell us about our future?

What, therefore, does this tell us in the uncertain time in which we now live? I think it reminds us that *whatever* happens, God has not lost the plot. Persecution clearly has no effect whatsoever on conversion growth, as our own times are showing us. False religions may *seem* very powerful, but in fact they are not, because they are on the losing side.

In relation to this book in particular, militant Islam may appear very frightening. One of the things we saw about Islamic terrorism is that, unlike most other terrorist groupings, they actually want maximum casualties, rather than just enough to prove their point or to get their case on television news. If, as some speculate, some Islamic groupings eventually get hold of nuclear weapons, they might well use them, with far more casualties created than we have seen so far. But *if* that happens – and one trusts that law enforcement agencies around the world are doing all they can to stop it – that does not mean that God has gone to sleep. People have been speculating as to where God is when tragedy strikes ever since the collapse of the wall of Siloam (Luke 13:4)! (And before, of course – as the book of Job reminds us.) As the apostle John reminds us in his epistle: "The one who is in you is greater than the one who is in the world" (1 John 4:4).

Humanist philosophers such as Voltaire were trying to use an earthquake in Lisbon in the eighteenth century to decry God's existence and power. In England there is a joke that goes: "The rain falls on the just and unjust, but more on the *just* because the unjust has stolen the just's umbrella!" Christians are not exempt from the results of the fall. My wife and I recently met a missionary lady whose husband was killed prematurely in a car wreck by a drunken driver, leaving his poor widow with four very small children. A good church friend of ours has just seen his wife die painfully of cancer, before she and her husband could enjoy their planned retirement together. For that matter, if I had hit the ground harder in a near-fatal accident I was involved in back in August 2001, you would not now be reading this book and my wife would be a widow.

What happens to us as individuals happens on a large scale as well. Global events might strike us as frightening or mysterious, but they are not a mystery to God! As Paul reminds Timothy: "In fact, everyone who wants to live a godly life in Christ Jesus will be persecuted, while evil men and impostors will go from bad to worse, deceiving and being deceived" (2 Timothy 3:12–13).

Maybe things will get worse. Perhaps Islam, in its extreme forms, will sweep over many countries. But God will not be defeated. On the other hand, revival could break out even in the Islamic world. Iraq, Egypt, Syria – all these could once again become Christian nations. And why should this *not* happen? Is God less powerful than some false religion? Can Satan beat God? To believe such things, one would have to have a very strange interpretation of large parts of the Bible! Even if you feel things will eventually get *much* worse, and many Christians do, there is no reason why things should not improve *before* they get worse. The astonishing global conversion growth that we are currently witnessing might indicate that the immediate future could go either way.

That is why I feel that I can end this book on an optimistic note. Whatever happens, Islamic extremism will fail and God's purposes will be worked out. The fear that many of us are now feeling in the West is, humanly speaking, quite understandable. But it is a sensation with which most Christians around the world have been very familiar for a long time.

Many a faithful Christian in, say, mid-Nigeria, must be getting out of bed each morning, wondering whether the new day will be their last on earth. Will the church service the following Sunday be the last one ever to which they can go freely, before the state authorities impose Islamic Sharia law? Such Christians are frail human beings like you or me, with all our weaknesses and failings. Yet God has not forsaken them! He is with them and will be so throughout eternity.

So it is with us, living in uncertain times. We have no idea how long the war on terror will last – but God does! Islam has been around for a very long time – in less than twenty years time it will have been around for fourteen hundred years. But if we recall the history of the twentieth century, both Fascism and Communism seemed most powerful and highly invincible at one time. The Third Reich and the Soviet Union no longer exist. Getting rid of the first took millions of lives; the second disintegrated without any war being needed to remove it.

We do not know whether we will live to see the demise of Islam. It took over seven centuries to reclaim Spain from Moorish rule. Egyptian Christians have been waiting over a millennium to see their country return to Christian faith – and we are all waiting still! Yet (South) Korea, a Buddhist country in 1900, is well on its way to becoming majority Christian in the twenty-first century.

We do not know the *particular* ways and purposes of God for individual countries or peoples. But we know God's *ultimate* purpose, because the Bible tells us! Christ will come again, God's church will prevail, and those who have been persecuted since the church began will be vindicated. As the apostle John reminds us: "They will make war against the Lamb, but the Lamb will overcome them because he is Lord of lords and King of kings – and with him will be his called, chosen and faithful followers" (Revelation 17:14).

That is why I am confident that we can end this book on an optimistic note. When Jesus Christ died upon the cross and rose again, the battle was won! God knows when the last battle will come, and we know what its outcome will be. Hallelujah!

Glossary and Index of Selected Words

caesaropapism – the practice in the Orthodox Christian Byzantine empire whereby the emperor (caesar) also had much of the authority that the pope alone exercised in the Catholic west: 66

Caliph/Caliphate – originally this meant Mohammed's successors, later it meant the prime Islamic ruler, down until its abolition in 1924; it is said that bin Laden wanted to revive this post, perhaps for himself; the Caliphates of the Ummayad dynasty in the Middle East and then in Spain, and the Abbasid Caliphate in Baghdad were the golden age of Islamic rule; the first four Caliphs are usually referred to as the "Four Rightly Guided Caliphs": 47–49, 59, 70, 76, 81, 85, 103, 105–6, 156, 197

Dar al-Harb – literally "the House or Abode of War," now used by Islamic extremists such as Osama bin Laden to mean any land not under Islamic rule, and in the past used to mean lands not conquered by Islamic armies or not converted to Muslim faith: 29, 114, 119, 121, 157, 177–78, 196, 244

Dar al-Islam – literally "the House or Abode of Islam," meaning a state under Islamic rule: 29, 51, 52, 64, 70, 85, 119, 121, 157, 160, 177–78, 196

Dar al-Salaam – literally "the House or Abode of Peace," meaning an area where there is no conflict: 113

dhimmi – literally "a protected monotheist," in practice a Christian or Jew living in an Islamic country and permitted by the Qu'ran to practice their faith: 44, 67, 76, 86, 144 *fatwa* – normally a formal legal opinion on Islamic law, though sometimes used by extremists for their own purposes: 128, 136, 178, 195, 212

Five Pillars of Islam – five basic Islamic practices common to all Muslims, the most famous of which is the Hajj, or pilgrimage to Mecca: 99–101

Four Schools – Islam being a religion of law, these are the four main schools of Sunni Islamic jurisprudence, the most famous of which today is the *Hanbali* interpretation of the law, practiced in Saudi Arabia: 107–8, 111–12, 113, 122–24, 136, 212

Hadith – a saying of Mohammed that does not have the full authority of the Qu'ran but is traditionally revered as authoritative: 95–96

imam – in majority Sunni Islam, the leader of the local mosque (Sunni Islam has no clergy); in Shiite Islam one of the righteous designated descendants of Mohammed, the last of whose return after many centuries is still eagerly awaited: 100, 106, 143, 184

ijtihad – literally "independent interpretation of Islamic law"; in Sunni Islam the "gate of ijtihad" has been closed to new interpretation for centuries, whereas in Shiite Islam it remains open: 110–111, 112, 184–15

islah – the possibility of reforming corrupted practices within Islam: 111

intifada – the uprising of Palestinians against Israeli occupation: 159

Islamicist – a technical Western term meaning someone who uses Islam as a political ideology as well as a faith: 28, 223

jahiliyya – literally "the time of unbelief in Arabia before Mohammed began his ministry," but in the twentieth century used by Islamic ideologues such as Sayyid Qutb to mean a Muslim state not living according to a strict interpretation of Qu'ranic principles, such as his own country, Egypt: 28, 51, 114–15, 117, 192

jihad – literally "struggle"; this is one of the most controversial words in Islamic terminology. There are two meanings: *greater jihad* or the struggle to live a pure life, the Muslim equivalent of holiness, and *lesser jihad* or Holy War, the military struggle against non-Muslims; moderate Muslims always prefer to use it in the first sense, Islamic terrorists like bin Laden in the second: 30, 46, 87, 89, 98, 101, 114, 141–44, 202–3, 214

Bibliography

Appearance in this bibliography does not necessarily mean an endorsement of what the book says, especially since several of these authors hold different viewpoints from each other. But all of them have useful insights whether or not one agrees with everything that an individual author writes. I have given the edition that I used – the publisher in the United States and United Kingdom may differ. The reason that I have listed so many books by Bernard Lewis is because they are so good. If you only have time to read a few of the books on this list, his are the best with which to begin.

AbuKhalil, As'ad. *Bin Laden, Islam and America's New "War on Terrorism."* New York: Seven Stories, 2002.

Ahmed, Akbar. *Islam Today.* 2d ed. London: IB Tauris, 2001.

Akbar, M.J. *The Shade of Swords: Jihad and the Conflict Between Islam and Christianity.* London: Routledge, 2002.

Ali, Tariq. *The Clash of Fundamentalisms: Crusades, Jihads, and Modernity.* London: Verso, 2002.

Anderson, Benedict. *Imagined Communities.* 2d ed. London: Verso, 1991.

Armstrong, Karen. *Islam: A Short History.* London: Weidenfeld and Nicolson, 2000.

Barber, Benjamin R. *Jihad vs. McWorld.* London: Times Books, 1995.

Baxter, Jenny, ed. *The Day That Shook the World.* London: BBC Books, 2001.

Bergen, Peter. *Holy War, Inc.* New York: Free Press, 2001.

Bloom, Jonathan and Sheila Blair. *Islam: A Thousand Years of Faith and Power.* New Haven, CT: Yale University Press, 2002.

Brzezinski, Zbigniew. *The Grand Chessboard.* New York: Basic Books, 1997.

Catherwood, Christopher. *Whose Side Is God On?* London: SPCK, 2003.

———. *Why the Nations Rage: Killing in the Name of God.* 2d ed. Lanham, MD: Rowman and Littlefield, 2002.

Chapman, Colin. *Cross and Crescent: Responding to the Challenge of Islam.* 2d ed. Leicester: InterVarsity Press, 2002.

Cigar, Norman. *Genocide in Bosnia: The Policy of Ethnic Cleansing.* College Station, TX: Texas A&M University Press, 1995.

Corbin, Jane. *The Base: In Search of Al Qaeda.* London: Simon and Schuster, 2002.

Cragg, Kenneth. *The Call of the Minaret.* Oxford: Oxford University Press, 1956.

Esposito, John. *Islam: The Straight Path.* 3d ed. Oxford: Oxford University Press, 1998.

———. *The Islam Threat: Myth or Reality?* 2d ed. Oxford: Oxford University Press, 1995.

———. *Unholy War: Terror in the Name of Islam.* Oxford: Oxford University Press, 2002.

———, ed. *The Oxford History of Islam.* Oxford: Oxford University Press, 1999.

Firestone, Reuven. *Jihad: The Origins of Holy War in Islam.* Oxford: Oxford University Press, 1999.

Friedman, Thomas. *From Beirut to Jerusalem.* 3d ed. New York: Anchor Books, 1995.

Fromkin, David. *A Peace to End All Peace: The Fall of the Ottoman Empire and the Creation of the Modern Middle East.* New York: Henry Holt, 1989.

Griffin, Michael. *Reaping the Worldwind: The Taliban Movement in Afghanistan.* London: Pluto Press, 2001.

Gunaratna, Rohan. *Inside Al Qaeda.* London: Hurst, 2002.

Halliday, Fred. *Two Hours That Shook the World.* London: Saqi Books, 2002.

Hanson, Victor Davis. *An Autumn of War.* New York: Basic Books, 2002.

Hiro, Dilip. *War Without End: The Rise of Islamic Terrorism and Global Response.* London: Routledge, 2002.

Hitti, Philip. *Islam: A Way of Life.* Minneapolis: University of Minnesota Press, 1970.

Hoge, James F., Jr. and Gideon Rose, eds. *How Did This Happen: Terrorism and the New War.* New York: Public Affairs, 2001.

Hoodbhoy, Pervez. *Islam and Science.* London: Zed, 1991.

Hourani, Albert. *A History of the Arab Peoples.* New York: Warner, 1991.

Huband, Mark. *Warriors of the Prophet: The Struggle for Islam.* Boulder, CO: Westview, 1999.

Hunter, Shireen. *The Future of Islam and the West.* Westport, CT: Praeger, 1999.

Huntington, Samuel P. *The Clash of Civilizations and the Remaking of World Order.* New York: Simon and Schuster, 1996.

Jacquard, Roland. *In the Name of Osama bin Laden.* Durham, NC: Duke University Press, 2002.

Johnson, Chalmers. *Blowback: The Costs and Consequences of American Empire.* New York: Henry Holt, 2000.

Juergensmeyer, Mark. *The New Cold War? Religious Nationalism Confronts the Secular State.* San Francisco: University of California Press, 1993.

———. *Terror in the Mind of God: The Global Rise of Religious Violence.* San Francisco: University of California Press, 2000

Kaplan, Robert. *Soldiers of God.* New York: Vintage, 2001.

Kennedy, Hugh. *Muslim Spain and Portugal.* Harlow: Longman, 1996.

———. *The Prophet and the Age of the Caliphates.* Harlow: Longman, 1986.

Kepel, Gilles. *Jihad: The Trail of Political Islam.* Cambridge, MA: Harvard University Press, 2002.

———. *The Revenge of God: The Resurgence of Islam, Christianity and Judaism in the Modern World.* Cambridge: Polity Press, 1994.

Lamb, David. *The Arabs: Journeys Beyond the Mirage.* 2d ed. New York: Vintage, 2002.

Lawrence, Bruce B. *Shattering the Myth: Islam Beyond Violence.* Princeton, NJ: Princeton University Press, 1998.

Lewis, Bernard. *The Arabs in History.* 6th ed. Oxford: Oxford University Press, 1993.

———. *Cultures in Conflict: Christians, Muslims, and Jews in the Age of Discovery.* Oxford: Oxford University Press, 1995.

———. *Islam and the West.* Oxford: Oxford University Press. 1993.

———. *Islam in History: Ideas, People, and Events in the Middle East.* 2d ed. Chicago: Open Court, 1993.

———. *The Jews of Islam.* Princeton, NJ: Princeton University Press, 1984.

———. *The Middle East.* London: Weidenfeld and Nicolson, 1995.

———. *A Middle East Mosaic.* New York: Random House, 2000.

———. *The Muslim Discovery of Europe.* 2d ed. New York: WW Norton, 2001.

———. *What Went Wrong?* Oxford: Oxford University Press, 2002

Lippman, Thomas W. *Understanding Islam.* 2d ed. Charlotte, NC: Meridian, 1995.

MacArthur, John F. *Terrorism, Jihad, and the Bible.* Nashville: W Publishing, 2001.

MacFie, A.L. *Orientalism.* Harlow: Longman, 2002.

Macmillan, Margaret. *Peacemakers.* London: John Murray, 2001.

Margolis, Eric. *War at the Top of the World.* 2d ed. London: Routledge, 2000.

McCarthy, Justin. *The Ottoman Peoples and the End of Empire.* South Harwich, MA: Arnold, 2001.

McDowell, Bruce and Anees Zaka. *Muslims and Christians at the Table.* Phillipsburg, NJ: Presbyterian and Reformed, 1999.

McNamara, Robert S. and James G. Blight. *Wilson's Ghost.* New York: Public Affairs, 2001.

Menocal, Maria Rosa. *The Ornament of the World: How Muslims, Jews, and Christians Created a Climate of Tolerance in Medieval Spain.* Boston: Little Brown, 2002.

Miller, Judith. *God Has Ninety-Nine Names: Reporting from a Militant Middle East.* New York: Simon and Schuster, 1996.

Mortimer, Edward. *Faith and Power: The Politics of Islam.* New York: Random House, 1982.

Moucarry, Chawkat. *Faith to Faith: Christianity and Islam in Dialogue.* Leicester: InterVarsity Press, 2001.

Naipaul, V.S. *Beyond Belief: Islamic Excursions Among the Converted Peoples.* Boston: Little Brown, 1998.

Ovendale, Ritchie. *The Middle East Since 1914.* 2d ed. Harlow: Longman, 1998.

Partner, Peter. *God of Battles: Holy Wars of Christianity and Islam.* New York: HarperCollins, 1997.

Peters, Ralph. *Beyond Terror.* Mechanicsburg, PA: Stackpole Books, 2002.

Pettifer, James. *The Turkish Labyrinth: Ataturk and the New Islam.* London: Viking, 1997.

Pipes, Daniel. *Militant Islam Reaches America.* New York: WW Norton, 2002.

Pryce-Jones, David. *The Closed Circle: An Interpretation of the Arabs.* 2d ed. Chicago: Ivan R. Dee, 2002.

Rashid, Ahmed. *Jihad: The Roots of Militant Islam in Central Asia.* New Haven, CT: Yale University Press, 2002.

———. *Taliban: Militant Islam, Oil, and Fundamentalism in Central Asia.* New Haven, CT: Yale University Press, 2001.

Reeve, Simon. *The New Jackals.* Boston: Northeastern University Press, 1999.

Reilly, Bernard. *The Medieval Spains.* Oxford: Oxford University Press, 1993.

Roberts, John. *Visions and Miracles: The Middle East in a New Era.* Edinburgh: Mainstream, 1995.

Robinson, Adam. *Bin Laden.* Edinburgh: Mainstream, 2001.

Robinson, Francis, ed. *The Cambridge Illustrated History of the Islamic World.* Cambridge: Cambridge University Press, 1996.

Roshwald, Aviel. *Ethnic Nationalism and the Fall of Empires: Central Europe, Russia, and the Middle East 1914–1923.* London: Routledge, 2001.

Ruthven, Malise. *A Fury for God: The Islamist Attack on America.* London: Granta, 2002.

———. *Islam in the World.* 2d ed. Oxford: Oxford University Press, 2000.

Said, Edward. *Covering Islam.* New York: Vintage, 2001.

Scruton, Roger. *The West and the Rest.* London: Continuum, 2002.

Shadid, Anthony. *Legacy of the Prophet: Despots, Democrats, and the New Politics of Islam.* Boulder, CO: Westview, 2001.

Talbott, Strobe and Nayan Chanda, eds. *The Age of Terror: America and the World After September 11.* New York: Perseus Press, 2001.

Tibi, Bassam. *Arab Nationalism Between Islam and the Nation State.* 3d ed. Basingstoke: Macmillan, 1997.

———. *The Challenge of Fundamentalism: Political Islam and the New World Disorder.* Los Angeles: University of California Press, 1998.

———. *Islam Between Culture and Politics.* Basingstoke: Palgrave, 2001.

Ullman, Harlan. *Unfinished Business: Afghanistan, the Middle East and Beyond.* New York: Citadel Press, 2002.

Viorst, Milton. *In the Shadow of the Prophet: The Struggle for the Soul of Islam.* Boulder, CO: Westview Press, 2001.

Waines, David. *An Introduction to Islam.* Cambridge: Cambridge University Press, 1995.

Wright, Robin. *Sacred Rage: The Wrath of Militant Islam.* 2d ed. New York: Touchstone, 2001.

Ye'or, Bat. *The Decline of Eastern Christianity under Islam: From Jihad to Dhimmitude.* Madison, WI: Farleigh Dickinson University Press, 1996.

If I listed all the articles that I read, this bibliography would be truly massive! I am grateful to: *Newsweek, Time, The Economist, Times, The Guardian, Independent, Financial Times, Daily Mail, The Sunday Times, The Sunday Telegraph, The Observer, International Herald Tribune, The New York Times, The Washington Post, Los Angeles Times, Foreign Affairs, Foreign Policy, The Weekly Standard, The National Interest, The New Republic, Commentary, Richmond Times-Dispatch, National Review, The American Spectator, The Spectator, Current History, Christianity Today, Evangelicals Now, First Things, The Jerusalem Post, The Tie,* and also to numerous online publications, for the countless articles that I read with such interest and profit. I am most grateful to those University search systems that enabled me to find them, especially at the Universities of Virginia and Richmond in the United States, and of Cambridge in Britain. *JSTOR* and *GaleGroup InfoTrac* are two invaluable search engines.